THE SPONSORSHIP MANUAL

Sponsorship Made Easy

EDWARD GELDARD
&
LAUREL SINCLAIR

The Sponsorship Unit Pty Ltd

Written by Edward Geldard & Laurel Sinclair

First Edition published 1996
Reprinted 1998
Second Edition published 2002
Reprinted 2005

Published by The Sponsorship Unit Pty Ltd,
1168 Burwood Highway, Upper Ferntree Gully, Victoria, Australia 3156
Phone + 61 3 9758 3700   Fax + 61 3 9758 5699
www.sponsorshipunit.com.au

Cover Design by: Initial Design work – Smartlook, Box Hill, Victoria, Australia. Final cover design - Peter Arnold Design, Croydon, Victoria, Australia
Printed by Taverner Printing, Nunawading, Victoria, Australia

National Library of Australia
Cataloguing-in-Publication Data

Geldard, E. (Edward), 1961- .
The sponsorship manual : sponsorship made easy.

2nd ed.
Includes index.
ISBN 0 9579948 0 X.

1. Corporate sponsorship - Australia. I. Sinclair, L. (Laurel), 1956- . II. Sponsorship Unit Pty. Ltd. III. Title.

658.820994

Contents

About The Authors

Edward Geldard is General Manager of The Sponsorship Unit, Australia's leading independent sponsorship consultancy. He is a visiting lecturer at Royal Melbourne Institute of Technology, and University of Technology Sydney. Edward is a founding judge of the Australian Financial Review National Sponsorship Awards and a past board member of the Australasian Sponsorship Marketing Association.

Edward has conducted more than 200 training workshops during the past ten years, and he has re-engineered sponsorship processes for a number of Top 100 companies in Australia.

His past positions have included National Sponsorship Manager at Telstra, and Manager – Sponsorships at Channel 9, Brisbane.

Laurel Sinclair is Managing Director of The Sponsorship Unit, an independent consultancy providing strategic advice, planning and evaluation, project management and training throughout Australia and the South Pacific. The Sponsorship Unit is the organiser of The Sponsorship Summit, the southern hemisphere's largest annual gathering of sponsorship professionals.

Laurel has extensive experience consulting to major corporations and project managing sponsorship programs. These programs have provided substantial return on investment, launches products, promoted services, increased sales and generated product usage.

Laurel's past positions were with large companies in corporate Australia, such as Coopers & Lybrand, Telstra and Gillette.

How to Use This Book for Maximum Benefit

This book has been divided into seven parts for ease of reading. Each part contains checklists, examples of documents, case studies, formulas for pricing and evaluating, and practical diagrams to help increase the sponsor's exposure. A fast find index and dictionary of terms is contained at the back.

Part One is a general introduction to sponsorship, and its role as a marketing and communications tool.

Part Two details the processes sponsorship seekers must undertake prior to seeking sponsorship. This includes the preparation of a policy and a strategy.

Part Three provides tips to help organisations gain sponsorship support. It covers methods of identifying benefits and packaging and pricing properties. It advises on the type of information required in a proposal, gives some hints on negotiating the deal and contains information relating to contracts.

Part Four details the processes sponsors must undertake to deliver a strategically planned sponsorship portfolio. This includes assessment procedures, preparation of policy and strategy documents, and interface with the public.

Part Five provides tips to help companies proactively select and purchase sponsorships that will deliver the company's marketing and communications objectives.

Part Six contains all the tips required to ensure sponsorship is successful. It provides assistance and 'handy hints' on everything from successful signage placement, right through to media management, ambush defence planning and evaluation.

Part Seven contains appendices referred to throughout text and a dictionary of terms

The **'Seeker'** (the recipient of sponsorship from a sponsor) could be an event, an organisation or an individual as an entrant.

The **'Sponsor'** (the purchaser of sponsorship rights). Either a business or a businesses representative.

The **'Property'**. Throughout this book we will refer to the opportunity (proposal) to be offered to a potential sponsor, whether it be an event, organisation or entrant as "the property".

Acknowledgments

The authors would especially like to acknowledge the following individuals and organisations for their assistance with the compilation of this publication.

Australian Commonwealth Games Association for allowing reproduction of the "Ambush" advertisement.

Australia Post for allowing reproduction of Australia Post's Sponsorship Guidelines.

Heather Sinclair - without her assistance and encouragement, the best selling first edition of this book would never have been written.

Sports Marketing and Management for arranging permission to reprint the 'Ambush' Commonwealth Games advertisement.

Terry Hearity, National Sponsorship Manager Australia Post for arranging permission to reprint Australia Post's Sponsorship Guidelines.

Tim Spargo, Project Manager, The Sponsorship Unit for his assistance with the graphics included in this publication.

Preface

The best-selling first edition of the Sponsorship Manual, published in 1996 came about as the result of many requests from clients, students and participants in the numerous workshops we have run, for recommended reading material on sponsorship. You will still find that most of the information contained in this book is original. We make no apologies for that. A lot of time was spent looking for reference material, and it was found there was a scarcity of useful written information on the sponsorship industry. This situation has improved somewhat in the past seven years.

The book talks a lot about human relationships, exploitation, profit and "win win" relationships because all of these occur in sponsorship relationships to varying degrees. Sponsorships, often based on human relationships will only succeed where there is a 'win win' relationship. This enables a sponsoring company to exploit their association with an organisation, event or individual to make a profit and return dividends to their owners and shareholders from sponsorship programs.

While reading this book, you will notice that we have emphasised some points more than once. The reason for this is because they are relevant to more than one area, and also because it was intended that the book will more often be used as a reference rather than a one off read.

This book differs from our original in that we have added a significant amount of information that relates specifically to sponsors in terms of purchasing and managing their sponsorships to gain maximum benefit for their company.

Gender bias is always a problem. For ease of reading we have alternated the use of the term 'he' or 'she', throughout the book, which is more practical than the use of combined pronouns such as he/she, her/him.

The sponsorship seeker will hereafter be known as the "seeker" regardless of whether the sponsorship has been sold/delivered – this is not a description that we particularly like, but it is universally understood.

Edward Geldard and Laurel Sinclair
Melbourne, Australia, 2002

Part 1

Introduction to Sponsorship

Chapter 1

Sponsorship Defined

Sponsorship - the Potential

Sponsorship, of all the marketing communications tools, has the greatest potential to allow a company to form a relationship with their customers via a personal medium. We are reading all the time how the world is becoming an impersonal place, and that people are yearning for a sense of community – of belonging. We email instead of talk; many of us no longer worship; stranger danger means that children are unable to play in their neighbourhood without supervision, and we are all so consumed with our careers, or just the business of living, that we do not have the time to make, and maintain those friendships that used to give us a sense of community and of belonging. Often the only sense of belonging comes from our interests – sport, arts, charitable beliefs, educational institutions and so on – each of us relate to at least one of these, often passionately. This is particularly so in the sports arena, where you are likely to see the same fans sitting in the same seats week after week.

It is not enough for a company to offer a brand to the market – even if it is an excellent one. The brand must now "stand for something" – in other words have some cultural meaning. People like to think that their purchases stand for something – consumers are informed and discriminating, and there is ample evidence available that they will change their purchase habits based on how they perceive the product/brand/company. Many companies have now realised that they need to invest their brand(s) with cultural meaning, and then communicate those values to their customers in a personal (and acceptable) manner. Sponsorship offers the opportunity to connect with people when they are experiencing or undertaking an activity that they enjoy and have chosen to be involved in.

In other words, sponsorship can offer the opportunity to communicate (or speak) *with or to* your desired target audience, rather than speaking *at*, which is often the way with conventional methods of marketing communication.

We have all seen the passion and excitement generated by sports and arts events, and the enthusiasm generated by the activities of major charities and medical research institutes. The hearts and minds of the public and the media alike can be captured by these events in a very positive manner. In becoming involved in sponsorship, companies are buying the right to associate themselves with these events, organisations and people; in order to positively impact on sales, release new products or perhaps heighten or improve company or corporate image. Many sponsorship properties offer the potential to gain both reach and frequency within a very targeted market, which as we all know is an integral part of getting the marketing message to stay with the consumer.

In our not too distant past, many companies just handed over the sponsorship money and then sat back waiting for the benefits to roll in. They either put no effort in, or expected the sponsored person or organisation to make it work for them. It will come as no surprise that the benefits did not ensue, and they never will, from such a lax arrangement.

Sponsorship has for many years now been a discipline in its own right. It is a business tool in competition for marketers and communicators budgets along with advertising, sales promotions, public relations and direct marketing. An effective marketing, communications or public relations program may use one or all of these tools for totally different effect. Sponsorship is now an integral part of almost every major company's marketing mix and can provide a substantial return on investment when well selected and managed to deliver objectives. However, it must be said that the added expense of human resources commitments and leverage dollars can disadvantage sponsorship when compared with other marketing and communications mediums.

Companies are seeking tangible benefits from their sponsorship programs such as: increased sales, access to hospitality, product sampling, signage rights, exclusivity (the ability to lock out the competitor), merchandising, networking, client entertainment, media coverage, publicity opportunities, use of personalities, image association, generation of awareness and goodwill, and retail and trade incentives.

Sponsorship's Effect on the Community

Sponsorship is vital to the survival of numerous non-profit sports, arts, charities, environmental organisations, events, and even professional sports and arts organisations and the like. Without sponsorship support ticket prices at many events would be forced up to exorbitant levels, and the events could well become non-viable. Sponsorship has become vitally significant to our community in a number of very important areas. Sponsorships help fund much of the entertainment we attend and view on television, from basketball to motor racing, to arts events and historical exhibitions. Sponsorship support is now making possible numerous environmental initiatives that do not enjoy government funding, and supporting the works of both charities and medical research institutes. Without significant sponsorship revenue many activities and events would not be made available to the community, and certainly not at the same level of expertise.

Sponsorship Defined

Sponsorship is generally recognised as the purchase of the, usually intangible, exploitable potential (rights and benefits), associated with an entrant, event or organisation which results in tangible benefits for the sponsoring company (image/profit enhancement).

New jargon/terms commonly come and go in the sponsorship arena. The common feature of all of the following is that they utilise a sponsorship relationship in order to achieve marketing and/or communications objectives:

- Cause related marketing activities
- Event marketing
- Sports marketing
- Arts marketing
- Experiential marketing

Sponsorship support can be of; an event, organisation, individual, team, object, television program, venue etc., and the benefits offered to the sponsor by the sponsored organisation can include:

- Exclusivity (the ability to lock out the competitor)
- Image association
- Product sampling at venues
- Sales rights
- Licensing rights
- Association with a lifestyle
- Signage rights
- Merchandising
- Hospitality for client entertainment
- Networking with people of importance
- Media coverage
- Publicity opportunities
- Use of personalities for advertising and promotions
- Retail and trade incentives to encourage your members to purchase the sponsor's product

The benefits, when leveraged can result in some or all of the following tangible results for the sponsor:

- Increase in brand, product and corporate awareness
- Significant media coverage
- The ability to influence opinion leaders
- Increase sales
- Generate awareness and goodwill within defined target audiences

Successful execution of sponsorship generally utilises most marketing and communications tools in its execution. Successful management of a sponsorship program can involve the use of advertising, public relations, sales promotions, cross promotions, television coverage, merchandising, licensing, media relations, on-pack promotions, and the creation of events.

It must be pointed out that **sponsorship is not a donation**. Donations are either free goods or money given with no return benefits expected. Sponsorship offers monetary support to an individual, team or organisation in return for an agreed benefit or list of benefits that are to be provided by the sponsored entity.

Grants are not sponsorship. Grants are most often a once only financial payment (assistance) provided by government, foundation or trust in order to assist in the development of a project, purchase of an artwork, educational endeavours or similar.

Grants are almost always non-commercial in nature, in fact in some places it is illegal to ask for commercial benefits in return for the bestowing of a grant, so it is worth checking local legislation. Generally the benefit is in the delivery of the activity or item supported by the grant.

The Beginning

The first documented sponsorships were of the arts during the renaissance period. These involved support of the arts and the artists of the time by rich and powerful persons who wanted to socialise and associate themselves with the artists' image and works.

The first modern sponsorships occurred at the turn of the century in the area of motor sport. The beginnings were humble, with a number of cars receiving contra support (free goods) from oil and tyre companies in exchange for signage and demonstrating the sponsor's product to the motor racing audience. Acknowledgement of that support was initially just a list of suppliers, not the brand signage that we now see on racing cars.

Of course, we went through a phase where some sponsors wanted a sign on everything that did (and didn't) move (the logo slap!). However, in most cases sanity has prevailed, and sponsors are now far more aware of whether their signage is appropriate and aesthetically acceptable.

Why Companies Use Sponsorship

Sponsorship in the past was in many cases a form of altruism by the Chief Executive and was a way of ensuring she got to play in the Pro-Am, or perhaps of pleasing their partner because they liked, for example, the Opera. This sort of altruistic (non marketing) sponsorship is on the decline due to the tightening economy and companies being accountable to Boards that are taking a far greater interest in justifying expenditure and getting a return for their shareholders.

Sponsorship is now more closely aligned to marketing and communications departments rather than the 'bosses' office. Too many companies, however, still have a few of the bosses 'pet' sponsorships lurking in their portfolio that are outside the scope of the company strategy and policy. (There are obviously still some advantages to being the boss!) However, increasingly even these have to be justified in terms of return on investment.

Companies undertake sponsorships to achieve or further many and varied objectives. The following are some reasons why companies become involved in sponsorship programs:

- **Change attitudes and behaviours** of trade, consumers, staff and corporate clients.

- **Generate consumer awareness** - used to introduce or build brands.

- **Purchase of a significant marketing advantage.** The right to exploit the sponsored organisation's or individual's image or lifestyle through: naming rights, use of mailing lists, creation of licensed and premium merchandise, on site concessions, exclusivity, signage, and use of personalities. A caution here – when a club, organization etc. gets personal name/address details from members, they should at the same time gain permission to pass these details on to sponsors. In some countries and states, significant privacy legislation exists, and it would be prudent to familiarise yourself with any requirements.

- **To generate goodwill towards the sponsor (company).** Relationship marketing, media coverage, lobbying, access to VIP's, ie., government ministers. There is increasing evidence that responsible corporate citizenship can and does result in an increase by consumers in propensity to purchase.

- **As a cost effective alternative** to mainstream advertising and other marketing tools, and a way to connect with your target audience in a more personal and lifestyle relevant manner.

- **Facilitate community activities/relations** – within the area of operation. Sponsorship is regularly undertaken by a company within its immediate area of operation in order to facilitate good relations within that community, and ultimately to assist it in operating within a climate of consent.

- **To generate or increase sales through utilising the relationship.** Directly, sales could be gained by selling product into related venues, such as sports stadiums and theatres. Indirectly, sales might be affected by change in audience attitude or knowledge, which leads to purchase.

- **To participate in relationship marketing.** Sponsorship often provides the platform to develop or strengthen relationships with clients or potential clients.

- **To generate brand awareness and acceptance.** Sponsorship is often used to raise the awareness of a company's brand or corporate identity, and to generate goodwill towards the sponsor.

- **To identify product with a lifestyle, through, for example, naming rights.** An example of this is Nikes sponsorship of high profile athletes, which sends a message that Nike products are both functional at a top level, and that they are desirable enough for high profile sports people to be seen wearing them.

- **Exclusivity - lock the competitor out of an activity.** With a high profile sponsorship such as soccer which receives many hours of television coverage, and has a huge number of fanatical supporters, it may be well worthwhile for a company (such as an airline for example) to ensure that their major competitor cannot get access to the supporter, (or for that matter the travel business of the teams and fans).

- **Access niche/target markets.** Sponsorship is often the only way to access a particular niche market. For example, a manufacturer of horse riding products would gain access to their target market if they undertook to sponsor all pony club activities, or cross country riding events.

- **Client entertainment/hospitality.** Sponsorship is often the only way to gain access to a large number of premium (A Reserve) seats at any given event, such as the Opera, the ballet, the Cricket and so on.

- **Demonstrate product attributes.** Sponsorship offers the opportunity to demonstrate product attributes in more than one way. You will often gain the right to sample your product in a venue if you are a sponsor.

Alternatively, you could have the team or stars actually use your product during an event, which clearly showcases it during use.

Initially sponsorship was not much more than a list of sponsors on a vehicle, but it has now developed into a sophisticated medium that can be a cost effective alternative to mainstream advertising and other marketing tools. Sponsorship should only be used as an alternative to conventional advertising and marketing programs when it is clearly the best or most cost effective method of achieving the sponsoring organisation's objectives and goals.

The Value of Sponsorship

The value of sponsorship can be measured by its effect on the sponsor's bottom line and their publics' perceptions of the company and its products. If the public and trade are unaware of, or disinterested in the sponsorship, attributable returns are likely to be minimal at best.

Sponsorship can be relatively inexpensive in comparison to other marketing tools, however companies using sponsorship in their armoury are only doing so if they are well serviced by the seeker and the relationship is rewarding and problem free. Far too often this is not the case – we could cite dozens of examples here – consultants tend to be invited on board when the going gets tough! To achieve and maintain a mutually beneficial relationship requires the sponsored organisation to initiate opportunities for the sponsor. These might include cross promotions, event promotions, or significant media coverage of the sponsor's key messages.

Marketing and Communications Defined

As mentioned, sponsorship is used as a marketing and communications tool therefore it is important that we define the terms marketing and communications:

Marketing is an activity that has existed for the past one and a half centuries. Marketing activities commenced when farmers and tradespeople had a surplus of goods and decided to barter those goods in exchange for an item or service owned by someone else.

Text Book Definition of Marketing:

Marketing is the process of planning and executing the conception, pricing, promotion, and distribution of ideas, goods, and services to create exchanges that satisfy individual and organisational goals.[1]

In essence, marketing involves the following elements:

1. Possessing or producing a product or service required by others that is surplus to your requirements (identifying product or service).

2. Locating potential customers for your product (research potential customers needs).

3. Pricing the product or service at market price.

4. Ensuring that potential customers are aware of your product (advertising).

5. Demonstrating how the product or service can help them and why they should purchase from you (distribution and selling).

Communications is defined in the Collins Dictionary as being:

"The imparting or exchange of information, ideas or feelings."

For effective communication to occur the communicator must decide on the information to be disseminated, select a medium via which to transmit the message and encode the message to ensure it is interesting and has relevance. The message then has to be decoded by a receiver who will act on the contents of the message. Depending on the effectiveness of the communication, the receiver may ignore the message, retain the information for future reference, or act on the message immediately by, for example, purchasing the goods mentioned.

---

[1]Bennett, Peter D., Ed., 1988, Marketing, American Marketing Association, p.54

Typlcal Company's Marketing Communications Mix

Marketing and communications tools are all regularly used in the execution of sponsorships to communicate key messages to the company's target audiences. The aim is to generate consumer interest that will motivate consumers to take in the sponsorship message. The marketing communications mix is usually made up of some or all of the following tools:

Advertising

Sponsorship communication often includes an advertising component that is paid for usually by the sponsor, sometimes by the seeker, but communication also takes place through general media coverage, editorial, press and video releases, and signage.

Sponsorship differs from advertising in that advertising is where a company pays a fee for the right to place advertising. In this instance, the company retains complete editorial control of the advertisement. This means that all messages are scripted and approved and appear as scheduled advertisements. Editorial control of the conventional advertising component of sponsorship is generally shared by both the sponsor and the seeker, and from time to time even a sub-sponsor.

Advertising has the capacity to be transmitted cheaply, on a cost per person basis, to vast audiences through non-personal mediums such as television radio and print. If, however, marketers are aiming to influence a 'niche' market, which consists of a relatively small number of people, television, radio and print can be very expensive on a cost per person basis. This is where a sponsorship property that delivers to that niche audience can be a very cost effective way of communicating to your desired audience.

Sales Promotions

Sales promotions are short-term marketing tactics designed to generate additional sales through the use of inducements, incentives, and/or added value. These include competitions, money back offers, sweepstakes, redemption's, two for one offers, etc. Sales promotions are regularly themed around a sponsorship program.

Public Relations

Public relations is the communication of information to consumers through the strategic use of non-cost mediums. Sponsorship can quite often be a catalyst for, or the subject of, public relations activities that will generate the necessary interest to communicate a message at no cost. This can be delivered through items such as news stories and editorial. Stories which are disseminated via public relations channels are often seen as being more credible than other sources, simply because they are not paid for advertising.

Niche Marketing

Niche marketing is often undertaken by a company or brand in order to gain a position of strength or give the appearance of being the dominant or only brand in their particular segment. Companies commonly have an identified target market (niche) for their activities, which will often match the audience provided by a particular organisation. Most events and organisations seeking sponsorship have strongly defined audiences (membership, publics and audience). These audiences have unique demographic and geographic trends, which can make sponsorship an ideal vehicle for accessing these niche markets. Identifying the niche markets a sponsorship property can deliver ensures you are able to match your target audience with a sponsorship property that can deliver that unique audience. Some examples of niche markets include:

- Various ethnic communities
- Youth
- Gay community
- Grey power (over 60's)
- Football Fans
- Punters

Categorising Sponsorship

Sponsorships can be broken down into three broad categories. These are **Corporate, Marketing and Philanthropic.** (The vast majority of sponsorships being signed are Marketing sponsorships.) The reason for this breakdown is based on the end use of the property by the sponsor, and to an extent, the budgets that they are funded from.

Marketing Sponsorships

Marketing sponsorships are the provision of cash or contra (free goods) in return for access to the exploitable potential associated with an entrant, event or organisation. These are used primarily to promote products and services to targeted market segments, and/or to reinforce a product or brand, or promote sales activities.

Sponsorships are often used in addition to advertising to ensure brand recognition. Examples of marketing sponsorships include the sponsorship of:

- Football teams
- Local festivals
- Pop concerts
- The Olympics

Marketing Sponsorships are taken out by businesses of all sizes for the *sole reason* that the sponsorship will have a positive quantifiable effect on the company's bottom line (ie, will generate profit, usually through increased sales).

Corporate Sponsorship

Corporate Sponsorship is the provision of financial or material support (cash, services, or product) by a company for an independent activity not directly linked to the company's normal business. Corporate Sponsorships are generally National or State sponsorships of major events or organisations. Examples include:

- The Arts
- The Environment
- Charitable sponsorships (not to be confused with philanthropy /donations)

The Objectives of Corporate Sponsorship can Include:

- Reinforcing the public's positive perceptions of a company, through positive media exposure and associating with the sponsored organisation's image.

- Communicating key corporate messages to defined target audiences.

- Supporting and reinforcing a company's corporate image.

- Building and/or maintaining the desired image of the company's identity.

- Establishing and maintaining a climate of consent for the company's activities by:

  o Providing opportunities to entertain key clients, opinion leaders and people with significant political and bureaucratic leverage.

  o Supporting worthy causes over prolonged periods.

  o Generating recognition within the general community that the company is a good corporate citizen and is supporting worthy causes.

Philanthropic Sponsorships

Philanthropy is the intersection of societal and corporate needs. Philanthropic support is provided by large companies or philanthropic foundations, and these are undertaken to give something back to the community in which a company operates. Philanthropy makes a company feel virtuous, can provide taxation concessions on occasion, and at times generates goodwill towards the company.

Philanthropic sponsorships are generally in the arts, education and medical research areas and generally yield little direct benefit to the sponsoring organisation. They are basically an investment by individuals or companies for the public good.

Cause Related Marketing

Cause related sponsorships involve the sponsorship of an organisation or cause that will generate emotion, or tug at consumer's heart strings. This type of sponsorship is designed to generate sales by linking a consumer purchase to funding or assisting the cause. In some cases the money spent on promoting the sponsorship will far exceed the donated amount.

Triple Bottom Line Reporting

In these days of triple-bottom line reporting, cause related programs are growing in popularity – they are being included in company strategies, and proving that expecting a return from "cause dollars" is indeed realistic. There is increasing evidence that people want to feel good about the company that they purchase their products from. Cause related marketing/sponsorship programs are being increasingly recognised as one way of achieving a feel good connection with the consumer.

The Triple-bottom line is a term coined by John Elkington (1997), author and management consultant, which refers to the three prongs of social, environmental and financial accountability. It is a term that has found increasing and widespread international acceptance within the corporate community and one that is informing and transforming corporate reporting practices.

The notion of reporting against the three components (or 'bottom lines') of economic, environmental and social performance is directly tied to the concept and goal of sustainable development. Triple-bottom line reporting, if properly implemented, will provide information to enable others to assess how sustainable an organisation's operations are.

The perspective taken is that for an organisation to be sustainable it must be financially secure; it must minimise (or ideally eliminate) its negative environmental impacts; and it must act in conformity with societal expectations. These three factors are obviously highly inter-related. (source:www.ecosteps.com.au/sustainabilitytree/3bl.html)

Integrated Marketing Programs

Integrated marketing is an attempt to stop the ambush marketer (a company that associates with an organisation or event when it has no right to do so). Integrated marketing eliminates competitive advertising and almost guarantees the sponsor wont be ambushed at any level.

Integrated marketing is an effective way of packaging sponsorships. This packaging sees media broadcast rights, advertising, and project and event management as a complete package. This form of packaging is being used extensively in prominent sports like Golf. It makes the outcome of the sponsorship far less risky for companies and requires less human resources input.

Integrated marketing programs incur a premium but they do have the definite advantage that competitors are deterred from attempting the ambush because of the complexity of the task, not to mention the expense of topping a well-planned integrated marketing program.

Television Sponsorship

Sponsorship is purchase of the exploitable rights associated with an event or organisation or entrant. Television sponsorship, on the other hand, is basically an advertising package with extra rights, ie - pull throughs, opening and closing billboards and exclusivity, which associate the advertiser more closely with the event being televised then, say, a one spot advertiser in the same segment. Television sponsorship costs a premium on normal advertising and is one way that television networks maximise advertising revenue during coverage of high profile events. However the viewing public is quite often left with the perception that the television sponsor is an actual sponsor of the event they are viewing, which may or may not be the case.

The danger for event sponsors is that, if they don't also purchase the television sponsorship package on top of the property purchase, they could be ambushed by a competitor and receive little or no coverage of their own logo or brand. It is very simple, and not uncommon, for a television crew to shoot an event and totally exclude the event sponsor's signage.

Growth of Sponsorship

Sponsorships have been embraced worldwide with even China and other Communist nations accepting and encouraging sponsorship. However, this medium has been widely utilised by the Australian, American, Japanese and European communities, as a legitimate and cost effective marketing tool. As long as sponsorship can be proven to be a value for money alternative to mainstream marketing mediums it will have a role in the marketing mix of companies. With sponsorships moving into the marketing plans of major companies, sponsors are increasingly demanding a proven return on investment.

The Advantages of Sponsorship

The value of sponsorships can be measured by the effect they have on the trade and the public. As mentioned earlier, if the public or trade, or worse still both, are not aware of, or uninterested in your sponsorship, returns will be disappointing at best. It is critical that the benefits offered within a sponsorship package can generate the desired returns for a sponsor. Sponsorship programs are proven effective in the following areas:

- **Relationship Marketing**. Sponsorships are an effective vehicle to use when you want to personally relate to a particular group or individual. They provide opportunities to meet at events, host high level client entertainment, entertain the trade, or meet with people of importance. Often an invitation to a high profile event is accepted, where a request for a formal meeting is not.

- **Cost Effective**. Sponsorship, if used properly, can be a very cost effective alternative to mainstream marketing tools such as advertising, direct marketing etc.

- **Self Funding**. Through on-site concessions. For example, beverage companies are unlikely to enter into a relationship that doesn't include vending rights at a major venue.

- **Community Involvement**. Sponsorship allows a company to get involved at the grass roots level, and offer positive benefits to the community it operates within. This obviously generates goodwill and projects a good image for the company involved.

- **Competitive Selling Advantage.** Can be gained through positively influencing the members of the target market provided by the sponsored organisation.

- **Customer Motivation.** Surveys that our company has undertaken have consistently supported the theory that customers are more likely to buy the sponsor's product than a competitors if they approve of the sponsorship. This is providing the product represents good value and is of comparative price to the competitors product.

- **Image Enhancement.** There is no doubt there is a significant rub off for sponsors. When it comes to sponsoring events like the Ballet, Opera, etc. a company's image can be 'refined' considerably.

- **Sell Product.** Most sponsorships offer the ability to sell product, either directly on-site at an event, via an order form in the program, or perhaps by using insertions in a medical charity's mail-out; for example, a medical supplier inserting advertising material and an order form in a medical charity's mail-out to subscribers.

- **Creation of Premium Products.** Premium products are normal products such as t-shirts, caps, key-rings, beer bottle holders, glasses, scarves – the list is virtually endless. These products have both the sponsors badging or association and the sponsored organisation featured on them. This makes them highly desirable items for fans, and an effective advertising medium for the sponsor.

- Sponsorships are excellent for **Niche Marketing** - targeting small defined markets, so it is very important to be able to identify your audiences.

- **Introducing Brands and Products.** Brand introduction works well under sponsorship. Australian telephone company Optus (Singtel) sponsored the opera event Turandot to launch its free call service, with all bookings made on the freecall service.

- **Reinforce Brand Position.** The perception of a consumer brand can be adjusted (positively or negatively) through the sponsorship of high profile events, activities, teams and individuals.

An early example is that tobacco companies' sponsorship of major sports and their stars in the 1970s reinforced the position that it was 'trendy' and 'the thing to do' to smoke the brand of cigarettes being promoted.

- **Associate With Winners**. If a company wants to be seen as a leader in its field, it definitely helps to associate themselves with the winner in another field – usually a sporting endeavour. It is particularly helpful if high profile, well thought of personalities affiliated with the sponsored property endorse the sponsors product or service.

- **Product Sampling**. Sponsorship can offer the opportunity to provide sampling programs at an event/ground etc. For example, a Dairy food supplier providing samples of its products at a major netball tournament.

- **Improve Corporate Image**. Through association. For example a company that sponsors, and therefore associates itself with, a major national counselling service is hoping to send a clear message that it cares for the people within its community.

- **Customer Hospitality**. VIP premium position ticketing is available through most sponsorships, whether it be tickets to a match, show, or an annual charity ball. Through sponsorship you would expect access to the best seats in the house, and usually verbal and visual acknowledgement at the event.

- **Media Exposure**. Can be of brand or company logos or key messages. There is little point in just placing a logo if your company already has very high recall. A "call to action" is of far more value in most cases than just a logo placement.

- **Communicate Product Attributes**. For example if a car is loaned to an international fashion model, the fact that she is using your product can communicate that car's attributes (desirability) to members of your target market.

- **Attitude and Behavioural Change.** Where a sponsorship property is well exploited and utilised, it has the ability to change consumer attitudes and behaviours. A good example of this is the affinity credit cards, whereby a purchase on a certain credit card accrues financial reward for an organisation (usually a charity) supported by the consumer and sponsored by the card issuer.

The Risks

Well selected and professionally managed sponsorships are unlikely to fail to deliver their benefits, or cause embarrassment. There are however exceptions to the rule - the sponsorship of individuals is always risky. Some individuals who have a high profile are hard to control and there is always the danger of the individual's personal habits bringing disrepute to the sponsoring organisation. These habits have, in past years, included: drug violations, allegations of child molestation and violence, to name just a few.

Association with any event or organisation exposes an element of risk through the possibility of accidents etc. To minimise possible damage, it is important to identify and predict all possible risks and then have a suitable crisis management plan in place.

Every sponsorship program is susceptible to risks, which include:

- **Cost blow out.** If a sponsorship is not well managed and does not have the appropriate budgets and plans completed, costs can blow out enormously, negating any benefits that may have been gained from the program.

- **Inappropriate image association.** A sponsorship program can send negative messages if, for example, the star you are sponsoring has a drug habit revealed or is caught cheating.

- **Sponsored organisation's lack of interest or knowledge.** On occasions, the only thing a sponsored organisation is interested in gaining is monetary support. On these occasions, the sponsored organisation does not get to know its sponsor, or their needs, much less deliver benefits to their sponsor/s.

- **Ambush.** It is becoming more and more common for companies to actively seek opportunities to ambush competitors' sponsorship programs.

- **Insufficient allocation of "leverage" funds.** All too often a company will fund the purchase price of a sponsorship, and then not allocate enough budget to allow for leveraging the program to achieve company objectives. (Which were of course in place prior to purchase?)

No sponsorship program will deliver benefits without a genuine effort being made by both sides.

Sponsorship and Company 'Downsizing'

Sponsorship can attract criticism, particularly in difficult economic climates or when a company is downsizing and shedding personnel. If the sponsorship portfolio has been selected for business reasons, and there are clearly stated objectives to be achieved by the program, and it is well managed, it is easy to demonstrate to unions, workforces and media that sponsorship is an integral part of the marketing mix and that the program is contributing to the health of the company.

It should also be remembered that most sponsorships are signed up for a period of 3-5 years. Therefore, a sponsorship may have been signed in a buoyant economic environment, and still be contracted when a company has a downturn, for whatever reason. To pull out of contracted sponsorships during such a period can have a twofold negative effect. Firstly, it gives a negative message to the financial market – when companies pull out of contracted obligations, this is an indication that things are really bad. Secondly, it can expose the company to legal costs that can only make the financial situation worse, and if you have signed a watertight contract, you will inevitably end up having to fulfil your financial obligations to your sponsorship partner.

Legal Entitlements

Sponsors expect, and are legally entitled to, certain rights and benefits with the purchase of a sponsorship. Sponsorship, for sponsors, is a method or a tool to assist them to increase either their bottom line or the public's perception of their organisation.

Sponsored organisations have a legal and moral obligation to deliver agreed rights, to protect their sponsor from ambush and to service their sponsor.

Sponsors have a legal and moral obligation to make payments as and when scheduled in the contract (or otherwise agreed), and to provide any other contracted benefits to the organization or individual they have sponsored.

Longevity

The benefits accruing from sponsorship programs generally accrue over time, and because of this a large number of sponsorships are signed for reasonably long periods. Commonly three-year contracts with the option to renew for a further three are undertaken. Unless you are particularly innovative, or your program/event is continually evolving, it would be unusual to see a sponsorship agreement run past 7 – 10 years.

Summary

- **The sponsor and seeker, on entering a sponsorship, have entered into a commercial agreement or partnership that allows the sponsor to exploit the relationship for commercial gain.**

- **Many activities come under the heading of sponsorship due to the sponsorship being the basis of the relationship. Examples are: cause related marketing, event marketing, sports marketing, arts marketing, experiential marketing etc.**

- **The value of sponsorship can be measured by the effect that they have on the target audience.**

- **So don't forget "SPONSORSHIP IS A BUSINESS TOOL" not a donation!**

Part 2

Streamlining Seekers Processes

Part 2

Streamlining Seekers Processes

Chapter 2

Sponsorship Processes for Seekers

The Processes

Over the past ten years, the costs of having a sponsor have risen quite dramatically. There are in fact many seeker organisations that have at least one sponsorship that is costing them money. Obviously there is no good reason to have a sponsor if you are not making money out of the deal – unless you have signed the sponsorship as a 'loss leader' with a view to increasing the sponsors commitment at the time of renewal.

Too many organisations have multiple sponsors, but do not have a process in place that places a value on those sponsors to their organisation. They have let their sponsorship program grow "willy-nilly", without putting a formal process or structure in place in order to ensure that any sponsorships they gain are adding value to their organisation.

It is our view that every organisation should undertake a review of current sponsorships to ascertain the value returned to the organisation. A sponsorship policy which sets the rules, and a sponsorship strategy detailing the number of sponsors at each level and the rights and benefits to be sold to each should then be written. Plans and evaluations should be completed on an annual basis at the commencement of the program.

The only successful way to manage sponsorships is within a process-orientated framework.

Why Write a Policy?

Prior to seeking sponsorship, an organisation should empower their Sponsorship Manager to do his job. This will require putting the abovementioned process and structure in place. This should mean that the manager can then do the job without having to refer back to senior management.

- The sponsorship policy should state the organisation's objectives for seeking sponsorships (financial, brand building, gain media coverage).

- It should set the rules for entering into sponsorship arrangements including who your organisation will and will not accept as sponsors. Remember – your sponsors must be acceptable to your membership.

- Ensure a uniform approach is taken to seeking and managing sponsorship throughout the organisation.

- State the level of accountability and responsibility required.

- Detail approval delegation(s).

Sponsorship should only be considered for use if it is the most cost effective means of achieving some or all of your organisation's objectives. This requires the ability to predict with some accuracy the impact having a sponsor will have on your organisation.

Sponsorship is not necessarily an easy method of fund raising. It requires a significant commitment both in terms of finances and human resources.

A structured selection process enables the organisation to select the most appropriate sponsor(s).

Policy Checklist

The policy document should be a brief document – only one or two pages. A policy would normally contain the following information:

- A definition of sponsorship as it relates to your organisation.

- Details of the approval process required in order to gain approval for a sponsorship deal.

- The position of the person delegated to approve sponsorship activity.

- Who will be accountable for the success of the sponsorship program.

- How formal the contract or letter of agreement needs to be.

- Statement that the sponsorship must comply with objectives listed in the Sponsorship Strategy document.

- Establish the rules for valuing and payment of sponsorships, including the use of contra/in-kind.

- State what categories of sponsors are acceptable to the membership of the organisation. (It is possible that gambling or alcohol sponsors, for example, may not be acceptable for certain activities. If this is the case, it should be stated in the policy.)

- Who must be informed about the signing of a sponsorship. These could include: the Board, membership, media and PR departments.

- Identify the budgets and accounts that will fund sponsor's expenses as per contract.

- What rights and benefits can or cannot be provided, ie, naming or title rights to the organisation may not be appropriate.

- The minimum profit to be recovered from each level of sponsorship.

- Describe the management process to be undertaken to ensure both parties have achieved their objectives. ie, the use of plans and evaluations.

- Budgetary approval levels. For example, branch level can approve up to $5000 sponsorship.

Sponsorship Policy (example only)

City Council Sponsorship Policy

Purpose

1. The purpose of this policy is to:

    1.1. State the City Council's objectives for entering into sponsorship
          agreements.

    1.2. Set the rules for entering into sponsorship agreements.

    1.3. Ensure a uniform approach is taken to sponsorship throughout the
          City Council.

    1.4. State the level of accountability and responsibility required.

Scope

2. The Sponsorship Policy applies to all of the City Council, including
    operating Departments and Units and associated independent operations.

3. The Sponsorship Policy covers all activities described as sponsorship in
    the definition below regardless of whether:

    -   The sponsorship is in kind (contra) or cash or the City Council is the
        sponsor or seeker (recipient).

Sponsorship Defined

Sponsorship is generally recognised as the purchase of the (usually) intangible exploitable potential rights and benefits associated with an event, entrant, or organisation, which results in tangible benefits (increased awareness of brand, communication of key messages, or sales) for the sponsor that exceeds the purchase price.

3.3   Sponsorship does not include the following:

Donations which are defined as free money with no benefits required, or

Grants that are defined as a sum of money provided or received by the City Council to an organisation for a specific purpose.

Sponsorship Policy for seeking sponsorship support

1.   The City Council has determined that sponsorships are to be sought to deliver the Council's Mission cost effectively, through:

- Reducing costs to the Council.
- Supplementing the existing budget to provide additional services.
- Demonstrating the Council's commitment to community service through community partnership described as payments made to Business Units for cost input or service delivery outputs that wouldn't normally occur in a business environment.
- Encouraging regional economic development.
- Adding value to Council activities.
- Achieving greater utilisation of tangible and intangible assets and increasing the Council's return on investment.
- Extending the ability to be a catalyst for projects and programs of benefit to the City.
- Contributing positively to the corporate image of the Council.

2.   All personnel involved in approaching potential sponsors on behalf of the Council must have been accredited as attending the City Council Sponsorship Workshop.

3.   All sponsorship activity is to be reported and registered to the Mayor's Office prior to canvassing potential sponsors:

- To avoid situations of conflict.
- To enable appropriate acknowledgment of sponsors by the Mayor and in Council publications, including the Annual Report.
- To ensure adequate return.

4.   A sponsorship agreement must not impose or imply conditions that would limit, or appear to limit, the City Council's ability to carry out its functions fully and impartially.

5.   Where a division of the Council has regulatory or inspectorial responsibilities, the area undertaking the policing should not seek sponsorship from parties likely to be subject to regulation or inspection during the life of the sponsorship.

6.   Sponsorship and explicit endorsement of products and or services of a sponsor must be in the public interest and must be approved by the Council or its delegate.

7.   Sponsorships that could involve the City Council in controversial issues or expose the Council to adverse criticism must be avoided. The following sponsors are regarded as being inappropriate:

- A sponsor that is at odds with local government policy directly or indirectly.

- A sponsor who does not meet community standards relating to "good taste".
- A sponsor whose products or services are at odds with the City Council's duty of care, aims or objectives
- No sponsorships should be received or sought from individuals or corporations who are party to significant tendering processes at the time. This is not to preclude existing contractors but only those where immediate or likely future benefit from tendering for Council business could accrue.

8. All sponsorship properties must have a detailed plan, which states the real cost of the sponsorship program to the City Council. As most sponsorship programs require extensive project management to enable the promised sponsor benefits to be delivered the anticipated staff costs must be detailed. The plan must detail who will be accountable for the overall success of the sponsorship program.

9. Contra (goods and or services in lieu of cash) received must be valued at the cost price the Council would have to pay for those goods and services. Benefits given from a sponsorship program must reflect the retail value of the products and services given.

10. Sponsorships must be approved by the Mayor or the delegated manager (listed below) on the Sponsorship approval form.

- Sponsorship programs with a value of up to $25,000 must be approved by the relevant Manager subject to the relevant business plan.
- Sponsorships valued in excess of $25,000 must be referred to the Chairman together with the Manager's recommendation for approval for consideration by the relevant Committee of Council.

11. All sponsorships must be subject to a written agreement which is formally recorded and must contain:

- Up to $25,000 - a letter of agreement signed by both parties.
- Over $25,000 - a contract must be prepared and approved by the Director of Legal Services.

Sponsorship Strategy - The Politics, The Benefits

The Sponsorship Strategy details the fundamental approach to procuring sponsorships. It details the packaging of rights and benefits to various levels of sponsors. It also details the overall amount of funding to be sought.

A Sponsorship Strategy has the potential to be a highly political document. It is written by the head of the sponsorship area and usually approved by the CEO, Marketing Director and sometimes the Board. It should be updated annually.

Once this document is approved by the relevant stakeholders it gives the Sponsorship Manager a free hand to get on with the job and provides an approved platform from which to get the job done.

The Contents

A sponsorship strategy generally contains the following:

- A **Situation Analysis** of the organisation and the environment it operates within and details current sponsorship agreements relative to the overall sponsorship structure.

- The broad **Objectives** for seeking sponsorship.

- Desired **Sponsors** to be targeted.

- An **action or implementation timetable** detailing when sponsorships are due for renewal, and those that are available to be sold.

- The overall **sponsorship budget,** detailing the level of funding required. It should also detail the costs associated with seeking and servicing a sponsor.

- Detail **the annual review process** (with respect to the overall sponsorship portfolio).

- The **Stakeholders** signature/s.

Guide to Writing the Strategy

1. Define your Objectives for seeking sponsorship.   Your objectives might include only one, or a number of the following:

- Fundraising
- Fund additional programs
- Generate brand awareness (media and publicity)
- Provide member benefits
- Provide contra (goods in kind) to facilitate planned activities.

2. Identify Sponsorship Structure

You will need to identify the number of levels of sponsorship you wish to offer, and how many sponsors you will have at each level to deliver the required level of funding. Do not forget to include your current sponsors in this process. It may be that you will decide not to pursue some of them at the end of the current contract period.

You will not have an infinite number of benefits to offer, and therefore your structure will, to a large extent, be dictated by what you have to offer.

In undertaking this exercise, you will need to keep in mind that the more sponsors you have, the more staff you will need to service them, and the more the servicing will cost. Also, sponsors almost always prefer to have a minimal number of co-sponsors at any given level.

It is important that your current sponsors are kept aware of where they will fit into your new structure, how many co-sponsors they will have at their level, and how many sponsors will be above them in the final hierarchy. (See Chapter 8, Packaging Sponsorships.)

3. Action Plan

The action plan in the strategy document details dates for renewal of sponsors and identifies available sponsorship properties to be offered to potential sponsors.

4. Budget

The strategy budget details gross revenues to be achieved and the costs of having a sponsor – including sales and service.

5. Annual Review

This segment of the strategy details the review process to be undertaken annually in terms of reviewing the strategic direction and make-up of the overall sponsorship program.

6. Identify stakeholders in this document

Getting the strategy document approved requires the identification of stakeholders and getting them on side prior to putting the document up for approval. Stakeholders could, and probably will, include the following:

- Board members. This will relate to both personal interest, and expenditure on behalf of shareholders.
- CEO
- Senior management must be committed to the portfolio.
- Sales team. They must support the program and believe in the value of sponsorship.

Summary

- Take time to make sure your processes are right – at the beginning, not as an afterthought.

- The policy sets the rules for successful sponsorship.

- The strategy determines the number of sponsors, the levels of sponsorship and how the rights and benefits will be divided between sponsors.

- Strategy should be revisited on an annual basis.

Part 3

The Art of Selling Sponsorship

Chapter 3

Is Sponsorship Right for Us?

Sponsorships are Hard Work!

Sponsorship should not be seen as an easy method of fund raising. Sourcing sponsorship is an expensive exercise in both time and money, with both perseverance and (often) a healthy ego required to succeed! Once you have successfully sold a sponsor your property the hard work starts! Legal contracts should be signed, and then the commitment of both financial and human resources servicing of the sponsor commences. On entering into a sponsorship agreement, you have entered into a commercial arrangement with a company. You have agreed to assign various rights to your sponsor or sponsors, and also to deliver certain benefits that will allow them to achieve the marketing and communication objectives they have assigned to the sponsorship program.

Donations

Sponsorships are often confused with donations. A donation is just that - a gift of product or cash with little or no expected return. Our definition of donation is 'free money' with no strings attached, and no return benefits or favours expected.

Those organisations seeking sponsorship that want cash to support their organisation's activities but are not prepared to provide tangible benefits in exchange are not seeking a sponsorship. They are seeking a donation in order to fund programs, or perhaps even stay viable. It is very important to distinguish between these two fundraising methods.

It is obviously dishonest to offer a menu of benefits to a sponsor, sign the agreement, take the money and then not deliver the benefits - in fact your organisation would be in breach of contract, whether or not a formal document was signed!

We cannot emphasise enough that sponsorship is not philanthropy (donating). Sponsorships are a business tool used by various companies to achieve defined marketing and communication objectives.

Grants

Grants are most often a once only financial payment (assistance) provided by government, foundation or trust in order to assist in the development of a project, purchase of an artwork, educational endeavours or similar. Grants are almost always non-commercial in nature, in fact in some places it is illegal to ask for commercial benefits in return for the bestowing of a grant, so it is worth checking local legislation. Generally the benefit is in the delivery of the activity or item supported by the grant.

Partner

A partner may be sought where an event or organisation requires substantial funds to underwrite a project. The partner will enter into an agreement with the seeker of the funds and will have rights to the project or venue for its useful life, or for an agreed lengthy period. Usually funding is via a once only payment at the commencement of the project.

Checklist - Is Sponsorship Right for Us?

To assist you to make the decision as to whether seeking sponsorship is the right direction for your organisation, it may be worth working through the points below.

Answer each question, and if unsure go to relevant chapter in this book. If any of your responses are negative it may be worth reconsidering trying to sell sponsorship?

1. Do you have rights or benefits that you can offer a sponsor?

Companies will only sponsor you if you are going to offer rights and/or benefits that will have a positive effect on their company, for example, improve their image, increase their sales, provide a competitive advantage, offer exclusivity, increase awareness of brand or product within a defined group, change attitudes of consumers. (For more detail see Chapter 5 - Identifying Benefits to Attract Sponsors.)

2. Are your members and/or target audience likely to approve of commercial sponsorship?

Commercial sponsorship is seen by some as 'selling out', although there is an increasing awareness of the benefits of sponsorship for the sponsored organisation within the community. Most organisations members are now aware that as government funding for a variety of organizations has decreased, sponsorship is necessary for survival. For sponsorship to work for both parties it must have the support of your members, staff, Board and target audiences. If any groups within your organisation are not positively disposed towards commercial sponsorship, or are not prepared to support the sponsor, sponsorship may not be appropriate for your organisation. Many sponsors may want to be active within your organisation, which could be seen as threat by some members. For a sponsorship to be successful it must have broad support from every level within your organisation.

3. Are you a hot property?

Selling sponsorships is like selling property. Those sponsorships that are seen as "hot properties" will be in high demand, even in down times. Mediocre sponsorship properties will usually sell, but may not receive the price you hoped for. The bottom of the market will always be hard to sell, and may not sell at all because it is difficult for potential sponsors to see the value now, or in the future.

A hot property traditionally has a known point of difference. It usually has one or more of the following:

- Avid fans (fans is an abbreviation for fanatics)
- High participation rates

- High reach and frequency (reach is the number of people affected, and frequency is how often they are affected)
- Significant sales returns
- Right timing
- High awareness of activity
- Extensive media/TV coverage of activity
- Regular occurrence

4. Are any companies not suitable sponsors for you?

Identify any potential sponsors who would be unacceptable to your group. For example, if your organisation were involved with children's issues, neither gaming companies nor producers of alcohol would be suitable sponsors. If you were to accept support from such companies, the relationship would be viewed very cynically by the public.

5. Do you have the human resources to sell and run the sponsorship?

Selling and servicing sponsors often proves to be very time consuming. If you are promising to deliver a number of rights and benefits to a sponsor make sure you have the people to deliver what you have promised.

6. To seek sponsorship, or not to seek sponsorship?

You should now make the decision whether or not to seek sponsorship based on the conclusions you have come to on the previous questions. Your next move may be to commission research or seek professional advice in order to ascertain the likelihood of selling your property.

Summary

- Sponsorship should not be seen as an easy method of fund raising.

- Sponsorship is a commercial arrangement providing tangible benefits to the sponsor – ensure you can offer them.

- Sourcing sponsorship is an expensive exercise in both time and money.

- Ensure your staff, membership and audience will be comfortable with the sponsor, and supportive of the sponsor's objectives.

- Determine if your property is saleable.

- In addition, be sure you have all the resources available to deliver the sponsorship rights and benefits promised to the sponsor.

Chapter 4

Guiding Principles for Selling Sponsorship

The Proposition

Assume you were attracted to a member of the opposite sex whom you have not met and vice versa. Would you consider writing to them seeking a relationship by detailing the assets that they might find attractive about you: Tall, beautiful, rich, the right family connections, drive a Mercedes convertible, etc? We would suggest if you attempted to facilitate a personal relationship in this manner there would only be an outside chance of a positive answer from a prospective beau.

Our contention is that the reason most sponsorship propositions that arrive as unsolicited mail result in a negative response is due to the fact that a potential sponsor is unlikely to enter into a business relationship when they don't personally know you; haven't been introduced and probably know little or nothing about your organisation or event.

We therefore suggest that the age old and most common method of soliciting sponsorship, the unsolicited letter, is flawed. Increasingly it appears that sponsorships are based on 'win win' commercial and human relationships, and that the relationship needs to be formed first, with the request for a sponsorship relationship coming later.

The Average Marriage

We would like to share an interesting statistic with you.

The average sponsorship lasts about the same length of time as the average marriage. Not so surprising really, when you consider that this is due mainly to the fact that sponsorships are based around human relationships.

The sponsorship relationship is between the sponsored organisation and the sponsoring company. The human relationships are usually between the sponsored organisation's marketing manager and the sponsor's sponsorship manager or marketing manager. The commercial relationship is between the sponsored organisation's image or lifestyle and the sponsor's image or product.

Sponsorships are a very sophisticated form of relationship marketing and offer the opportunity for the sponsor to undertake experiential marketing. In the sponsorship relationship, two parties get together to further their own goals through the sponsorship union. This occurs through the parties exploiting the sponsorship relationship or association, with the sponsor exploiting the benefits to maximise the return to the sponsor's bottom line profit, and the seeker exploiting the association through financial gain and the kudos of associating with the sponsor's image and reputation.

The Sponsorship Unit Relationship Model

Let's now turn our minds to the order in which personal, and sponsorship, relationships generally unfold:

The Attraction

Initially one party is attracted to the other. Either the potential sponsor is attracted to the benefits an organisation has to offer, or an organisation is attracted to the sponsors money and image.

The Approach

This phase is not dissimilar to the human relationship where one party has to make the bold move of introducing themselves to the other party. This is often the most difficult part of the entire process.

Courting

During the courting process you and the potential sponsor determine whether or not you can both achieve your individual organisation's goals through a sponsorship relationship. If you both decide that you "like the look of each other" you will then get to know each other and the information exchange will commence.

Proposal

The question is asked, usually verbally, and in the sponsorship relationship, this is followed up in writing. It should be noted that the vast majority of successful sponsorship proposals occur following the approach and the courting phases of the relationship, not directly after the initial attraction.

Engagement

If the response is yes, you then have a verbal agreement to enter into a marriage. This is when the date is set, and the contracts are drawn up. The agreement has occurred.

Marriage

The marriage occurs, and for it to work the relationship has to be 'win win'. The old saying it takes 'two to make it work' applies to sponsorships as much as it does to human relationships. The one problem with most sponsorship relationships is that all the parties are bigamous, and they tend to look after those partners who they personally prefer.

Affairs

Sponsorship affairs are reasonably common, and just like personal relationships, they are damaging. This is where a property owner (the seeker) sets their sights on a new partner, and in doing so, their attention is diverted away from their current partner. The addition of new partners often makes the sponsor feel less valued, and they may leave and look for a new partner elsewhere.

Divorce

Sadly, marriages are breaking down regularly, and, not to trivialise divorce, probably for many of the same reasons as sponsorship relationships fail. The sponsorship breakdown, or divorce, can occur for a multitude of reasons, but the majority are due to either a breakdown in communications between the parties or a change of personnel or objectives by either side.

The majority of sponsorships are based on human relationships that form between the two parties involved, and in fact most fail due to the departure of either the Seeker's or sponsor's representative; the two parties not getting on or, sometimes, because the sponsor's objectives have been achieved, and there is nothing to be gained by extending the relationship.

The Sponsorship Unit's Rules of Selling Sponsorships

Selling sponsorship may be considered an art (if not a downright gift!) but there are a number of guiding rules that can dramatically improve your chance of achieving the elusive sale. The overall principal to keep in mind is provide value for money and be creative!

Rule One - offer an opportunity and not a problem!

Putting it in a different way: Ask not what your sponsor can do for you, but demonstrate what you can do for your sponsor!

Offering the sponsor an opportunity and not a problem is the single most important rule to successfully selling sponsorships! The reason for the outstanding success of this rule is the fact that the overwhelming majority of sponsorship proposals sent to companies are presenting the potential sponsor with a major problem, or at the very least a great deal of additional work.

What is the Problem?

Many proposals offer a very standard package, containing an endless list of possible benefits for the sponsor.

These might include naming rights, signage, media coverage, access to national heroes etc. In return for granting the use of these benefits, the organisation or individual wants to be paid - preferably in cash, if not in contra (free goods and services). The value placed on the sponsorship package has usually been unscientifically, but very artfully, packaged to give the impression of value for money. We hear you say *"So what is the problem"?* Well the problem is that you want the potential sponsor's money. Sadly for those seeking sponsorship support, the days of money being handed out with gay abandon are well and truly over.

Most companies have one person charged with responding to sponsorship requests. That person is aware of budget constraints and the need for all money spent to impact positively on their company's bottom line. They will spend considerable time perusing your proposal (and up to fifty others each day) and in the majority of cases will decline your request. Should your proposal look to be particularly good value for money, or appear to be targeting this company's critical target market, it is far more likely that this person will research your proposal further, and the odds are much higher that your proposal will eventually be taken up.

So how do you beat the odds and use the rule to your advantage? The secret is to offer a solution to a company's problems. This could be anything from returning a positive bottom line result through increased sales, to influencing a person of importance to the company. Let me give you an example:

Seagulls Generate Sponsorship Funds

A major car manufacturer had a problem. Their manufacturing plant was situated near a substantial outdoor rubbish dump. Said dump was the feeding ground for over ten thousand seagulls that had made the adjacent factory roof their home. The seagulls had to commute from home to the dump and back, and the most direct route was directly over the car park used for storage of brand new vehicles that had just been rolled off the assembly line. Following feeding, the return trip required a toilet stop, commonly over the new cars, causing the car manufacturer to spend significant time, money and effort cleaning the cars.

The car company tried all the usual methods of discouraging the birds, from scarecrows, chilli painted on the roof to scatter guns borrowed from the local airport - all to little or no avail.

The saga was reported in the local press and an entrepreneurial zoo marketeer contacted the car manufacturer with an offer of a solution to their problem - in exchange for a modest sponsorship. A deal was struck and the zoo, which nursed birds of prey back to health, flew their birds of prey over the factory on a regular basis with the result that the seagulls have now taken up residence elsewhere, resulting in a half million dollar a year saving in cleaning cars. The zoo struck up a happy association with the car manufacturer.

As companies are in business to return a dividend to their shareholders or owners you have to be able to offer potential sponsors opportunities that are too good to refuse. This requires you to identify how your organisation can provide the potential sponsor with a bottom line saving or profit.

Don't forget you must be able to make the sponsor's investment of time and money in your organisation justifiable in measurable returns to their company's bottom line.

Rule Two - Target the right companies with the right Target audience fit.

Make Sure It Fits! It is critically important that your organisation can clearly detail to potential sponsors the make up of your audience demographics, psychographics and geographic location, and you may need to commission research to gain this information.

It is a general rule that international companies will sponsor large international events (for example, look at Soccer sponsors), national companies will sponsor national events (for example, National Leagues) and local businesses will focus on local activities within their region (ie, the local footy club). The exception to this is where a large international or national company will sponsor activities within the areas of their plants and operations. (See Chapter 7 – Methods of Identifying Potential Sponsors.)

Rule Three – Offer benefits the company can exploit

Every company undertakes sponsorship for a slightly different reason and may therefore require substantially different rights. Keep in mind that these requirements can change within the same company over time. (See Chapter 5 – Identifying Benefits to Attract Sponsors.)

Rule Four – Price your property competitively and offer value for money

Price your property to ensure your organisation is going to benefit from the relationship and that the sponsor will succeed in making a profit from the association. Make sure your property is priced similarly to comparable properties.

The package should be priced realistically (at market value). The old adage that any house will sell at the market price does not hold with sponsorship, due to the constant over supply of sponsorship properties. Price the property competitively - not at what you require to run your event or organisation, or what you <u>think</u> the property is worth, but at market price. Make sure any potential sponsor being approached can afford the sponsorship. (See Chapter 6 –'Methods for Valuing Your Sponsorship'.)

Rule Five – Stand out from the clutter

Large companies receive many proposals each day and the vast majority of those receive little more than a cursory glance. Therefore you must ensure that the right person reads your proposal. That is the person who has the power to say yes. There are commonly many people with the power to say no but only one or two who can say yes, so make sure your proposal is addressed or delivered to the appropriate person (often the contents of a courier bag are treated with more respect than an envelope received in the mail.)

There are a couple of methods that deliver more favourable results. One involves having a relationship and knowing the person you are applying for sponsorship from, and the other involves a stunt to catch the attention of the recipient of your request. A couple of stunts that come to mind include:

- A food and wine festival that originally sent in excess of fifty sponsorship requests to various companies and had a 100% fail rate. They subsequently sent a bottle of wine to the same companies, this time featuring the sponsorship proposal on the wine label. This resulted in a very high positive response rate.

- A company already sponsored by Reebok despatched one running shoe to a number of potential sponsors and stated if they wanted the other they had to attend a meeting to be briefed about the sponsorship. It will probably come as no surprise to learn that the vast majority of invitees accepted the invitation.

If you are going to use a stunt make sure it is interesting and relevant, and not annoying or dangerous. (See Chapter 9 – Approaching Potential Sponsors and Understanding the Request Process.)

Rule Six – Be professional and credible

Your organisation may be made up of volunteers, however, a company is unlikely to allocate funds to your organisation if your operation appears amateurish, much less forge a close relationship with you. Make sure your representatives always present themselves in a professional manner, and portray an understanding of what is required of a commercial relationship.

It is important your organisation has credibility in the community and a track record of delivering value for money will make it significantly easier to gain sponsorship support.

Rule Seven – Be persistent – not a pest

There is a fine line between being persistent and being a pest. It will take time for a potential sponsor to come to grips with what you are offering and for a relationship to grow and develop. Without developing the relationship there is less chance of a sponsorship deal being struck. It is quite acceptable to be professionally persistent in your follow up to your sponsorship request, but never be so persistent that you interrupt the recipient's ability to do their job.

If you have been denied sponsorship support, on most occasions, you must accept that there are very good reasons why your request has been declined, such as; the budget already having been allocated elsewhere; the money is simply not there; your proposal clashes with something else the company is doing, and so on.

The Sales Process

The successful sale of a sponsorship property depends on you and your organisation providing the potential sponsor with an opportunity to have a mutually rewarding business relationship. You can build this relationship by offering opportunities to generate awareness, build sales, reduce costs or provide some other benefit that is of direct value to your potential sponsor. When an advertising agency recommends and sells the space for a commercial on television to a client, the recommendation is not generally made on the basis of a statement such as, "this is a really good program, therefore you should purchase advertising space during it". It is sold on the basis of how many people are viewing the program and the make up of that audience in terms of demographics, therefore it is imperative that, wherever possible, you sell your sponsorship in terms of the type and make up of the audience you can provide to the sponsor.

The corporate reaction to a request for sponsorship

On receipt of a request for sponsorship, companies seek the answers to three questions, so make sure you have provided the answers.

1. **What am I being asked to sponsor** (event, organisation description). When and where does it happen?

2. **What benefits will my company receive** (list of possible tangible benefits)?

3. **How much this going to cost?**

The answers to these three questions will enable a potential sponsor to understand what they are being asked to sponsor, and if the potential results justify the cash outlay.

Let's have a quick look at some tactics that have successfully assisted Seekers to obtain the sponsor of their choice.

Free sponsorships - performance based sponsorships

If you have a potential sponsor who is interested in sponsoring you or your organisation, but is worried about some aspect of the property, (usually your lack of track record in managing sponsorships) consider giving the potential sponsor a free trial *with the proviso* that if you meet pre-set criteria the sponsor will pay you on achieving those pre-set goals.

Another option is to base the fee to be paid by the sponsor on your success in delivering the sponsor's objectives (make sure you get these – in writing – up front!).

This option removes the risk factor for the sponsor and may help you clinch a long-term sponsor.

Ballot sponsorships

This form of sponsorship selling is not uncommon in small organisations like regional football clubs. This process sees a relatively large number of sponsorships sold for a relatively small amount. Once all sponsors have been secured, a draw will take place with one of the purchasers receiving all the major rights, including naming rights. The losers commonly receive benefits that are equivalent to their outlay in tickets and advertising in club newsletters and ground signage.

Summary

The Sponsorship Unit's Rules of Selling Sponsorships

- Offer an opportunity and not a problem - demonstrate what you can do for your sponsor!

- Target the right companies with the right target audience fit

- Offer benefits the company can exploit

- Price your property competitively and offer value for money

- Stand out from the clutter

- Be professional

- Be persistent - not a pest

- Prove to a potential sponsor that you are sound financial managers and are credible

Chapter 5

Identifying Benefits to Attract Sponsors

As we keep stressing, sponsorship is, above all else, about offering a second party (the potential sponsor) an opportunity to commercially gain from the sponsorship relationship with your organisation. It is therefore important that the potential sponsor is able to identify your organisation's composition, probable effect on its audiences and public, and the opportunities you can provide through assigning rights and benefits to them. You consequently need to be able to identify and convey the following information to the sponsor. This requires an accurate analysis of your property to be undertaken by you or perhaps an independent third party.

1. **Organisation's composition.** You must be able to clearly demonstrate your organisation's membership and its audiences make up in terms of demographics, psychographic, and geographic data.

2. **General public's perceptions.** You must also be able to demonstrate that the general public perceive your organisation's activities in a positive manner.

3. **Potential rights and benefits.** Your proposal must convince a potential sponsor that the rights and benefits you can provide will result in either a positive commercial return, or improved public perception of their company's image.

Identifying Your Organisation's Composition

If your organisation doesn't already have this information, it is imperative that some research is conducted. This could be achieved by surveying both your members and your organisation's audiences via a questionnaire. Depending on the size of your organisation, usually between one and two hundred respondents will give you a fairly accurate overview of your organisation.

The following information is required for a sponsor to make an informed judgement about your organisation: (As mentioned above, this can be gained from a simple, voluntary survey.)

- **Demographics.** The vital and social statistics of populations. Might include information relating to your membership such as: age, education, ethnic back ground, family size, income, occupation, sex, and social class

- **Geographic make up.** Pertains to the geographic characteristics of your audience. Would indicate where the audience and your membership reside by region or regions, in your state only, nationally or internationally.

- **Psychographic.** This would give an overall indication of your group's lifestyles and personalities.

Other information to be included (obviously if this information is insignificant, leave it out.)

1. Number of participants in a given period
2. Frequency of contact with your organisation in a given period
3. Members attitudes to current sponsors and their products
4. Attitudes to your organisation and its activities held by the general public and media

Public's Attitude To Your Organisation, Personalities, And Its Membership

If you are offering as a benefit the probability of attracting the attention of your organisation or activity's audiences, as mentioned in point 3. above, you need to know how they actually feel about your activities, and whether in fact they will be positively disposed towards a sponsor. Perceptions may not always in fact be accurate but they are real in the mind of the audience and therefore valid.

1. Who are your fans?
2. Are they prepared to support your sponsor?
3. What is your public profile?

Individuals

1. Are you an individual or a team athlete, and if a team member, who are your team's sponsors?
2. Indicate that you are presentable and will be an asset to a sponsor.
3. Where do you train, reside and work, and where are most of your events held, ie, in the one state, nationally or internationally?

Organisational Profile (example)

South Alligator River Yacht Club

The South Alligator River Yacht Club has 2036 active members. Of these 80 % sail in club races every weekend. The majority of the members are made up of family groups of high disposable income ($50,000pa plus). 93% of members are able to name our club's major sponsor and their products, and 78% state that they will choose a sponsors product in preference to a non sponsors product, assuming the sponsor's products are of a similar quality and value.

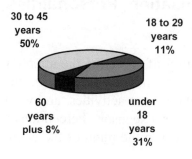

30 to 45 years 50%

18 to 29 years 11%

60 years plus 8%

under 18 years 31%

Age

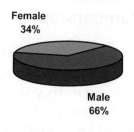

Female 34%

Male 66%

Gender

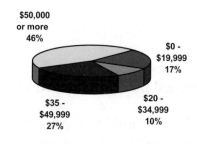

$50,000 or more 46%

$0 - $19,999 17%

$35 - $49,999 27%

$20 - $34,999 10%

Income

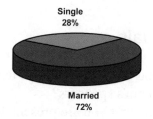

Single 28%

Married 72%

Marital Status

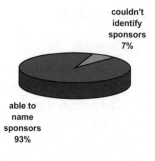

couldn't identify sponsors 7%

able to name sponsors 93%

Awareness of sponsors

Undecided 22%

Choose Sponsors Product 78%

Propensity to choose sponsors products

Some important questions you must ask are included in the attached sample questionnaire. The information on this survey can not only be used in the pursuit of new sponsors but also during the evaluation and renegotiation period for existing sponsors by demonstrating your success in promoting the sponsorship to your membership and audiences.

The Sponsorship Unit Awareness Questionnaire
(A clean copy of this questionnaire can be found in Appendix 1.)

The following questions may be asked at any time with no charge provided the copyright held by The Sponsorship Unit is displayed at the bottom of your questionnaire as follows © The Sponsorship Unit 1994.

1. Can you name any sponsor(s) of your organisation?

1 _____ 2 _____

3 _____ 4 _____

This question is asked to demonstrate the current awareness of your sponsors. This enables you to gauge your effectiveness at promoting your sponsors to your audience and membership. If this rating is high you can use this information to demonstrate to a potential sponsor that you are capable of promoting awareness to your group and its audiences. (Note: If the rating is low, you are doing something wrong - perhaps you are not putting in the required effort!)

Please indicate how you feel about the following statements:

2. When I see products made by companies who sponsor (your organisation, event, or sporting team), it makes me more likely to choose that brand?

    ❑ Agree Strongly
    ❑ Agree Somewhat
    ❑ Neutral
    ❑ Disagree Somewhat
    ❑ Disagree Strongly

Assuming your research agrees with that undertaken by The Sponsorship Unit, these research results can become a very powerful selling tool, as you are able to demonstrate that your membership and its audience are more likely to buy a sponsor's product over a non sponsor's provided they are aware of the sponsorship relationship.

Regular research conducted by The Sponsorship Unit Pty Ltd indicates that an organisation's members and their audiences are likely to react in the following manner: Agree strongly (25 to 40%), Agree somewhat (30 to 55 %), neutral (0 to 20 %), Disagree somewhat (0%), Disagree strongly, (0 to 10%).

3. **When I see products made by companies who sponsor and support (the category, ie., charities, the environment, particular sports), it makes me more likely to choose that brand?**

    ❑   Agree Strongly
    ❑   Agree Somewhat
    ❑   Neutral
    ❑   Disagree Somewhat
    ❑   Disagree Strongly

Regular research conducted by The Sponsorship Unit Pty Ltd indicates that an organisation's members and their audiences are likely to react in the following manner: Agree strongly (20 to 35%), Agree somewhat (20 to 55 %), neutral (0 to 30 %), Disagree somewhat (0), Disagree strongly, (0 to 10%).

4. **When I see products made by companies who sponsor (opposition organisations or sporting teams) I don't support, it makes me less likely to choose that brand?**

    ❑   Agree Strongly
    ❑   Agree Somewhat
    ❑   Neutral
    ❑   Disagree Somewhat
    ❑   Disagree Strongly

This question is particularly useful where your organisation is a team competing against other teams in a competition. These results should demonstrate that your audiences and members are not one eyed and will not cause a negative impact for the sponsor in the eyes of competing organisations.

In regular research conducted by The Sponsorship Unit Pty Ltd, an organisation's members and their audiences are likely to react in the following manner: Agree strongly (20 to 35%), Agree somewhat (20 to 55 %), neutral (0 to 30 %), Disagree somewhat (0), Disagree strongly, (0 to 10%).

5. **Can you name any sponsors in the (insert potential sponsors product) category.**

This will provide an indication of awareness of various potential sponsors.

6. **Have you used (insert potential sponsors product category), if so, how long ago?**

❑   Last week
❑   This month
❑   This year

This will provide information that could be relevant to selling your sponsorship.

If relevant, include questions relating to demographic and geographic information.

Demographics

- age
- education
- ethnic background
- family size
- income
- occupation
- sex
- income bracket

Geographic

- local
- state wide
- nationally
- internationally

Methods for Identifying Benefits

The question you should ask while preparing your proposal will be: *"What do we own that someone else wants"?* The best method of answering this question is to organise a group of people who are very familiar with your organisation and hold a brainstorming session to identify all activities, events, advertising mediums and networking opportunities that a sponsor could exploit to reinforce the relationship and promote products and services to your organisations market.

Rules for Your Brainstorming Session

1. Every person to suggest ideas and every idea must be written down no matter how ridiculous or outrageous it may be.

2. Any group member can add to, or change, any idea to improve it.

3. Once all ideas have been written down, the group should discuss the viability of each idea and place a rating against it (eg, 1 = high, 5 = low) based on ease of implementing and its appeal to potential sponsors.

List of Possible Benefits

Some, or all, of the following list of rights and benefits can be provided through sponsorship. Bear in mind that, depending on the sponsor and their commercial needs, they may only want one of these benefits, or they may want 'the lot'.

Sales

Your organisation and/or its members guaranteed purchase of product can be a powerful incentive for a sponsor to come on board, especially if there are multiple providers of product in the category. For example, with banks now being deregulated your assurance that you would use the services of the targeted bank would be an attractive benefit to offer. Similarly, telecommunications is now a competitive field, and set to become even more so in the future, so if you offered as a benefit that you would shift your business to a new telecommunications operation, that would be a point in your favour.

In other words, indicate that you would always choose a sponsor's product, whether it be food, beverage or services, over a non sponsor's goods. Also indicate that you would actively lobby your members to choose a sponsor's product.

Naming Rights / Title Sponsorship

This is the situation where the sponsored organisation has the right to have their identity included as part of your organisation's name. ie, "Jays Joggers Football Club", or, "The Volvo Round The World Yacht Race".

The value of naming rights can be questionable, or the very least slow in being recognised by the media, when offered to an event that is well known. For example, the sponsor's name, Fosters, is not required to identify The Melbourne Cup, although over time the recognition will grow - but it can take some years. Wherever possible make the sponsors name the identifier, ie, The Optus Oval - you can't just call it 'the oval'. To do so does not identify which oval you are talking about, so in that instance naming rights work well.

Exclusivity

The ability of a sponsor to lock out their competitors from a high profile event is often regarded as a powerful marketing tool in its own right. This means that the organisation and its members will use the sponsor's product exclusively, and only the sponsor will have the right to advertise in the organisation's publications, and only the sponsor's name and logo will be displayed on any signage.

The level of exclusivity can vary substantially from total exclusivity (only one sponsor) to category exclusivity, ie the only beverage sponsoring, only financial institution sponsoring, etc.

Networking

Can your membership or its management provide opportunities for the sponsor to meet people of importance to their business. For example, potential clients or government and regulatory representatives who you are able to introduce either formally or informally. There is no doubt that personal relationships help companies to succeed in business.

Merchandising Rights

This is the right of sponsor(s) to market their product to your organisation's members and audience. This is a common category for, say, a beverage company to take in a sporting club. For example, you may offer Coca Cola the right to be the only beverage in that category to be sold at your venues and events. You can only offer this benefit if you hold the rights to do so, eg, if you have not sold the venue rights to a catering company.

Media and Publicity

Is your organisation able to provide favourable media and publicity exposure of the sponsors corporate and product identity? If so, how much? You will need to be able to quantify this by producing articles that have been published historically that include coverage of current or past sponsors' products and identity. Do not forget that any articles that feature your organisation but do not feature a sponsor's image or identity are of no value whatsoever to your sponsor.

Signage

Signage is a regularly offered benefit and can be offered on an endless variety of items, ranging from your members' apparel, your stationary, venue signage, vehicles, drink coasters, flags, tickets, grass signage – the list is endless.

Advertising

Can your organisation or event be tied in with the sponsor's conventional advertising? This will not only promote your event but also reinforce the association between the sponsor and your organisation.

The provision of exclusive advertising in your publications, through your mailing list or during your regular media coverage adds a significant point of difference. If you have sold the rights to your programs and publications to a third party, you will need to have, prior to offering this benefit to a sponsor, agreed with the third party that they will honour these exclusive rights.

If you allow non-advertisers to advertise in your publications and programs, you are minimising the benefits of being a sponsor, because obviously advertising non-exclusivity will allow competitors of your sponsor entree to the very same audience that your sponsor has paid a premium to access.

Sampling

Is there the opportunity for the sponsor to demonstrate their products attributes to your audience and your members at events, meetings, annual dinner dances, etc?

Personality Availability

The use of personalities, patrons, stars and their likenesses and success stories, can be used by the sponsor for advertising their product. Personalities may make appearances at promotions, client meetings, public meetings, for staff motivation purposes, demonstrating product use, and one many other occasions. Any third party use (sponsor) of personalities or their likenesses needs to be contracted and approved prior to use.

Client Entertainment Facilities

Does your organisation have events at which your sponsor can entertain important clients? If so can you provide a meal, refreshments, the best seat(s) in the house, VIP entrance, VIP parking, gifts that will remind the clients of the experience? Creating something special and unique can be very popular – for example dinner on a theatre set, back of house tours and visits to areas the general public cannot normally get to, such as the pits at a car race or the dressing rooms at a theatre.

You may be very familiar and comfortable with your facilities, but before you offer them as a benefit to a potential sponsor, cast a jaundiced eye over them, and ensure that they don't need a 'spruce up' before they are of a suitable standard for business entertaining.

Function Facilities

If you have venues or facilities that your sponsor could utilise for functions, such as staff training sessions, conventions and conferences or staff parties make sure you include this as a no cost benefit in your contract.

It may result in unused facilities being used and additional food and beverage sales accruing to your organisation. By doing this you are offering the potential sponsor a saving in room charges at a hotel.

Ticketing

Offer your sponsors the best seats in the house. Also offer your sponsor's staff discount ticketing or membership. Staff involvement is often important to companies as it helps with staff morale and therefore productivity. It can also help maintain a positive atmosphere within the company with regards to the sponsorship, heighten the likelihood of a long term relationship, fill empty venues and introduce potential new patrons to your activity.

Publicly Identifying With Your Organisation

Emphasise the right of the sponsors to call themselves a sponsor of your organisation and promote that fact, including the use of your logo on their advertising material, letterhead. This can be particularly important if a company needs to improve its image within the wider community.

Endorsement

Many sponsorships include the benefit of the seeker endorsing or approving the sponsors products. A common example is sports people approving of, or endorsing sports drinks, health foods, vitamins, sports gear. Or, for example, botanical gardens endorsing the use of particular garden equipment and fertilisers.

Use of Imagery

Sponsorship of an organisation will generally allow you to utilise their imagery in your advertising. You will however need to ensure this is included in the contract if required, and that there are no associations above the one you are dealing with who might hold the authority to preclude such use.

What Benefits Does a Sponsor Want?

When you get to the stage of negotiating a sponsorship agreement with a potential sponsor, they may request extra benefits and rights in order to achieve their objectives. It is important at this stage to be open minded to make sure you have the right mix. If you don't get the benefits package right at this point, it is not likely that the sponsor will achieve their objectives, and therefore it is likely that they will terminate at the end of the first contract period. It is also important, however, to ensure that you do not compromise any current sponsor's rights, or the objectives of your organisation.

Summary

- **Identify Your Organisation's Composition**

    Potential sponsors require an accurate picture of who your organisation represents, so you must be able to identify your organisation's membership in terms of demographic, geographic and psychographic make up.

- **Identify Benefits That Can Help A Sponsor**

    What do you own or control that someone else wants?

Chapter 6

Methods of Valuing Your Sponsorship

How Much are We Worth?

We have talked a lot about the benefits that must accrue to the sponsor, but never forget, you, or your organisation, must be making money (a profit – after the cost of having a sponsor is deducted) out of the arrangement otherwise there is no point in entering into it.

It is essential that you do your homework and accurately cost your property to ensure that both your organisation and the sponsor will benefit from the agreement.

Never overprice your proposal with a view to discounting later. Ambit claims don't work. Companies will value the benefits being offered against the amount being requested, and if it is not immediately and obviously cost efficient in comparison to other marketing and communications mediums, such as advertising and direct marketing, they will stick with conventional marketing activities. If your proposal is just patently overpriced, the potential sponsor is likely to assume the proposer doesn't understand the value of sponsorship and they will reject the proposal outright, without even giving you the opportunity to negotiate.

It is very important that you nominate the cost of your proposal to the potential sponsor, to enable the property to be properly assessed. If that cost is not immediately evident, the potential sponsor will be unable to assess the proposal in relation to their budget constraints, and in most cases they will assume the worst. Remember, they have a pretty accurate idea of how much advertising and direct marketing have cost them in the past, and they know what the returns have been. You are therefore very unlikely to receive any interest from a potential sponsor if they don't know what you are requesting in dollar terms.

The only exception to this would be if you were selling a *very* high profile "hot property", organisation, individual or event, with a highly negotiable package of benefits.

The Sponsorship Unit's Valuation Method

Applying the following method should help to determine not only the value of the sponsorship to the sponsor, but also the real cost to your organisation of having a sponsor. This should enable you to place a sensible price on your property.

There is no point in entering into a sponsorship agreement that will end up costing your organisation money. Each sponsorship has a real cost in terms of both time and financial output by the organisation selling the sponsorship.

The first phase of putting a value on the sponsorship is to identify the real cost of the sponsorship package to you, ie, what is the cost of having a sponsor? This may well be a lot more expensive than you would realise.

The following formula should be utilised to value your sponsorship.

1. Determine the sum of all the costs of having a sponsor.

2. Determine profit required. (This is the surplus of sponsorship fee left for your organisation's use, after all sponsor costs are paid.)

3. Cost + profit = minimum sales price. (This is the lowest price that you can afford to accept for your property.)

4. Determine market value through independent market analysis.

5. If minimum sales price is less than market value, go to market. If minimum sales price is greater than market value, your sponsorship is not likely to sell.

To apply the Sponsorship Unit Valuation Method follow the instructions below:

Sponsorship Unit Cost Sheet- Instructions for Use

(Blank copies of sponsorship cost and benefits sheet can be found in Appendix 2.)

1. List on the sponsorship cost sheet every benefit being provided to a sponsor.

2. Add in the real cost of each item. (The amount it will cost your organisation to provide these items).

3. The items, 'Cost of Selling Sponsorship' and 'Cost of Servicing Sponsorship' listed near the bottom of the form are where you should put a value on your time and energy, in terms of human resources.

   o Note: If you are employed by this organisation the time spent selling and servicing the sponsor will be to the detriment of your other duties. If you have not previously had a sponsor, the time spent liaising with and servicing the sponsor would normally have been spent on other activities of value to your organisation, so this should be costed into the sponsorship.

   (If you are selling multiple sponsorships this information may justify a request for extra staff that can be costed into the selling price of the sponsorships.)

   If you are a volunteer for an organisation it is vital you put a figure representing the value of your time and effort so that the organisation obtains that value in real dollars through the sponsorship.

   You will note that there is a multiplier of 1.9 included in this calculation. This represents the additional costs that are traditionally paid by an employer. These are such items as superannuation, sick leave, work stations, computers, coffee and tea, soap and toilet paper and so on.

4. Determine the profit margin you require. Usually the larger the sponsorship the more the profit margin for the seeker after the costs of having a sponsor are deducted. History proves that generally the sponsor costs do not vary greatly between small and large sponsorships. Calculate the profit margin and list it in the relevant column.

5. Add the total real cost to the profit margin required and this will result in the "minimum sponsorship sale price". The maximum sales price represents the highest market value achievable, and takes into account a number of environmental factors.

Sponsorship Unit Cost Sheet List all items that will incur either financial expenditure or person hours	
Item and quantity	**Real Cost**
Tickets 6 games X 10 tickets at $10 each	$ 600
Hospitality Food and Beverages for 60 people at $30 per head	$ 1,800
VIP parking passes 3 passes X 6 games	nil
Event programs 60 at $5 each	$ 300
Additional printing, ie., ads in magazine 10 Ads	$ 1,000
Signage production 5 signs	$ 500
Signage erection	nil
Support Advertising	nil
Apparel for competitors, officials, media etc featuring sponsor	$ 2,500
Evaluation research	nil
Media monitoring	nil
Fax's and phone calls	$ 180
Public relations support	
Legal costs contract preparation	$ 240
Cost of selling sponsorship staff time and expenses based on 60 hours at $10 per hour X 1.9 for real cost of salary	$1,140
Cost of servicing sponsorship in staff time based on 80 hours over the season $10 X 1.9 for real cost of staff member	$1,520
Total Costs	**$9,780**
Plus tax if applicable	$
Plus profit margin	$10,000
Minimum Sponsorship Sale Price	**$ 19,780**

Minimum Sponsorship Sale Price

Completion of the Sponsorship Cost Sheet will identify the real cost to your organisation of having a sponsor, in this case that figure is *$9,780.00*. It would obviously be financially disastrous to sell the sponsorship for less than this cost.

The minimum sale price that has been calculated includes the minimum profit margin that your organisation wishes to make from this sponsorship activity.

Keep the Accountant At Bay

On receipt of the sponsorship cheque, more often than not an organisation's Board has already identified where those dollars are going to be used. Their calculations are on the full amount and do not take into account the actual expenditure that will have to be undertaken to service the sponsor. This amount regularly falls into the cracks, resulting in either a search for additional funds or the sponsor not receiving the benefits it has been promised.

It is important that your Board members and accountants are aware of the commitments that have been made to the sponsor, and provide an appropriate amount to enable you to service the sponsor. Obviously the remainder will go to the allocated project or into consolidated revenue.

How to Determine Market Price?

The bottom line in setting the market sponsorship sale price is to:

1. **Determine the lowest price acceptable.** Complete the Sponsorship Cost Sheet in order to determine the actual cost to your organisation of seeking and running a sponsorship. Any fee sought must be above minimum sales price.

2. Ensure that the sponsor knows the price is fair and will provide a value for money return on their sponsorship investment.

3. Make sure that the sponsorship property is saleable.

The following process should assist you to determine a fair market price for your property.

a) *Value all the tangible benefits in your proposal,* including the value of:

- o Ticketing
- o Hospitality
- o Advertising spend promoting the event that features the sponsor/s
- o Likely media coverage
- o Use of personalties

b) *Calculate premium factors,* including:

- o Merchandising rights being offered and the likely sales to be returned to the sponsor.

- o The difference in value of various categories. For example in highly competitive categories you may be able to negotiate a higher priced based on the fact more than one buyer is interested in the property. (Never threaten that you are going to the competitor though. This will just cause bad feeling.)

c) *Apply price adjusters,* which include items such as:

- o Sponsor's promotional commitment - if the sponsor is prepared to spend significant sums promoting your organisation this should result in you lowering the price being sought.

- o Be aware of the extra costs that companies incur with sponsorship. Sometimes these below the line costs are as much or more than the original purchase price of the sponsorship. If you can offer some, or all, of the following, the sponsor's outlay will be reduced:

  - ▪ Signage production
  - ▪ Signage erection
  - ▪ Client entertainment, food and beverages, car parking etc
  - ▪ Support advertising
  - ▪ Television production costs
  - ▪ Apparel for competitors, officials, media etc

- Trophies and awards
- Evaluation research
- Media monitoring
- Sponsorship project management costs
- Public relations
- Trade and consumer promotions
- Staff time
- Merchandise
- Promotional items
- Exclusivity naturally commands a higher price as, this will limit the number of sponsors you can seek, and there will be no competition for the sponsor striving to associate with your organisation.

d) *Competitive factors.* Make sure that the property is correctly valued, not the value you think it is worth or the money you need, but valued at market value. Once you have set the price be prepared to negotiate. Companies will value the property independently and will only pay what they think its worth; the market value.

To calculate market value, compare the cost of similar properties in the market place. To find this out ask other seekers what they are getting for their proposals. Most people are happy to discuss how they package their sponsorships and approximately how much they get.

If you do not own a "Hot Property" it will be difficult to get a high price as supply invariably outstrips demand for all but the most desirable sponsorships available.

e) *Compare to mainstream marketing costs.* As sponsorship is a marketing and communications tool, once again, we stress that it is important to compare the cost of your sponsorship against the cost of either direct marketing or advertising. This calculation should be on a cost per person affected basis. The following simple calculation will determine your property's cost per person.

Sponsorship

*Total cost of sponsorship # ÷ number of people effected * = Cost per person*

\# (Don't forget the actual cost to the company for your sponsorship will be significantly more than your sponsorship fee. Companies have to pay for all below the line costs such as signage, advertising and staff time to manage the property etc.)

* (organisation members and live and TV audience)

Direct Marketing

The cost of a direct marketing campaign can be calculated as follows:

(Cost of postage + production of material + cost of mail list) x number of people targeted = cost per person

Advertising Campaign

The cost of advertising can be calculated as follows:

(Cost of production + cost of airtime) ÷ number of people in audience = cost per person

Don't Forget

• Price the property realistically so that you make a profit and potential sponsors can afford to buy.

• Make sure that the property is priced at market value.

Once you have set the price, be prepared to negotiate. Companies will value the property independently and will only pay what they think its worth. If you are getting close to your break-even figure, it may be necessary to reduce the benefits being offered.

A rule of thumb is that the bigger the company, the less negotiation on price, however, there is significantly more negotiation on achieving the right mix of benefits. The smaller the company, the more negotiation on price, but they tend to accept the benefits on offer without argument.

Prior to approaching a company it is important to make sure the sponsorship is within their price range. The most efficient way is to estimate their expenditure on advertising and promotions. If it is significantly more than you are requesting, you are in the ballpark as far as price is concerned. As mentioned, the only occasion on which you might get away with overpricing your property, to some extent, is if your property is absolutely unique and very high profile. Then it is open to the highest bidder – demand exceeds supply for premium properties.

The Dilemma of Contra

Contra or in-kind support or value in kind or goods in kind is where a company's products or services are provided in lieu of, or as well as, cash for the payment of a sponsorship. Sometimes contra can suit both parties, however it is often problematic, and can be difficult to value.

Not all companies offer contra due to difficulties relating to taxation and transfer pricing within a company. Quite often, particularly within large companies, the sponsorship budget or department does not have access to product unless they purchase it.

As a seeker you have to decide whether contra is acceptable to you.

If a company wishes to pay for its major sponsorship with 60,000 bricks and you are about to build a brick clubhouse made up of 59,990 bricks, contra is probably acceptable - assuming you can agree on how to value the bricks.

However if a cosmetics company wants to pay for a $50,000 sponsorship with hair conditioner, you need to establish what you are going to do with the product, and how you can use it, trade it or sell it. Where you are going to store the goods? There would be a strong possibility in such a case that you might end up paying for the product to be dumped. If you are lucky enough to find a market for the product and decide to sell it, the revenue from the sale may be subject to taxation!

Get professional advice when agreeing to receive contra in lieu of cash, and be sure your organisation has a use for the product or can off load it in a manner beneficial to your organisation.

Valuing Contra

Valuing contra depends on how valuable the goods are to your normal operations. If you were going to have to buy the product anyway with cash received in a sponsorship agreement, you can probably value the contra at retail value, but be extremely careful. Personally we would value the goods based on the price the company would normally sell them at, for example:

Source	Value
Manufacturer	Manufacturer's sale price
Wholesaler	Wholesale price
Retailer	Retail price

If you accept contra from a wholesaler at retail price they are effectively purchasing your sponsorship for a discount - that discount being the difference in price between wholesale and retail price.

The Underwriter

For those organisations holding events, sponsorship is sometimes sought on the basis of the sponsor underwriting the set up costs and receiving a return from the profits made on the gate, which provides the potential for the sponsorship to either be cost neutral or even return a profit, however, there is of course the risk that the event will flop. Potential sponsors would be wise to cover themselves for this eventuality!

Can I Have Some More?

Make sure you ask for enough money to cover your needs at the time of sale. It is very bad form to go back to a sponsor asking for more on the basis that you didn't get your figures right at the outset. This immediately alerts the sponsor to the fact that they are dealing with amateurs who may be in financial trouble.

The Acid Test

When you have put your proposal together, ask yourself if you received the proposal **would you buy it**? Does it represent value for money? **If not fix the price before you send it**.

Summary

The secret to valuing your sponsorship is:

- **Determining the real cost of having a sponsor and add on to that the minimum profit you require. This will result in the identification of a realistic Minimum Sponsorship Sale Price.**

- **The Market Price is the highest figure attainable. It must be higher or equal to the Minimum Sponsorship Sale Price to ensure your organisation is going to make money, and must be low enough for the sponsor to know that the price represents good value.**

- **Make sure the potential sponsor can afford your price.**

- **If your proposal does not immediately strike the person evaluating it as either very good value, or a unique opportunity, your chances of gaining their support will be minimal.**

Chapter 7

Methods of Identifying Potential Sponsors

Selecting Potential Sponsors

How do you decide on who will be your sponsor? Do you pick up the phone book and start dialling; do you look out the window to see which companies are local; or do you ask friends and acquaintances if they know of any company with the necessary cash? Well all of the above have worked, but let's detail a more structured process which should eliminate a lot of wasted time and successfully capture the odd sponsor or two.

Research – the Need

The first part of the process - and the most important knowledge that you need - is to know exactly who you (your organisation) are. You will need to know your audience in terms of composition. You will also need to know what the public thinks of your organisation, what your fans think of you, and the opinion of any existing sponsors. This will provide useful information to enable a potential sponsor to know what your property offers, and whether or not there is a fit between the two organisations.

In terms of your audience, you will need to know the following:

- Audience size
- Demographics
- Geographic spread
- Third party audiences (media)

- Audience interests
- Audience spending power
- Awareness of organisation within the community
- Attitudes to organisation within the community
- High profile supporters/patrons/people of influence in supporter base
- Awareness of existing sponsors
- Attitudes to existing sponsors and their products
- Propensity to purchase – existing sponsors' goods and services

Make Sure It Fits!

When identifying potential sponsors start by getting the right fit for your organisation and the target company. If there is natural synergy between the two parties, the target company is going to be far more interested in building a commercial relationship with you.

In this instance, natural synergy means that you share common target audiences, common goals and common geographic reach. For example if your audience is predominantly female under 18 years of age you wouldn't be approaching a menswear company for sponsorship - it just doesn't fit, and the benefits aren't there for either party. Similarly, there is little point in going to a major national company based in another capital city for sponsorship if your event is very local and has no relevance to the company.

Strategic Fit. Strategic fit is all about ensuring a good match between your organisation's target audiences and the sponsoring company's target audience. The two audiences need to match in terms of geography (local, state, national, international) and demographics (age group, education level, ethnicity, family groupings, income, occupation, gender and social standing) to enable the sponsor to use the sponsorship as a cost effective marketing and communications tool.

Some Examples Of A Bad Fit

- **A health food shop sponsoring a rally car** - it just doesn't fit. The audiences are likely to be very different. People who buy from health food shops are normally environmentally aware and rally cars are seen by many as definitely not being in the environmentally aware category.

- **Children's sport sponsored by an alcohol supplier**. A relationship of this type would be illegal in most cases and would certainly be quite inappropriate. The alcohol company would not be helping its image in the community and it would be marketing to an audience that isn't able to purchase/consume alcohol.

Some Examples of a Natural Fit

- **A prestige car maker sponsoring the opera.** These two organisations would fit perfectly because they share a common audience – educated, older age group (35+) with a high disposable income.

- **Swimwear manufacturer sponsoring competitive swimming.** This also fits. The swimwear manufacturer would be marketing directly to their target audience, and the use of fit, healthy athletes to market their range of swim wear would obviously be beneficial to them.

Identifying Potential Sponsors

The best method of identifying potential sponsors is to have a number of your organisation's members brainstorm and identify companies that have the 'right fit'. A list of suggested aids are listed below:

- Check through the list of companies your organisation does business with.

- Check all members' employers.

- Use personal contacts at companies and businesses in the relevant area.

- The internet is a useful tool in identifying potential sponsors – many companies are now including information about their sponsorship program on their web site and also have posted guidelines for seekers of sponsorship detailing the company's preferred method of receiving applications and their requirements.

- Annual reports of publicly listed companies often provide detailed information of current and future marketing programs.

- Check the community phone book if applicable, ie, if you are looking in your local area only.

- Complete the sponsor identification checklist.

Geographic Match

Ensure your target company actually operates in the geographical area of your organisation or event. Many national companies will only sponsor national events or organisations and local companies are only likely to sponsor organisations in the region where they market their product. The exception to this rule is that national companies will often sponsor organisations operating in the community where they are headquartered.

Product Seasonality

Ensure that your organisation's season matches the product life cycle of the business you are targeting. It would be rather pointless to request a swimwear company to sponsor you at the end of summer when all their energies will be devoted to getting their new range prepared for the following season.

The Sponsor Identification Checklist
(A clean copy of this checklist is contained in Appendix 3.)

This check-list is designed to assist you in identifying potential sponsors in the market place.

1. **Does your property have synergy with a particular company or industry?** For example a baby food manufacturer with new mothers.

2. **Does the target market of any company exactly match the make up of your organisation's members or event audience?** For example, tennis ball manufacturers and tennis tournaments.

3. **Would your organisation's members be relevant to any company's products and services?** Polo Clubs (high money earners) and Prestige Cars.

4. **Can you offer on site concessions or vending rights to food or beverage manufacturers?** For example, all beer sold at your club will be ABC brand.

5. **Does your sponsorship have the capacity to help any particular business sell product or make money?** Bank with your sponsor.

6. **Does your geographic reach match that of any potential sponsors' specific market area?** For example, a statewide dairy food supplier, and a state-wide netball association.

7. **What does your sponsorship offer that other mediums (advertising, sales promotion, direct marketing) cannot?** Networking, media exposure, a particular niche market.

8. **Will your property attract potential clients for any potential sponsors?** Can the sponsor do business with your organisation or other sponsor's organisations.

9. **Will your property directly sell product and /or services for any potential sponsors?** For example, vending rights.

10. **Will this property increase a sponsor's visibility in the eyes of your members/audience?** For example, through signage, internal advertising, etc

11. **Will your property buy a piece of the 'good guy' image for a potential sponsor?** Will this sponsorship improve a company's standing in the community?

12. **Do you want your organisation sponsored by this company?** For example, an environmental organisation would need to be very careful when approaching a company that had recently been involved in an environmental incident. The benefits would definitely be there for the company involved, but your organisation could be viewed very cynically for accepting funds from that particular source.

The 'Shot Gun' Approach

The shotgun approach is not as violent as it sounds. The shotgun method is a quick and easy way to get your opportunity (proposal) out to numerous prospects and gauge the interest. If you can produce a proposal that stands out from the clutter, it can maximise your chances of gaining the interest of a sponsor. However, if you have used base standard document, and then personalised each proposal, *check it again and again* - make sure that the address, recipient's name, and text in the body of the proposal are all relevant to the company you are sending it to.

Taking the shotgun approach within one company is not a good idea. However many managers you approach within a company, sponsorship proposals are generally all channelled to the one area.

Introductory Brochures can be Useful

One method that high-level seekers have used with some success is to produce a brochure that contains background information on their organisation, standard sponsorship packages and contact details. This brochure is not a substitute for a formal proposal – it serves to identify potential sponsors by "sounding them out" in this relatively low cost manner.

Advertise for a Sponsor

Another method of identifying sponsors is to place an advertisement calling for expressions of interest from potential sponsors. The advertisement must detail who your audiences (demographics, psychographics, etc.) are and what you can offer a potential sponsor.

Note: If you are a public body, it may in fact be mandatory that you do advertise the availability of a sponsorship widely.

If your sponsorship provides advertising opportunities like fence signage (at a venue), car signage (motor racing team), apparel signage (a cyclist), advertise that you want a sponsor rather than waste the space.

Sponsorship Brokers

Retaining the services of a Sponsorship Broker is one option for selling your sponsorship. A broker will take on your property to sell, along with others that he has on his books – not unlike a real estate agent. He will then approach companies that he thinks are likely to purchase your property. If he is successful, he will take a commission of anywhere between 20% and 40% of the fee received, depending on your initial agreement.

There are good brokerage companies in every field of sponsorship – but in our opinion, very few of them! Do make sure that you ask for references – and check them.

There are numbers of individuals who feel that selling sponsorship is easy money – these people generally operate on a monthly retainer basis, and offer no guarantee of success – and you guessed it – they often don't succeed.

Pros and Cons of Appointing a Broker

The Pros of appointing a Broker are as follows:

- You don't have to do it yourself.
- A good Broker has his own network.
- A good Broker has a track record of selling, which you may not have.
- They will prepare a professional, tailored proposal for each potential sponsor – (this will require your input).

The Cons of appointing a Broker are as follows:

- The costs (fee, plus monthly retainer prior to sale). Do not forget that the fee is generally payable on every payment made until the sponsor is no longer associated with your organisation – which could be many years.

- You lack control over the sale process, and it is difficult to know how much effort is being put in to the sale for the money being paid, or what priority is being placed on your sale.

- They do not know your organisation as well as you do.

- The unscrupulous among them tend to promise anything requested to a potential sponsor in order to get the sale (and the commission). This needs to be strictly controlled – you may end up with an expectation of benefits that you are unable to deliver.

- If you provide the Broker with exclusivity, and then a sponsor (who may be a personal contact of yours) approaches you, you can't do the deal without paying the broker a commission – make sure this is covered in your written agreement with the broker.

Choosing a Broker

- Track record is critical! Do not just accept what they say – CHECK that they actually sold the properties claimed and that both organisations were happy with their performance. Credible brokers will not mind giving you this information.

- Set the terms and conditions that you are comfortable with. Make sure that you can still do business with potential sponsors, particularly those you have already approached.

Renumerating a Broker

- The ideal is to pay only on success, with limited pre-approved expenses paid.

- If a retainer is to be paid (to a broker with a good track record) you would expect weekly progress reports detailing how many companies have been approached, and the progress that she is making with each.

- Ensure that you have the ability to discontinue the retainer if you are not happy with the performance.

- Expect to pay more than 20% as a success fee – year on year – and anything up to 50%, with 40% being quite common.

Sponsors as Brokers

Speak to existing or retiring sponsors and ask if they know of any companies that may be interested in sponsoring your event.

One method that has been employed successfully overseas, but to my knowledge never in this country, is offering sponsors a discount on their package for every other sponsor they bring to the event.

Ethical Dilemmas

In identifying sponsors you may also identify companies that you don't want as a sponsors. For example, if your group is of an environmental nature, you probably don't want to be sponsored by a company that is the biggest polluter in the area. (However, if you chose to be sponsored by the polluter you may open the doors for your group to speak to the decision makers and help them to clean up their processes.) You do need to make a decision as to whether there are there any companies you won't approach for sponsorship support, or accept sponsorship from.

Conflict of Interest

Obviously it may be seen as a conflict of interest if you were to accept sponsorship from a company tendering for work within your organisation, or which is subject to regulation by your organisation.

Summary

- Undertake research –know who you are

- Ensure that potential sponsors have a fit with your organisation

- Utilise all resources available to you to identify sponsors, including your members, the internet, annual reports

- Consider using a sponsorship broker with a good track record, but be aware of the pitfalls

Chapter 8

Packaging Sponsorships

The Alternatives

The method in which you choose to package or structure your sponsorship portfolio will to some extent be determined by your organisation/event structure. It is important when packaging your assets to maximise potential revenue by making the packages saleable, therefore it is necessary to decide what assets you can offer for sale and which are most saleable. You then need to decide how many sponsors you want and at what levels. It is important to define the multiple levels and ensure that benefits don't overlap.

Don't forget to be realistic and consistent in the pricing. Sponsors do talk to each other, and are often dismayed to find out that their package has been priced on their ability to pay, rather than in relation to other sponsors' packages. Ask yourself, would you buy the package for the benefits being offered?

Packaging will also partly be based on supply and demand, the money you require, the number of potential sponsors available and the number of levels of sponsorship you have available.

A caution – packaging is a critical element of your ongoing sales process. If you sell all your benefits to one sponsor, it effectively precludes you from having another sponsor. If you want more than one sponsor, you need to have the benefits packages and levels defined prior to approaching any potential sponsors.

If you already have a sponsor(s), and you wish to rearrange the sponsor hierarchy, you need to ensure that you are not infringing on rights that you have already sold exclusively, and also you will need to advise your current sponsor as to what is happening, and where they are going to fit in the new sponsorship structure.

The Five Common Methods of Packaging Sponsorships

1. The Level Playing Field

2. The Hierarchical Package

3. The Pyramid

4. The Sole Sponsorship

5. Ad Hoc

Level Playing Field

The level playing field is probably the fairest of method of dividing up the benefits of all the methods employed. The level playing field is used by the Olympic movement and it provides each sponsor (at each level) with identical rights and benefits (use of the Olympic logo and mascot, and the right to associate with the team as a whole). In each industry category there is only ever one sponsor. For example, one bank, one telecommunications company, one beverage company, one apparel sponsor and so on.

Finance	Telecommunications	Beverage	Apparel	Food

It should, however, be noted that with this type of package sponsors may be charged significantly different amounts and payment levels are usually based on competition within each category. If a number of potential sponsors in a single category are interested in the property, obviously you can ask for more money. Also, to some extent, the program is based on capacity to pay, the bigger the sponsor the more it is likely to cost them.

This method provides sponsors with 'a level playing field' in terms of rights and benefits received, and it is up to each sponsor to maximise their own returns. It is fascinating to see the varied ways each sponsor maximises their returns. When all sponsors are created equal the only difference in the outcome is a result of the time, creativity and money invested.

The negative aspect of this package is the number of sponsorships to be sold.

The positive with this package is that if one sponsor withdraws the effect of the loss of income is minimised by having a number of sponsors in other categories contributing to the organisation. As the benefits are delivered with minimal servicing required, the workload is reduced.

Note: This type of package can usually only be sold to sought after and/or high profile events. The advantage that the Olympic Games have is that they are very high profile, and absolutely unique, so as mentioned earlier, they can successfully use the level playing field method of selling sponsorships.

Hierarchical Package

This is probably the most common package of them all. Basically it is based on amount paid - the more you pay the more you get. Let's take the example of an arts organisation like a high profile ballet company. Normally the structure of sponsors would be as follows: One principal sponsor, two or three major sponsors, numerous minor sponsors and official suppliers.

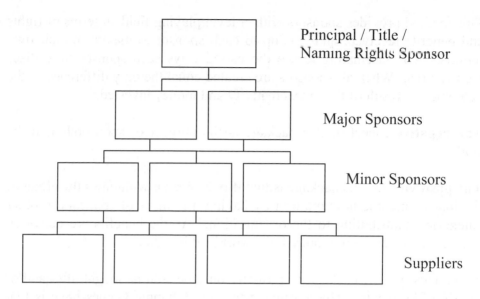

- **Naming/Title Rights Sponsor.** Naming or title rights sponsor is the same as a principal rights sponsor and with the exception that a naming/title rights sponsor receives identical rights and benefits, with the addition of having the right to have their name added as a prefix to the organisation or event name. An organisation would not have both a naming rights sponsor and a principal sponsor.

- **Major Sponsor.** This is the level directly below the principal sponsor and in an arts organisation could either be a Production Sponsor (who has the rights to have their logo displayed with the principal sponsors every time a particular ballet is danced, for example, Swan Lake) or a Tour Sponsor (who sponsors a particular tour where a number of ballets will be danced). Obviously there can be a number of sponsors at this level.

- **Minor Sponsor.** A Minor Sponsor provides funding to sponsor particular necessary items, such as ballet shoes for the entire company. A Minor Sponsor may also sponsor an individual performer. Naturally there could be multiple sponsors at this level.

- **Official Supplier.** This status provides the sponsor with the right to make the claim that they are an official supplier to the organisation, in return for providing free or discounted services and goods.

- Alternatively, they may simply have the right to be the sole purveyor of goods in a particular category, for example the right to supply vitamins to the organisation.

The negative aspect of this type of packaging is the number of sponsorships to be sold and the large amount of work – not to mention budget and human resources - that is required to service sponsor needs.

The positive with this type of packaging is that if one sponsor withdraws, the effect of the loss of income is minimised by having a number of sponsors contributing to the organisation. It also allows for natural ascendancy of minor sponsors into more major sponsorship roles.

The Pyramid

This is an interesting adaptation of the hierarchical method in that it is very structured and most importantly each level of sponsorship benefits and revenue adds up to one complete major package.

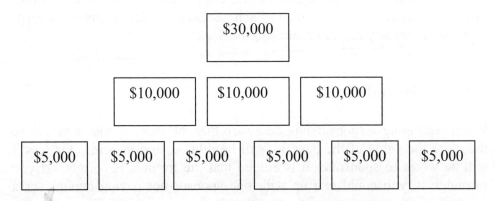

For example you would have one principal sponsor who would receive a complete range of benefits for say $30,000. You would then have a certain number of major sponsors, say three, who would pay $10,000 each (total $30,000) who would equally divide exactly the same benefits the principal sponsor received. The minor sponsors, say six, would each pay $5,000 (total 6 x $5,000 = $30,000) and divide exactly the same benefits as the principal sponsor between them.

The pyramid method ensures fairness at every level.

Sole Sponsor

This is the most valuable sponsorship for any sponsor as they are not competing with other sponsors and they have absolute exclusivity. An exclusive sponsorship should provide a premium due to its exclusivity. (In other words, the sponsor should pay more.)

The negative aspect of this sponsorship package is that if the sponsor decides not to renew the sponsorship, an organisation's entire funding base is removed at one time.

The positive aspect is that your organisation only has to convince one sponsor to sign up and it also means taking care of only one sponsor's interests, which significantly cuts down the amount of work involved.

Ad Hoc

Ad Hoc sponsorship packaging sees no formal structure, and bits and pieces are sold as required, either by the seeker organisation for financial reasons, or when approached by a sponsor. Each package provides different benefits to the sponsors and varying returns to the Seeker.

Diluting Benefits

When packaging a sponsorship, be aware that the more sponsors you have the more the value of the benefits will be diluted, and therefore the less it will be worth to sponsors. It is crucial that the formula is correct. If you misjudge it, you could end up with one sponsor not paying enough, or a number of sponsors paying too much. Either way it will not help your cause.

Sponsor's Needs

The structure of each sponsorship package and the individual benefits you are offering each sponsor will largely be determined by each individual sponsor's needs.

Generally sponsors are looking for involvement on a medium to long-term basis rather than with the once-off event that comes and goes quickly.

Media exposure is an important element of a sponsorship for the majority of companies, so wherever possible provide some or all of the following elements in a sponsorship package:

- Radio
- Television
- Print
- Community access

Increasing The Value of Your Package

There are various ways of increasing the value of your package, and they include:

- **Think Big.** Expand the scope of your organisation by forming alliances with similar bodies in other states to make a national property rather than a regional property.

- **Build/Create a "Hot" Property**. We can all think of organisations which have started small, built a very successful brand over the years, and have become a hot property in this way (many popular music festivals have started this way – small and local, and after a few years are so well known that people flock from all corners of the country to attend).

- **Form Alliances With Media.** This is one of the most effective ways of dramatically increasing the value of your sponsorship. Providing coverage of your event or organisation's activities and providing the sponsors with exposure through your media articles. When seeking a media sponsor it is worth providing the sponsorship at little or no cost to get the free exposure: this could include free commercial spots that could be given as a benefit to major sponsors.

- **Exclusivity.** Offering category exclusivity offers your sponsor the ability to lock out their competitor. This is something that most sponsors demand and is one way of adding a premium to your value.

- **Create A Multi Dimensional Offer.** Offer a whole range or menu of benefits, not just use of a logo or signage.

- **Cross Promotions.** Arranging cross promotions with other prominent sponsors is a successful way of increasing your sponsors' returns. Cross promotions involve two sponsors promoting each others products, commonly through either a competition, advertising in each others outlets or on each other's products, or devising an on-pack promotion that is beneficial to both parties.

- **Sponsors Like To Stand Out From The Clutter.** Sponsors don't like a situation where their logo is lost in a plethora of other companies logos - this situation is known in the trade as 'duelling logos'. Keeping the number of sponsors to a minimum is a balancing act, however remember small sponsors cost almost as much to service as big sponsors.

- **Be Flexible.** Be prepared to negotiate and adjust the package, to some extent, to provide the sponsor with the package they need to achieve their own objectives. However, as mentioned previously, it is important during the negotiation process not to compromise your own organisation in any way.

- **Create Events.** By creating events you can provide extra avenues for sponsorship funding and extra benefits for sponsors.

- **Deliver Opportunities.** When setting up the sponsorship packages for your organisation always think of the needs of the potential sponsors, and structure the packages to fulfil those needs. Don't simply look at what you have to offer and try to sell it. If you do, it may well end up looking like a problem that needs funding rather than a cost effective business opportunity.

- **Prove Your Sponsorship Changes Attitudes and Behaviours.** Measure your target audiences attitudes towards your sponsors, and if they are prepared to choose a sponsors product over a non-sponsor, make sure potential sponsors are aware of this.

Summary

- The method in which you choose to package your sponsorship property will, to some extent, be determined by your organisation/event structure. It is important when packaging your assets to maximise potential revenue by making the packages saleable, therefore it is necessary to decide what assets you can/will offer for sale, and that are most saleable.

- You then need to decide how many sponsors you require at what levels. It is important to define the multiple levels and ensure that benefits don't overlap. Don't forget to be realistic in the pricing be consistent. Ask yourself, would you buy the package for the benefits being offered?

- There are five common methods of packaging sponsorships:

  - The Level Playing Field
  - The Hierarchical Package
  - The Pyramid
  - The Sole Sponsorship, and
  - Ad Hoc, where each provides different benefits to the sponsors and varying returns to the Seeker.

Chapter 9

Approaching Potential Sponsors

The Assessment Process

Many companies do not have a dedicated Sponsorship Manager. Customarily this role would be shared with another role, which could be the marketing manager, publicity manager or the Marketing Manager's secretary. Consequently sponsorship is often a chore that can be a nuisance, particularly responding to unsolicited requests for sponsorship! Many large companies are receiving up to fifty proposals (requests) for sponsorship a week. Every one of these requires perusal and answering. Therefore every extra proposal received requires them spending more of their time on a, generally, unproductive job. Following are the usual steps once your proposal has been received within a company.

Step One

On receipt of the sponsorship proposal it is usually skimmed to see if there is any interest at all. Depending on the company and its resources, this process may take less than thirty seconds. Those properties that 'just don't fit', or 'don't feel right', are immediately declined.

Step Two

If there is some interest the second stage involves reading the document in its entirety to assess whether this property is a possibility for sponsorship funding. If it proves not to be, it also gets declined.

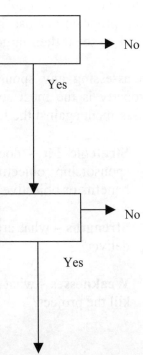

Step Three

If there is still interest the sponsorship manager may undertake some research to see if the proposal can deliver everything it promises. This could include following up with past sponsors, checking industry sources and so on.

Yes

No

Step Four

Assuming the proposal and your organisation checks out they may call you and ask for a meeting to discuss your proposal. If all goes well, negotiations will commence culminating, hopefully, in a contract.

No

Comparing Oranges And Apples

When receiving proposals and requests for sponsorship companies are being asked to compare sponsorships in different price brackets that target totally different demographic groups and offer varying benefits and costs. To effectively sift through the proposals received, companies usually assess your proposal against their marketing and communications objectives, and check to see if their target audience matches the audience(s) you can deliver.

In assessing any sponsorship the company is determining whether that property is the most suitable for their unique needs. To do this requires assessment against the following criteria.

- **Strategic Fit** - does the sponsorship property match the company's sponsorship objectives and can this property deliver the required benefits or objectives cost effectively.

- **Strengths** - what are the property's strengths and what benefits does it deliver?

- **Weaknesses** - what are the property's weaknesses - are they enough to kill the project?

- **Opportunities** - what are the opportunities that this property presents. (For example, could it be used to influence policy makers or gain exclusive supply rights, if that is what the company needs to do?)

- **Risks** - what risks exist and are they minimal?

- **Uncontrollable Factors** - which items are beyond the sponsor's control and are they comfortable with the situation.

- **Controllable Factors** - which factors are within their control, and are you comfortable with the effect these factors could have on your organisation.

Plan in Advance

This process is rarely instant and assessment can take up to several months. This is another good reason for preparing well in advance. You may miss out on a sponsor simply because you have not given them enough time to observe their procedures before your season or event commences.

The majority of sponsors have to adhere to formal processes during the assessment of potential sponsorships. The internal documents involved generally include the following:

The Sponsorship Policy

The Policy details the rules as to what is allowed to be sponsored and what isn't. This document is an internal document and details items such as levels of expenditure and the approval processes required.

Sponsorship Policy
(example only)

Sponsorship is the provision of cash or contra in return for access to the exploitable potential associated with an event, organisation or individual. Sponsorships are to be used to achieve the marketing objectives of the company.

1. All requests for sponsorship must be approved by the delegated Manager.

2. All sponsorships must achieve quantifiable marketing objectives as demonstrated by a detailed plan.

3. All sponsorships must be evaluated against planned objectives.

4. Sponsorships of political parties must not be undertaken.

5. Contra must be costed at customer retail price, not at the cost price. Benefits from a sponsorship must reflect the retail value of the products and services given.

6. Sponsorships must be within the operating area (geographic boundaries) of the company.

7. Sponsorships which have the potential to create precedents beyond the local geographic area are not permitted, eg, the sponsorship of local branches of national organisations or community bodies.

8. Sponsorships must be consistent with the company's desired corporate image and identity.

9. Sponsorship of staff is permitted if there are justifiable business reasons to do so, and there are tangible benefits for the company.

10. Sponsorships that could involve the company in controversial issues or expose the company to adverse criticism must be avoided.

11. Sponsorship requests of more than $X must be approved by the Managing Director. Those between $X and $X require the signature of the Marketing Director. Those below $X require the signature of the Group Product Manager.

The Sponsorship Strategy

The sponsorship strategy outlines the basic approach to sponsorships within a company. It sets the overall course for achieving the company's stated marketing and communications objectives through the use of sponsorship. It provides the basis for selecting the individual sponsorships that make up the companies sponsorship program.

The sponsorship strategy typically changes from year to year based on the company's strategic marketing and communications objectives.

Company Sponsorship Strategy
(example only)

Situation Analysis

Our organisation XYZ Company, is the market leader in its category in Australia and will be introducing its products into Europe during the next 12 months. BCD Limited, our major competitor, currently holds 100% of the European market.

Company Objectives For Sponsorship

To utilise sponsorship to gain awareness within the identified target audiences, through the use of dominant signage, sampling, and use of personalities.

Company's Target Audiences

The target audiences for our sponsorship programs will be aimed at our product's target markets. Those target markets consist of all women aged 18 to 40, with the secondary audience being women aged 40 plus.

Sponsorship Guidelines

Sponsorship proposals are generally evaluated against pre-set sponsorship guidelines, which are increasingly being formalised and becoming available to the public.

These guidelines take the relevant sponsorship information contained in the policy and strategy documents and present the information in a checklist fashion. If these are available to you read them, so you don't waste your opportunity.

Companies often use an assessment checklist similar to that detailed below. This list would typically be utilised when there is some interest in your property.

The assessment checklist takes into account all the factors listed above (policy, strategy), and you may wish to add some to suit your particular needs and check your proposal against it.

Assessment Checklist
Example only
(From the company/sponsor perspective)

Fit:

❑   Is the property consistent with our company's objectives?

❑   Does the lifestyle of the event fit the product, brand or company?

❑   Do audience demographics match those of the product(s) to be promoted?

❑   Does the event's geographic reach match your product's requirements?

❑   Does it fit with existing sponsorships - is there synergy?

❑   Is your organisation compatible with current or future sub-sponsors?

❑   Does the property reach the target audience numbers required?

❑   Is this cost effective in comparison to other marketing mediums?

❑   Is it a sustained activity (longevity)?

❑   Will the target audience receive multiple impacts (ie, be exposed to our message more than once)? What is the frequency?

❑   Will it attract consumer attention? Is it an issue of importance?

General:

❑   Is category exclusivity guaranteed?

❑   Degree of clutter - how many other sponsors are there?

❑   What is the likelihood of ambush?

❑   Is the event in a growth or decline cycle?

❑ Does the package provide the benefits required? If not, can it be tailored?

❑ Does it have long term potential?

❑ Can the benefits promised be delivered?

❑ Does it enhance our corporate image?

❑ Are we backing winners?

❑ Is the event unique?

❑ Will this activity have staff and shareholder appeal?

❑ Will it open doors to prospects, government departments, legislators and the media?

❑ Is there sufficient time to complete the planning processes prior to the event/season commencing? (Usually at least three months.)

Seekers Credibility And Track Record:

❑ Is the Seeker responsible, able to work with sponsors, flexible, creative, motivated to succeed?

❑ Does the organisation want a sponsor or is it simply desperate for funds?

❑ Will the seeker win in its competition/be best in its category?

❑ Does the seeker have the resources to run a sponsorship and look after our company's interests?

❑ What is their record with finances?

❑ Will it be easy to implement and execute a program which will achieve our objectives?

Costs:

❑ Is sponsorship the most cost effective means to achieve the company's objectives? If not, consider advertising, direct marketing or sales promotions.

❑ Is the cost realistic in comparison to other similar events on the market?

❑ What are the below the line costs?

❏　　Are there any hidden costs?

❏　　Will costs be justified by results?

❏　　Cost of not sponsoring (will the competitor grab it)?

Awareness:

❏　　Will it reach and favourably influence opinion leaders?

❏　　Will the Sponsorship broaden product awareness, and therefore stimulate sales?

❏　　Is the community interested in this activity? (Check research.)

Promotional Extensions:

❏　　Can in-store promotions be used?

❏　　Can local promotions be created?

❏　　Can trade incentives be introduced?

❏　　Are compatible co-sponsors interested in cross promotions?

❏　　Can advertising programs be created using the event or its personalities?

❏　　Are there opportunities to create event merchandise?

❏　　Are there opportunities for sampling?

❏　　Are there display opportunities?

❏　　Are there opportunities to get on site concessions?

❏　　Is there access to data-bases for direct marketing?

Signage:

❏　　Television?

❏　　Uniforms/apparel?

❏　　Site?

❏　　What is the clutter like? (ie will there be a duelling logos situation?)

Hospitality:

❑ Is it available?

❑ Is the standard of client facilities acceptable? (Make sure *you* physically check – don't take anyone elses word!)

Media Coverage:

❑ Will the media see the sponsorship or the event as newsworthy?

❑ Are there opportunities to get the brand or logo in all media stories?

❑ Is the event broadcast? Are there opportunities for advertising or on air promotions?

Staff Involvement:

❑ Are there opportunities to involve staff?

❑ Will staff be proud to be associated with this sponsorship?

❑ Is there an opportunity for staff discounts?

How Long Will it Take to Evaluate?

Ensure sponsorship proposals are sent a minimum of four, and preferably six, months prior to an event. This enables companies to consider the sponsorship and if they are interested it allows time to enter negotiations, sign the deal, prepare business plans to exploit the relationship and organise resources and budgets to implement the event.

Many companies plan their sponsorship programs a year in advance and it is therefore imperative that your proposal reaches potential sponsors well in advance of the event. (It is true – the wheels do move slowly in most big companies!)

You are almost guaranteed that you will not receive sponsorship for an event happening in a fortnight.

Your offer will be declined for three reasons. a) There simply will not be enough time for a company to evaluate your proposal and enter into negotiations; b) they will wonder at the credibility of an event that has not secured any sponsors only a fortnight before the event commences;

Sponsorship proposals will take anywhere from one to six weeks to be assessed and responded to depending, once again, on the resources of the company involved. It is strongly recommended that you don't harass the recipient of your proposal for at least the first three weeks.

During our time assessing sponsorships potential Seekers have often phoned us, asking if we had received and assessed their proposal - often twice before we had even received the proposal.

Put yourself in the shoes of the assessor. They are assessing a number of proposals every week, commonly 20 to 50, but anything up to 300 in some cases. Imagine getting 150 telephone calls a week from self interested people asking how their proposal was going. For one thing, it becomes difficult to get the assessments done when you are either on the phone, or searching through your in tray for a specific proposal. For another, it is quite possible that the assessor will see your interest as harassment, and give your proposal less attention than it deserves when they get to it. If a company does sponsor you, you want the relationship to be on the best possible footing, so do not get them offside by harassing. One call, pleasantly asking if they require further information would be quite sufficient in most cases.

Timing Your Run

Companies who have chosen to be sponsors are generally proactive in finding properties that fit. They actively go and canvas potential Seekers and look for the right sponsorship. However they are always hopeful the right proposal will arrive unsolicited.

Most companies budget for their sponsorship program once a year with 70 to 80% of the budget being committed to identified or ongoing sponsorships.

It is therefore important to time your run. To do this you need to know when the company's budget year starts.

Generally the budgeting process takes place at least three months prior to the start of the new financial cycle, so to be considered in the 20 to 30% of available funding you should approach the company in either February/March or August/September depending on the individual company's budget cycle.

The easiest way to gain this information is look at the annual report if it is a public company. If you are dealing with a private company, the receptionist or accounts staff will be able to provide this information.

Who is the Decision Maker - Who Can Say Yes?

Deciding what level to pitch your sponsorship at gets more difficult as the company gets bigger. In most small companies the sponsorship decisions are made by the 'Boss', (the manager or the owner). As the company starts to grow either the Manager's Secretary or the Sales and Marketing Manager will be the person running the sponsorship area. In medium sized companies the PR, or Corporate Affairs or Marketing Department will handle the sponsorships.

Large companies, however, generally have dedicated staff in the sponsorship area who receive *many* proposals for sponsorship per week. These people are responsible for setting guidelines, evaluating proposals and recommending which sponsorship should be purchased. They usually manage Sponsorships and make the decision as to whether to renew at the end of the contract. They are often under the auspices of the Marketing Department or the Public Relations/Corporate Affairs Department.

In some very large companies this function is contracted out to an outside company, such as a sponsorship consultancy or possibly an advertising agency.

To ensure you go to the right person, do your homework. Ring the company and ask the telephonist for the name, title, department, mailing address and correct spelling of the appropriate contact's name.

In a large number of companies there may be many people who have the right to decline your opportunity.

However, whereas many people can decline your proposal, very few have the power to approve it – it is therefore a very good idea to ensure your correspondence is received by this person or people.

Making Contact With the Decision Maker

If you are able to speak to the decision maker or their representative prior to sending in a proposal, make sure you do so.

Don't forget, personal contact does provide a significant advantage, however, if you don't have a personal contact ring reception and ask for the correct spelling of his or her name and their correct title. At that point you should also enquire if they have sponsorship guidelines available to the public, if they do get them and read them. Don't ask to be put through to that person at this time.

Step One

Once you have determined who the decision maker is ring back and ask for that person by name and ask for assistance with what they sponsor. Most people are happy to provide advice. Don't attempt to sell your proposal at this point, as no one likes to feel they have been taken advantage of.

Step Two

Send in your proposal. Don't follow up immediately - give the assessor time to go through their decision making process.

Step Three

If your proposal is rejected this is another opportunity to grow the relationship. Ring and thank them for taking the time to assess your proposal. This is your opportunity to ask whether there was a specific reason why your proposal was declined, and also whether it would be worth reapplying at a specified time in the future.

If not, ask if they know of any other company that may be interested in your opportunity. If you have been pleasant to deal with, they may take the trouble to recommend a possible sponsor.

Getting a Personal Meeting

The easiest way of getting sponsorship is to approach personal friends or acquaintances, who are well placed in companies, and who understand the nature of the sponsorship. If you have friends, business associates or club members who know the appropriate person in a company, ask them to either introduce you or arrange a meeting.

As in any business deal there is no doubt that the personal touch reaps big dividends – many smaller sponsorships are undertaken by companies that have staff members personally involved with the seeker organisation. The downside with this approach is that if you are not offering very tangible benefits you may well stretch a good friendship, so tread cautiously.

If you are lucky enough to get a personal presentation, keep it short and sweet. This is a business meeting – not a social occasion.

Present verbally and authoritatively without using the proposal, and then at the end of the presentation ask for questions and deliver the document for private reading.

Successful Meetings

If you are fortunate enough to get a meeting with the decision maker, you are generally more than halfway to getting your sponsorship signed.

The golden rule to remember is that this will be a business meeting of probably no more than half an hour, so be well prepared! Our rules of meetings are as follows:

1. Ensure the appropriate person from your organisation attends the meeting. This should be someone with the authority to agree to benefits and price. Don't take more than one person unless they can usefully add to the discussions.

2. If you require the use of equipment, ensure it is available in the room you are meeting in. If it is not, hire and take it yourself if necessary. Allow enough time for set-up over and above the time allocated to the meeting.

3. Prepare your fall back position in any negotiations and prepare a list of questions you want to ask.

4. Present yourself in a professional manner. Dress to suit the organisation you are visiting – not yourself. You may well wear jeans every day, but it is not appropriate to wear jeans to an office where everyone else is attired in business suits.

5. Familiarise yourself with the company's products and services. Usually a read of their annual report will suffice. If this is not readily available, try the company website, or ask for brochures on company products/services.

6. Arrive ten minutes prior to the meeting time, unless setting up audio-visual equipment or the like, when you will require more time.

7. Remember to *listen* to what the potential sponsor says. Don't be rigid – they may want to adjust what you are offering for very good business reasons, so be prepared to be flexible.

8. Don't assume the sponsor knows a lot about your organisation. Give a 'thumb nail sketch', and perhaps leave some relevant documentation for their perusal at a later date.

9. Find out what information they require to make a decision in regards to your proposal, and have it with you at the meeting. If further questions arise at the meeting, tell them that you will provide them with the answers by a specific date, *and make sure you do*.

10. Follow up in writing, thanking them for taking the time to speak to you personally, and invite further questions.

11. Persistence pays off. Keep talking to a potential sponsor for as long as is appropriate, and grow the relationship. Don't forget to ask them along to any event or function you hold during the negotiation period. (See Chapter 11 "Negotiating the Deal".)

Never Turn Up Without an Appointment

One thing that is guaranteed to irritate a sponsorship manager is someone turning up at the reception desk and asking if he is available to look at a proposal on the spot. I remember one such case, where a couple had caught a flight from interstate to do just that. I was in another meeting, and indicated that I was not available. They then pointed out to the receptionist (aggressively) that they had paid for airfares to get there. She felt obliged to find someone to speak to them, and eventually one of my staff had to leave her duties, find an appropriate meeting area, and shelve her planned activities to speak to them.

Their proposal, as it happens, had no synergy with our company at all, and was of no interest whatsoever - we had been chosen on our ability to pay. Their behaviour displayed a total lack of courtesy and also guaranteed that their organisation's name *was* memorable - but not quite in the way they had hoped!

The Written Approach

This is the most common way of applying for sponsorship, with the proposal document normally being prefaced by a short letter outlining the attached proposal. How do you send it? By email, fax, post, courier or personally deliver it to the company?   Faxes, we believe, are still treated with a little more urgency than a letter, and a courier bag is generally opened by the person it is addressed to, guaranteeing that they will at least be aware of the contents.

We are not so sure that emails are a great idea, unless you have been able to speak to the person and establish that they will not mind receiving a proposal on their desktop in this manner. It is too easy to have a quick glance at an email, and intend to get back to it …. later ….. much later. Another problem with email is that, because of the risk of viruses, an increasing number of companies have a policy of not opening any attachments unless they are from a known business contact.

The important thing is to have done your homework, and made sure your proposal will be received by the appropriate person.

Telephone Contact

Making cold calls is never easy, but if after researching the target company, you feel your proposition is ideal for them, the cold call will occasionally work. If you are fortunate enough to get put through to the right person, don't immediately sell – ask for general information relating to objectives, budget and type of properties currently sponsored. Indicate that you are seeking sponsorship, and that you will follow up with a written proposal.

The Knock Back

If you get knocked back it could be for one of many reasons, including a lack of money. Don't get the sponsorship person offside, don't threaten and don't go above his or her head. It is possible if you handle this rejection gracefully that you may be considered at some time in the future. If you have been promised support (say at a cocktail party) by a more senior person in the organisation, you should mention this, and ask the sponsorship person to check with their manager.

Climbing the Ladder

Some Seekers feel that they have a right to sponsorship from a particular company and if they are declined they then hassle the assessor demanding to know why their proposal was turned down. Companies have no obligation to tell you why they declined your opportunity, although most will, if asked in a polite and non-demanding manner.

The less professional Seekers start climbing the ladder after the initial refusal. They go to the Sponsorship Manager's boss, the Marketing Manager or the Corporate Affairs Director, who generally refers it to the person paid to look after sponsorships - the person who initially declined the proposal, and who will again. The really persistent Seeker goes to the CEO who refers it down the line and guess who has to say no again? The final try is writing to a board member or the Chairman who once again refers it down the line.

Reapplying

Quite often your proposal may suit the company but it is presented too late or there just isn't the budget available, so it does no harm to ring the company and politely ask why you were declined and if you should resubmit in future years. If they indicate that you may reapply, it would then be prudent to ask what aspects of your proposal they liked or disliked.

Summary

- **Time your run - make sure you are applying for sponsorship when the company has the ability to fund it. In other words before they have allocated their sponsorship budget for the year, and many months prior to your event/season start etc.**

- **Identify the decision maker who can say yes and if possible get to know them and identify their views on the benefits of sponsorship prior to sending your proposal.**

- **Don't forget to ask yourself the value question - does it make good business sense to sponsor your opportunity, does your sponsorship have the capacity to help a business, is it cost effective?**

Chapter 10

Constructing the Proposal

The Proposal

The majority of successful proposals will be presented to a potential sponsor following verbal acceptance that there is interest. This is generally after the attraction, introduction, friendship and courtship phases of the relationship. (See Chapter 4, "Guiding Principles for Selling Sponsorship".)

Ideally, the sponsorship proposal will be tailored to individual sponsors, addressing the delivery of their marketing and communication objectives.

A detailed proposal containing all the information covered in the previous chapters, for example, benefits, package, price and contact details will then be presented in a business document.

This proposal is an offer to do business and it is vitally important that the document:

- Is well presented, in the form of a business document.
- Contains enough information for a company to gain a thorough understanding of what they are being offered.
- Indicates how much it will cost, and who they are dealing with.

Your proposal should however be as brief as possible without omitting important information, or you run the risk that it will not be read! A creative essay is not appropriate!

Standing Out From the Clutter

Due to the enormous number of sponsorship requests received by companies you need to make your sponsorship proposal stand out from all of the others. The best method for standing out from the clutter is to know the recipient of the proposal and hand it to them personally. It is also important, wherever possible, to tailor the proposal to the individual needs of the company being approached. To be able to do this successfully requires some background research being undertaken on the company to be approached, its desired image, products and services, prior to constructing your proposal.

Allocating Resources

Writing proposals, contacting companies and making your pitch is a time consuming and often thankless task. It is important, early on, to decide how much tailoring of the proposal will take place to meet the specific requirements of potential sponsors. Be aware of how much time is required per proposal and decide whether you will change it for each potential sponsor, or whether you are going to offer a standard package of benefits to all, and stick to that policy. (Be aware, though, that most companies will expect some negotiation of the benefits package in order to be able to achieve their specific objectives.)

Proposal Structure and Size

Structure your proposal document in an orderly business like manner. Ensure it is easy to read and the relevant information can be found. As mentioned earlier, it may also pay to do some research on the company you are targeting (requesting a copy of their Annual Report and reading it should suffice).

The following information is important in developing a proposal that sells:

- Communicate key rights and benefits.
- Demonstrate how your property will help improve the sponsor's bottom line.
- Offer a menu of benefits – a small choice allows a sponsor to pick an appropriate package.

- Present various cost options.
- Identify deal killers, such as over pricing.

Proposal length should be proportional to the value of the sponsorship. Remember – most proposals get a very quick initial perusal – the shorter and more succinct the initial document the better. Attempt to minimise the number of paragraphs you write – use short, snappy dot points. Sponsorship proposals over three pages are very unlikely to be read from cover to cover, so ensure headings are clear. Unsolicited proposals over ten pages will definitely not be read from cover to cover - who has the time? Remember, sponsorship proposals are most often sent to companies unsolicited and therefore they are under no obligation to return the proposal or any attachments, so don't include any items you want returned (photos, videotapes, certificates etc). Videotapes are rarely viewed unless you have a personal meeting with the organisation, or perhaps if they have a *very* intriguing, cute or catchy cover, and the assessor has both a spare moment <u>and</u> a VCR readily available.

Use of Endorsements

If you have happy past or present sponsors, ask them to write an endorsement of your organisation. This will provide you with credibility and indicate a track record of delivering benefits successfully to sponsors. Organisations like the Olympics use endorsements by their sponsors to elicit the sponsorship of other companies - if it works for them there is no reason why it can't for your organisation!

Use of Statistics

Many proposals promise benefits that aren't or cannot be quantified and quote media figures that aren't backed up with independent media advice or examples. The use of relevant statistical information and graphical presentation where appropriate in proposals can help the assessor get a picture of your organisation or event and can help identify cost benefit and demographic fit in relation to his own target audiences. It also indicates that your organisation is professional and serious about providing benefits. This information should help the assessor make a decision.

Past Sponsor Checks

The first check most potential sponsors should make is to ring your past and current sponsors to see how you delivered in terms of both benefits contracted, and sponsor servicing.

Disgruntled sponsors always let potential sponsors know what they think of the way they were treated in their relationship. Sponsorship is relationship marketing and where the relationship has problems both parties often take it extremely personally, particularly the party that has outlaid large amounts of money - the sponsor.

Media Monitors Checks

Media exposure is an important element of a sponsorship for 99% of companies, so wherever possible provide some or all of the following elements in a sponsorship package:

- Radio
- Television
- Print
- Community access

If you make claims of receiving significant media coverage make sure you can substantiate them, and make sure the coverage includes sponsor mention in all claimed stories.

If you received huge coverage but your past sponsor was never mentioned don't bother trying to claim the sponsor will receive massive coverage. Remember, media coverage which mentions your organisation, but not the sponsor, is of *no value whatsoever to your sponsor*!

The Proposal's Key Messages

The Proposal should communicate succinctly to the reader (potential sponsor) initially answering three questions quickly, which are:

1. **What am I being asked to sponsor** (event, organisation description). When and where does it happen?

2. **What will my company receive for sponsorship** (list of possible tangible benefits)?

3. **What is this going to cost**? If you don't include the cost, the assessor is likely to assume the cost is high, and it is very difficult for them to make a comparison with other proposals received.

The Proposal's Executive Summary

The executive summary should be less than one page and should clearly provide the following information:

- A *brief* description of what you are offering.
- Applicable date or dates for an event, or the contract period for an organisation.
- A summary of benefits
- Cost
- Your name, address, phone (business and after hours) and fax number.

The Proposal's Property Description

The property or activity description should provide all relevant information about the opportunity. Remember, the assessor probably has no knowledge of your activity and needs the following information:

Proposal Checklist

❏ Concise description of the opportunity.

❏ History - is it a long term event (they may want to be in for the long haul)?

❏ Name current or past sponsors.

❏ Provide the geographic location, and list local state or national extensions.

❑   Dates or times the sponsorship will be valid (If an event, does the timing match their product's life cycle)?

❑   Staffing of the event/organisation.

❑   Estimated attendance if applicable.

❑   Demographics - it is important to be able to define who your membership, publics and audience. By identifying the niche markets your organisation can deliver, it then becomes easy to match your audience with a product or company that markets to this unique audience. These should be presented graphically wherever possible.

❑   Estimated exposure; state actual number of media stories received in previous years where applicable. (ie, Where a sponsor was mentioned, or how many you estimate you could gain coverage of your sponsor in.)

❑   Estimate value of all exposure including, television coverage, spot packages, radio, press, signage, backup with statistics

❑   A brief background on the rights holder listing their experience, mission statement and long term goals for your organisation or event.

❑   What rights are being offered, quantify, provide value for money.

❑   Does the sponsorship have a strategic fit with the potential sponsor.

❑   How difficult is this sponsorship going to be to run, will it be well run, and take minimal time? Who is the promoter, rights holder, concession operator, and what is their experience?

❑   Who will look after the event PR?

❑   Is there opportunity for client entertainment?

❑   Is exclusivity being offered?

❑   What are the signage opportunities?

❑   Are heroes or personalities available?

❑   Is there media interest?

❑   Will our competitors want this property?

❏   The officiating body's track record experience, media handling, professionalism, marketing ability, human resources?

❏   Will this sponsorship grow sales - if so how?

❏   Will involvement with your organisation help enhance the sponsor's image?

❏   How much will market share increase and how will this be facilitated?

❏   Does your organisation have credibility? (The last thing a sponsor wants is for you to disappear with her money, or have the event fold and receive negative publicity.)

❏   Can the sponsor trust you and your organisation? They are about to pay you a significant sum of money.

The Proposal - Benefits Being Offered

The benefits section is the most important section of the document and is where you identify what benefits you are selling to potential sponsors. (See Chapter 7 'Identifying Benefits to Attract Sponsors'.) The rules are:

1. Under sell and over deliver when it comes to sponsor benefits.

2. Make sure the benefits you are offering are realistic and you have the ability to deliver them. Remember, you will be entering into a legal contract.

Keep in mind that each of your sponsors may not be interested in the same benefits. Some sponsors may want the signage or media coverage, where others may only want your membership mailing list or for you to stock their product.

(Remember to check privacy legislation in your area prior to promising membership details – in many places this is either illegal, or you must receive your member's permission to provide their details to a third party.)

The Proposal - The Property Cost

Putting a price on a proposal is a very difficult thing to do. (See Chapter 6 – 'Methods of Valuing Your Sponsorship'.) Is your opportunity, (organisation, event, team, activity) unique? If not, know what similar properties are selling for. Ask around and price yourself competitively. (If there is a sponsorship industry group operating in your area, this may be a good source of information.)

Any price listed may be subject to negotiation. Prior to signing, a potential sponsor will independently put a value on your proposal. If your offer is cost effective or unique - you are in the running - if not you do not stand much of a chance. Do not inflate the original asking price with a view to significantly lowering it at some later point.

If you are prepared to take contra (goods instead of cash) make sure you indicate this and state the value of goods you are prepared to accept and at what valuation - retail or cost. Commonly, only a small number of companies are prepared to offer contra, and be flexible in relation to costing that contra. Goods and Sales taxes can make contra a more complicated option than cash.

Proposal - Final Check

1. Allow ample lead-time. Last minute requests almost always get a negative response.

2. Is the correct person targeted (ring and check)? The Receptionist will give you the correct spelling, title and address.

3. Your proposal must convince the potential sponsor your property will work for him. Demonstrate the following:

   o   Commitment
   o   Willingness to compromise if necessary
   o   Shared vision
   o   What constitutes success

Prior to presenting the proposal ask yourself these questions:

- o Does it make good business sense to sponsor this opportunity?
- o Does this sponsorship have the capacity to help a business?
- o Is this a cost effective way for the sponsor to achieve their objectives?

Standard Base Documents

The various software packages available ensure that putting together a professional, striking proposal is within the reach of anyone who is computer literate. You can take the original document and personalise it, tailoring the benefits so they fit the client, but beware of the inherent dangers! If you are personalising a document make sure every time the company name appears it has the correct name, make sure every time you name the recipient it is the same person. There is nothing worse than being a sponsor who has received a proposal and on the last page it refers to your competitor. This is not professional, and very off-putting for a potential sponsor. Check and double-check the document prior to despatch/delivery. It never ceases to amaze us how often we still see this happen.

Copyright

How do you protect the ideas in your proposal? A common phrase amongst marketers is: "There is no such thing as an original idea", and it is in fact impossible to legally protect ideas, however it is possible to protect the document they are contained in through the law of copyright. For further information on the law of copyright contact your local Copyright Council.

Summary

- Tailor the proposal to the sponsors requirements whenever possible! Highlight your event's or organisation's strengths. Beware of weaknesses; price realistically; provide reliable statistics and demographic details with regard to your organisation or event.

- Less is better – keep the proposal short and succinct

- Undersell and over deliver the benefits!

- Make sure the benefits are realistic and you have the ability to deliver them. Remember you will be entering into a legal contract. Servicing sponsorship is an extremely time consuming exercise, so ensure you are able to identify certain staff members who will be responsible for the success of the sponsorship.

- Check company and contacts name spelling.

- The assessment, negotiation and planning involved to successfully manage a sponsorship takes substantial time, so allow a minimum of six months prior to the event to have sponsors tied up.

- Ask yourself this question:

  "Does it make good business sense to sponsor this opportunity, does our sponsorship have the capacity to help a business? Is it cost effective?"

Chapter 11

Negotiating the Deal

It is pointless becoming involved in a sponsorship arrangement where the outcome isn't 'win win'. The best deals are where a good relationship is created and both parties benefit from the relationship. The ideal situation is where a sponsor re-signs, which means that you (the one responsible for procuring sponsorship support) will not have to go out selling your organisation to sponsors for, hopefully, a very long time. Sponsors tend to re-sign only if they feel they got value for money and have been able to demonstrate that they achieved their objectives.

Some Negotiating Points to Remember

Following is some good advice from Tim Clarke, a Freelance Journalist who wrote a particularly useful article on negotiating for Discover magazine (Jan/Feb 2001).

> "When we think of negotiating, we assume one of two things will happen: either we'll win or we'll lose. But skilled negotiators don't see it that way – they know a successful negotiation is one where both sides feel like winners.
>
> Don't feel you have to win on every issue: score major victories but concede small points. Ask yourself "What can I give up that will please the other person without putting a major dent in what I want out of this?"
>
> Many people think that certain company policies and procedures are unchangeable, but the fact is that nothing is unchangeable and everything is negotiable."

Tim had some **handy hints to keep in mind when negotiating,** which are:

- A successful negotiation is one where both sides emerge feeling like winners.
- Never assume that just because something is written down on paper, it's therefore not negotiable.
- Before you sit down to negotiate, have three figures clearly in mind: the maximum you are prepared to ask for, the minimum you are prepared to settle for, and the actual figure you are aiming to agree on.
- The person who controls the negotiation is usually the one who has set the guidelines for it.
- To succeed in negotiation, you need to be prepared. Avoid surprise negotiations.
- Gather all the facts that support your position.
- Learn as much as you can about your opponents before you sit down to negotiate.
- Keep your cool if you are on the defensive.
- Try to highlight the common goals and points of agreement.

We have a couple of our own to add:

- *Always* be honest about the property.
- Be fair.
- Undersell the property's benefits and over deliver the benefits once signed.
- Be realistic with what you are offering, make sure someone with decision-making power is available to service the sponsor, and answer any queries they may have in a timely fashion.

Prior to entering negotiations you will have identified the minimum amount that you are prepared to accept for your property. If a potential sponsor is determined to force the price below that figure, you will have to consider withdrawing some of the benefits offered, or perhaps bringing on board a sub-sponsor – but don't forget, two sponsors will cost more to service than one.

Try to create renewal incentives that make it difficult for the sponsor to withdraw. Incentives such as on-site concessions are valuable tools at negotiation time.

Never oversell your property. Make sure that you are able to deliver every item that you promise in your proposal, during the negotiations and in the contract. Be aware that when servicing sponsors, underselling and over delivering in respect to benefits makes for a happy sponsor. To be able to do this successfully is an extremely time consuming exercise, always keep the following in mind; **"Undersell and over deliver - it makes for happy sponsors and long relationships."**

The Company Angle

The aim of the negotiations is to complete a favourable commercial agreement and in doing so obtain the right mix of benefits, value for money and minimise any competition or ambush by competitors.

The proposal is exactly that, a proposal, or a suggestion to do business and is only the starting point. Most companies consider that everything is negotiable. Some benefits offered will not be of interest, others will be perceived as valuable and, possibly, others not mentioned in the original proposal will be added to the melting pot. Companies enter negotiations with the view that if they don't get a package that is attractive they will go elsewhere, and we all know that there are many, many organisations out there seeking sponsorship support.

The relationship begins with the negotiations and if those negotiations don't result in both parties feeling satisfied with the outcome they should proceed no further. A bad deal for either side spells disaster and will result in resentment that will be detrimental to both the company and you as the seeker.

Payment of Fees

Most sponsorships have terms of payment set in the contract and it is normal that the first payment will be on signing of the contract document, with further payments happening at various milestones. These could include: after a specified period, or on commencement of the event. It is normal to have a payment near the end of the contract (which could well be performance driven). The terms are often used in negotiating the final outcome.

Market Price

Make sure that your property is priced at market value.   Even though you have set the price you must be be prepared to negotiate (within reason). Companies will value the property independently and will only pay what they consider it is worth. (See Chapter 6 'Methods for Valuing Your Sponsorship')

Overpricing

Never overprice your proposal initially, with a view to dropping the price. Ambit claims don't work. Companies will value the property against the benefits being offered in the proposal, and if they consider it overpriced they will assume the proposer doesn't understand the value of sponsorship will usually not even consider the proposal any further. The only occasion on which you can charge a premium, to some extent, is if your property is absolutely unique and very high profile – in other words, a 'hot property'.

Ask yourself if you received the proposal would you buy it?   Does it represent value for money? If not fix it before you send it.

The Bargain Hunter

Beware the bargain hunter! A tactic used by these people, who like to negotiate the price down below its market value, is to ask for each benefit to be individually priced. They might then pick out the one or two benefits that interest them and offer to pay the price marked along side. If you are after a single sponsor for the all of the rights being offered, it is not in your interests to individually value each item.

Listen

It is important during negotiations that you listen to what the other party is saying and that you commit to paper any proposal to expand or reduce the benefits.

When to Make Concessions

Keep in mind that what you are offering should be negotiable. If it doesn't suit the potential purchaser, an opportunity may disappear, so it is important that you are flexible enough to catch the potential sponsor.

Third Party Approval (Good Guy - Bad Guy)

A ploy used successfully in negotiations is for a third party, who is not present at the negotiations, to have the power to make the final approval on any amendments to the proposal. This allows for someone, without the emotion of being involved face to face, to look at the amended proposal with a clear head. This is generally undertaken on the sponsor's side of the equation, where often the sponsorship manager genuinely does not have the authority to sign off the expenditure required.

Time is on the Sponsor's Side!

Negotiations will become more problematic the closer you are to the event. The potential sponsor will be aware that they hold the chequebook, and that you are in a hurry to secure sponsorship. This enables them to hold a position of power and to negotiate the price down.

Free or Performance Based Sponsorships

A proven method of signing a wavering sponsor is to offer the potential sponsor the first year's sponsorship at a discount, or even free of charge, to enable the sponsor to get a taste of the benefits that can accrue for them. A similar method is the 'pay if you are happy' offer, where if pre-set benchmarks for delivery are achieved the sponsor pays for the deal at the end of the year.

Be Sure of What You Are Offering

When conducting negotiations make sure you are aware of exactly what you are offering.

If you do not have the right to negotiate on behalf of, or offer for example, the use of personalities in the package do not make the offer. In other words, make sure you have the ability to deliver every single benefit that you have offered. If you are in doubt do not promise – say that you will check and give an answer within a short (stated) time frame.

Don't Threaten

Never state that you are going to the competition or threaten a company that their main competitor is interested in sponsoring you.

This approach is almost guaranteed to ensure that you don't get the sponsorship money - after all, how often have you heard of a Dutch auction being held over a sponsorship?

Prove the Property's Worth

Be prepared to demonstrate how your sponsorship property can provide a return on investment for the potential sponsor.

Summary

Some points to remember in any negotiations are:
- **Always be honest about the property**
- **Be fair**
- **Understand that a potential sponsor *will* want to negotiate**
- **Make sure there will be no surprises**
- **Undersell the property's benefits and over deliver the benefits once signed**
- **Be realistic with what you are offering, make sure someone is available to service the sponsor, and answer any queries they may have in a timely fashion.**

Part 4

Streamlining Sponsors Processes

Chapter 12

Streamlining Sponsors Processes

Managing the Sponsorship Cycle

Sponsorship should only be considered for use if it is the most cost effective means of achieving some or all of your company's corporate or marketing objectives. This requires the ability to predict with some accuracy the impact the sponsorship program will have on the company, brand or product's bottom line. Having predicted the company's return on sponsorship investment, it can then be compared to the return other mainstream marketing and communications mediums provide, giving an indication of sponsorships' cost effectiveness.

An effective sponsorship program only occurs when a formal business process is in place. This process requires direction, strategic planning, proactive selection of sponsorship properties that will deliver strategic marketing and communications objectives, formal contracts being in place and effective sponsorship management which has its own sets of processes including planning, budgeting, review, evaluation and benchmarking. The final process is to undertake an annual review of the portfolio as a whole. Strategy for the following year should be set (or re-set) based on the outcome of the review.

The bottom line here is that a structured selection process enables companies to select the most appropriate and cost effective property, and usually results in the company becoming proactive in seeking appropriate sponsorship properties.

The formal process of selecting, planning, reviewing and post evaluating sponsorship programs provides a process of continuous improvement and through documenting the company's return on sponsorship investment and its impact on the bottom - line.

The Sponsorship Policy

To deliver a structured sponsorship program within a controlled process that will deliver accountability requires the production and approval of a formal sponsorship policy.

The sponsorship policy details the rules as to what your company will sponsor, and what they wont. This document is an internal document and tends to survive changes of management, budget and strategic management. The policy details items such as levels of expenditure and the approval processes required. (See Chapter 13 "The Sponsorship Policy".)

Sponsorship Policy
(Example only)

Sponsorship is the provision of cash or contra in return for access to the exploitable potential associated with a sponsorship property. Sponsorships are to be used to achieve the marketing objectives of the company. No sponsorships must be undertaken without the prior (written) approval of the delegated manager.

1. All sponsorships must achieve quantifiable marketing objectives as detailed in a written planning document.

2. All sponsorships must be (post) evaluated against planned objectives.

3. Sponsorships of political parties must not be undertaken.

4. Contra must be costed at customer retail price, not at the cost price. Benefits from a sponsorship must reflect the retail value of the products and services given.

5. Sponsorships must be undertaken only within the operating area (geographic boundaries) of the company.

6. Any sponsorship having the potential to create precedents beyond the local geographic area is not permitted. As an example: the sponsorship of local branches of national organisations or community bodies.

7. Sponsorships must be consistent with the company's desired corporate image and identity.

8. Sponsorship of staff is permitted if there are justifiable business reasons to do so, and tangible benefits accrue to the company.

9. Any sponsorship that has the potential to involve the company in controversial issues, or expose the company to adverse criticism, must be avoided.

10. Sponsorship requests of more than $X must be approved by the Managing Director.

11. Those between $X and $X require the signature of the Marketing Director. Those below $X require the signature of the Group Product Manager.

The Sponsorship Strategy

This document outlines the company or brand objectives for entering into a sponsorship arrangement. The strategy should determine the overall direction of the company's sponsorship portfolio and is based on strategic marketing and communications direction, current portfolio and future budget. (See Chapter 14 for "The Sponsorship Strategy".)

The strategy typically is updated with the marketing and communications strategy and does change with any change of management, company direction, budgets and available human resources.

Sponsorship Strategy
(Example only)

Situation Analysis

XYZ company is the market leader in its category in Australia and will be introducing its products into Europe during the next 12 months. BCD Limited, our major competitor, currently holds 100% of the European market.

Company Objectives for Sponsorship

To utilise sponsorship to gain awareness within the identified target audiences, through the use of personalities, sampling and dominant signage.

Company's Target Audiences

The target audiences for our sponsorship programs will be aimed at our product's target markets. Those target markets consist of all women aged 18 to 40 years, with the secondary audience being women aged 40 years or more.

Current Sponsorship Portfolio

Nil.

Proposed Acquisitions

Market research has determined that the company's objectives will be best achieved by associating with a property that is fashionable and personality based, with common appeal across Europe.

Budget

A purchase budget of $1,000,000, plus $600,000 leverage (below the line) has been allocated for the ensuing three years.

Public Sponsorship Guidelines

Sponsorship proposals are generally evaluated against pre-set guidelines, which are increasingly being formalised and partially made available to the public. These guidelines take the information contained in the sponsorship policy and sponsorship strategy documents, and present it in a checklist fashion. Preparing public sponsorship guidelines, and posting them on your website, or making them available to phone enquirers will, save your company having to respond to many totally unsuitable proposals. (See Chapter 16 for "Sponsorship Public Guidelines".)

Internal Assessment Guidelines

Companies often make use of an internal assessment checklist similar to that detailed below. The assessment checklist takes into account all the factors listed in the policy and strategy. It is utilised for assessing sponsorships that are being positively considered. (See Chapter 15 for "Streamlining Assessment Procedures".)

Assessment Checklist
(example only – from a company perspective)

Fit:

❑   Is the property consistent with our company's objectives?
❑   Do audience demographics match those of the product(s) to be promoted?
❑   Does the event's geographic reach match our product's requirements?

General:

❑   Is category exclusivity guaranteed?
❑   Is the package tailored with the benefits required? If not, can it be?
❑   Does it enhance our corporate image?
❑   Is there sufficient time to complete the planning processes prior to the event/season commencing? (Usually at least three months.)

Seeker Credibility and Track Record:

❑   Is the seeker responsible, able to work with sponsors, flexible, creative, motivated to succeed?
❑   Does the seeker have the resources to run a sponsorship and look after our company's interests?
❑   Will it be easy to implement and execute a program which will achieve our objectives?

Costs:

❑   Is sponsorship the most cost effective means to achieve the company's objectives? (If not, consider advertising, direct marketing or sales promotions.)

❑   Is the cost realistic in comparison to other similar events on the market?

❑   What are the below the line costs?

Awareness:

❑   Will it reach and favourably influence opinion leaders?

❑   Is the community interested in this activity? (Check research.)

❑   Does the property reach the target audience numbers required?

Promotional Extensions:

❑   Can trade incentives be introduced?

❑   Are compatible co-sponsors interested in cross promotions?

❑   Are there display opportunities?

❑   Are there opportunities to get on site concessions?

Signage:

❑   Television?

❑   Uniforms/apparel?

Hospitality:

❑   Is it available?

❑   Are the facilities of a suitable standard for corporate entertaining?

Media Coverage:

❑   Are there opportunities to get the brand or logo in all media stories?

❑   Is the event broadcast? Are there opportunities for advertising or on air promotions?

The Sponsorship Budget

This document dictates how much money is available for expenditure on property (sponsorship) purchase and below the line or support expenditure for the company's sponsorship program. (See Chapter 24 for "Creating the Sponsorship Plan".)

The Sponsorship Contract

Without any doubt, the most important document of all is the contract. The foundation for a good relationship is a tight contract. It details all rights and benefits to accrue to the sponsor, payment dates and details, renewal options and covers the obligations of both the sponsored organisation and the sponsor in relation to the property. (See Chapter 23 for 'The Contract and its Implications'.)

Sponsorship Business Plans

A sponsorship business or leverage plan should be written for each sponsorship in your portfolio, and it should contain the following:

- Set sales or volume targets to be directly achieved by the sponsorship program
- Define corporate and brand objectives to be achieved by the sponsorship program
- Identify promotional extensions and their cost and value
- Detail planned leverage activities, allocating responsibilities
- Accurately predict, the program's below the line costs
- Outline the man-hours required
- Detail the review and post evaluation methods to be undertaken.

(See Chapter 24 for 'Creating the Sponsorship Business Plan'.)

Continuous Review

The minimum evaluation to be undertaken should be a post evaluation, which should happen at least annually, however, if you wait until the end of the year to look at your results, you may be shocked to find that people, at best, are unaware of the association, and at worst have been negatively impacted or influenced by the sponsorship. It is therefore recommended that a process of continuous review be undertaken, whereby you would measure all sponsorships against objectives at least quarterly.

Post Evaluation

The Post Evaluation will determine the accuracy of the business plan, detail the actual return on investment, and, when the results are compared to benchmarks, will provide an indication of the performance of the management of the sponsorship by Project Manager(s) and consultancies involved. (See Chapter 31 for 'Evaluating the Results and Benchmarking'.)

Summary

- **Good sponsorship programs do not happen by accident – they are the result of a structured selection process, strategic planning and implementation, continuous review and formal post evaluation**

- **The following documents must be produced and approved by senior management *prior* to considering sponsorship:**

  - **Policy**
  - **Strategy**
  - **Internal Guidelines and Public Guidelines**
  - **Internal Assessment Checklist**
  - **Sponsorship Budget**
  - **Contracts**
  - **Sponsorship Business Plans – for each sponsorship**
  - **Formal Post Evaluation**

Chapter 13

The Sponsorship Policy

Why Write a Policy?

The Sponsorship Policy provides the company's ground rules for entering into sponsorship agreements. A policy is most valuable where multiple people are able to sign sponsorship agreements. This typically occurs where a company is national and has regional offices or branches.

The policy ensures that all sponsorships are handled in a uniform manner and assessed fairly within a company. Policy procedures will ensure that people who need to know about sponsorships in progress are informed.

The policy is usually promulgated by the CEO or the Board. It delegates the authority to purchase and manage the sponsorship program to the Sponsorship Manager, and delivers accountability and control to the organisation's overall sponsorship program.

Some companies may need more than one policy - particularly if they are engaging in more than one category of sponsorship in order to achieve differing objectives. There may be one policy for national or corporate sponsorship and another for marketing and/or regional sponsorships.

Policy Checklist

The policy document should be brief– only two or three pages. A policy would normally contain the following information:

- The approval process required in order to gain approval for a sponsorship deal.

- The position of the person delegated to approve sponsorship activity.

- Who will be accountable for the success of the sponsorship program.

- How formal the contract or letter of agreement needs to be.

- Statement that the sponsorship must comply with corporate objectives listed in the Sponsorship Strategy document

- Establish the rules for valuing and paying for sponsorships, including the use of contra/in-kind to pay for properties.

- State what categories of sponsorship may be sponsored at a local and at a national level. For example, events that are of a local nature may be sponsored by a local branch.

- Detail whether or not staff and staff teams can be sponsored and list any conditions.

- List properties that must not be sponsored, these could include. For example, political parties or religious groups.

- Who must be informed about the signing of a sponsorship. For example, Media and PR departments.

- Identify the budgets and accounts sponsorships are to be funded from.

- The company's requirements for exclusivity (usually category at least).

- Sponsorship must comply with corporate identity policy.

- Prescribed levels of benefits required.

- Criteria with which to value sponsorship properties.

- Budgetary approval levels. For example, branch level can approve up to $5000 sponsorship.

Guide to a Writing Sponsorship Policy

Policy - Identify Purpose

- State the organisation's objectives for entering into sponsorship agreements.
- Set the rules for entering into sponsorship agreements.
- Ensure a uniform approach is taken to sponsorship throughout the organisation.
- State the level of accountability and responsibility required.

Identify Scope

- Detail which areas The Sponsorship Policy applies to, ie, the entire organisation, including operating Departments and Units and associated independent operations.

- The Sponsorship Policy covers all activities described as sponsorship in the definition below regardless of whether the sponsorship is in kind (contra) or cash or the organisation is the sponsor or seeker (recipient).

Define Sponsorship

- Describe clearly what constitutes a sponsorship arrangement. A definition of sponsorship can be found in the glossary of terms at the end of this book.

- Describe clearly what a sponsorship is not. This may include donations hospitality and grants.

Describe Use of Sponsorship

Describe clearly the use of sponsorships within the company. Uses could include:

- Providing a financial return on investment to the organisation through incremental sales growth.

- Increasing awareness of the brand or products.

- Improving the organisations image.

- Developing relationships with the community and community groups.

- Communicating key messages and/or facilitating change in community attitudes towards the organisation.

Describe Reporting

Describe all reporting requirements. For example, "all sponsorship activity is to be registered in the sponsorship database".

- To avoid situations of conflict
- To ensure adequate recognition of recipients by the CEO.

List Limitations

Most organisations will avoid becoming involved with those sponsorships that could involve them in controversy or expose the organisation to adverse criticism.

The following sponsorships would be regarded by many organisations as being inappropriate.

- Political or religious organisations.
- Programs that denigrate, exclude, or offend minority community groups.
- Programs that may present a hazard to the community.
- Programs that create environmental hazards.
- Programs that do not reflect community standards.

Describe Management Process

This section of the policy should describe other policies to be adhered to and the general principles of managing the organisation's sponsorship program. Examples are:

- Sponsorship programs undertaken should normally be within the operating area (geographic boundaries) of the organisation.

- Sponsorships must be consistent with the organisations desired corporate image and identity.

- Sponsorship of staff is permitted if there are justifiable business reasons, and tangible benefits are returned to the organisation. (Refer to HR Policy).

- Sponsorships are to be funded and managed by the relevant business group as a component of the group's business plan.

- All sponsorship properties must be able to achieve quantifiable marketing and/or communications objectives as demonstrated by a detailed sponsorship plan, which states the real cost of the sponsorship program to the organisation.

- As most sponsorship programs require extensive project management to enable the benefits to be delivered, the anticipated staff costs must be detailed.

- The plan must detail who will be accountable for the overall success of the sponsorship program.

- All sponsorships must be post evaluated against planned marketing and communication objectives (a minimum of once per year).

- Contra (goods and/or services in lieu of cash) given must be valued at cost price. The resulting benefits received from a sponsorship program must reflect the retail value of the products and services given.

Describe Delegation Limits

Often delegation limits are significantly reduced for sponsorships due to the potential (and unfortunately the likelihood in a lot of cases) for unsuitable properties to be funded.

- Sponsorship programs with a value of up to $25,000 must be approved by the relevant Manager subject to the relevant business plan.

- Sponsorships valued in excess of $25,000 must be referred to the CEO together with the Manager's recommendation for approval.

Example Policy

Pineapple People of Australia
Sponsorship Policy

Purpose of Policy

➤   To state Pineapple People of Australia's objectives for entering into all sponsorship agreements.

➤   To set the rules for entering into sponsorship agreements.

➤   To ensure a uniform approach is taken to sponsorship throughout the company.

➤   To state the level of accountability and responsibility required in the purchase and management of sponsorship programs including shows.

Scope of the Policy

➤   The Sponsorship Policy applies to all of Pineapple People of Australia, including operating Departments and Units and associated independent operations that use Pineapple People of Australia Brands.

➤   The Sponsorship Policy covers all activities described as sponsorship in the definition below regardless of whether the sponsorship is in kind (contra) or cash.

Sponsorship is defined as:

➤ Any relationship that Pineapple People of
Australia has with another organisation event
or individual which results in any one of the
company's brands being exposed or linked in
conjunction with that event, organisation or
individual and/or provides intangible
exploitable potential rights and benefits
associated with an event, entrant, or
organisation, which results in tangible
benefits (which could include increased
awareness of brand, communication of key
messages, sales, hospitality, signage,
goodwill,) to the company in return for
payment or contra.

➤ Sponsorship does not include donations, which
are defined as free money given with no
benefits required.

Use of Sponsorship

➤ Sponsorships are to be purchased to deliver the
objectives detailed in the Sponsorship
Strategy.

Reporting Requirements

➤ All sponsorship activity is to be reported to
the Manager Sponsorship and registered in
Sponsorcom prior to commitment. This will ensure
accountability and responsibility and avoid
situations of conflict.

Limitations

➤ Sponsorships that could involve Pineapple
People of Australia in controversial issues or
expose the organisation to adverse criticism
must be avoided. The following sponsorships
are regarded as being inappropriate:

- political parties or religious organisations;
- programs that denigrate, exclude, or offend minority community groups;
- programs that may present a hazard to the community;
- programs that create environmental hazards;
- programs that do not reflect community standards;
- programs sponsored by competitors.

Management Process

➤ Sponsorships must be consistent with Pineapple People of Australia desired corporate image and identity.

➤ Sponsorships are to be funded and managed by the Sponsorship Manager or delegated representative as a component of Pineapple People of Australia business plan.

➤ All sponsorship properties must be able to achieve quantifiable marketing and/or communications objectives as demonstrated by a detailed sponsorship plan and budget, which states the real cost of the sponsorship program to Pineapple People of Australia.

➤ Unbudgeted sponsorships are not to be undertaken without approval of the Sponsorship Manager.

➤ As most sponsorship programs require extensive project management to enable all benefits to be delivered, the anticipated leverage costs must be detailed the sponsorship plan.

➢ The plan must detail who will be accountable for the overall success of the sponsorship program.

➢ All sponsorships must be post evaluated against planned marketing and communication objectives (a minimum of once per year).

➢ Contra (goods and/or services in lieu of cash) given must be valued at retail price. The resulting benefits received from a sponsorship program must reflect the retail value of the products and services given.

➢ The cost of sale to win an account should not be linked to sponsorship activity unless sponsorship of the particular organisation fits strategy, is budgeted for and approved, prior to agreement, by the Sponsorship Manager.

➢ Otherwise the cost of sale (cash or contra) should be funded by the sales area and sponsorship benefits such as use of the brand, receipt of ticketing and hospitality should not be agreed to.

Delegation Limits

➢ All sponsorship programs must be recommended for approval by the Sponsorship Manager and approved by the Marketing Manager.

Summary

- Take time to make sure your processes are right – at the beginning, not as an afterthought.

- The policy sets the rules for entering into sponsorship agreements.

- Sponsorship policy delegates the responsibility and accountability for the success of the sponsorship program to the Sponsorship Manager

Chapter 14

The Sponsorship Strategy

Sponsorship Strategy

+ Business/Marketing Plan for each sponsorship

+ Implementation

+ Evaluation

= Demonstrated Return on Investment (a successful sponsorship)

The Sponsorship Strategy details the fundamental approach to sponsorships within a company, as part of the overall marketing and communication strategy for the company. It sets the overall course for achieving stated objectives and provides the foundation of all sponsorship business plans. The strategy document should detail:

- The company or brands target market (demographics)
- The company's (desired) image
- The company's mission statement
- Company's objectives for entering into sponsorship
- Identify ideal sponsorship portfolio
- Identify sponsorships to be divested
- Identify sponsorships to be purchased
- Allocated budget
- Available human resources
- Identify review process to be undertaken
- Gain approval of relevant stakeholders

The sponsorship strategy should not be confused with the sponsorship policy. Each document has a separate role. The sponsorship policy is an internal document and contains information such as the approval processes required, levels of expenditure and the rules as to what the company will sponsor, and what it will not. The policy rarely changes, however the strategy will change with changes of:

- Company direction
- Product lines
- Management
- Budget
- Human resource availability

The Politics, the Benefits

A Corporate Sponsorship Strategy has the potential to be a highly political document. It is written by the head of the sponsorship area and usually approved by the Marketing Director and sometimes the CEO. It should be updated on at least an annual basis, or more often if there is a strategic marketing and communications change within the company.

Once this document is approved by the relevant stakeholders it gives the Sponsorship Manager a free hand to get on with the job and provides an approved platform from which to get the job done.

The Contents

A corporate sponsorship strategy usually contains the following:

- A **Situation Analysis** of the company and the environment it operates within.

- A description of the company's **desired corporate image.** A company's image is essentially its personality, and indicates how the company is perceived externally. Corporate image is affected by the way a company communicates and relates with its publics and can change from time to time, and can be directly affected by the company's marketing and communications program.

- The company's **mission statement**. This states the company values and reason for trading.

- The broad **company objectives** for undertaking sponsorship programs.

- Desired **target audiences** including stakeholders, external and internal audiences.

- Broad **key messages** to be transmitted by the company's sponsorship program.

- Identify **ideal sponsorship portfolio.** This will detail the categories of sponsorship that will best achieve the company's marketing and communications objectives as detailed in the overall marketing and communications strategy.

- Identify **sponsorships to be divested**. Identify sponsorships within the existing sponsorship portfolio that need to be divested in order to move forward to the ideal sponsorship portfolio.

- Identify **sponsorships to be purchased**. This will identify any gaps in the portfolio, and identify those sponsorship properties that are capable of delivering the sponsorship strategy.

- An **action or implementation timetable** detailing what sponsorships to purchase, option dates, and those to discontinue.

- The overall company **sponsorship budget, including purchase and leverage funding.** In many cases there is no set specific sponsorship budget, as sponsorship activity is funded through the marketing or advertising accounts.

- **Available human resources.** It is impossible to successfully deliver a sponsorship program without the necessary staff.

- Detail e**valuation** Mechanisms to be employed to measure results and quantify return on sponsorship investment.

- The **stakeholders** signature/s.

Guide to Writing the Strategy

1. **The Situation Analysis should contain:**

    *   A concise description of the environment the company is currently operating within.
    *   Details of any significant competitors in the category.
    *   The broad existing use of sponsorship.
    *   The markets the company operates within.
    *   Any changes to the marketing and communications direction of the company.

2. **A description of the company's desired corporate image.**

    *   This would generally be provided by the Director of Marketing.

3. **The company's mission statement.**

    *   Insert a copy of your company's mission statement. This would come from the CEO's office in most cases. All sponsorship activity should adhere to the principles contained in the mission statement.

4. **Define your broad objectives for the use of Sponsorships. Your objectives could include one or a number of the following:**

    *   Generate goodwill (PR)
    *   Increase sale (bottom line)
    *   Generate brand/product or corporate awareness (media and publicity)
    *   Relationship marketing (hospitality/client entertainment)
    *   Identify a product with a lifestyle (position a brand)
    *   Exclusivity (the ability to lock the opposition out)
    *   Narrow-casting (communicate to niche markets)
    *   Create merchandising opportunities (on-site concessions)
    *   Demonstrate product attributes (sampling)

5. **Identify Target Audiences of the Sponsorship Program.**
   Sponsorships are an ideal vehicle to communicate to defined market
   segments (niches) whether that be by geography, demography, or
   psychographics. It is important to define who the target group(s) of your
   sponsorship program is. They could include:

   - Customers
   - General Public
   - Stakeholders (shareholders, regulators)
   - Trade
   - Staff and families
   - Media
   - Government
   - Lobby Groups
   - International audience
   - National audience
   - Regional audience
   - Local audience
   - Specific age group(s)
   - Lifestyles

6. **Broad key messages to be transmitted by the company's
   sponsorship program. These could include:**

   1. Sales messages/call to action
   2. Brand attributes
   3. Corporate positioning

7. **Identify the ideal sponsorship portfolio.** The portfolio chosen must be
   compatible with the target audiences and its values, and also compatible
   with the company's image and products. The portfolio could include
   one or more of the following.

   - Arts
   - Education
   - Environment
   - Sports - Professional
   - Sports - Amateur
   - Sports - National
   - Charity/Cause Related

- Community
- Popular Arts (Theatre - Concerts)
- Individuals (sports people, artists, musicians etc)

8. **Identify sponsorship properties to be divested.** List those sponsorship properties that are currently contained within the portfolio, and no longer fit strategy.

9. **Identify Sponsorship properties to be acquired.** List those sponsorship properties that will deliver strategy.

10. **Timetable of acquisitions and divestments**. This should detail:

- Expiry dates of current sponsorships (to be divested)
- Option dates of those properties that will be retained
- Relevant dates relating to acquisition of new properties.

11. **Identify Sponsorship Budget.** Insert overall sponsorship budget including purchase and leverage funds.

12. **Detail human resources required to enable delivery of the planned sponsorship program.**

13. **Evaluation. Detail evaluation methods to be utilised and date annual review due. The Evaluation can:**

- Measure the effectiveness and accuracy of the communicated messages.
- Identify target audiences reached, their size and what messages are received.
- Interpret the overall tone of the coverage: ie, positive, neutral, or negative.
- Identify return on investment versus advertising.
- Measure sponsor recognition and the sponsor's key messages.
- Identify how effectively sponsors are linked to the sponsorship.
- Compare sponsors return on investment.
- Compare events for value for money.
- Measure cost per impact.

14. **Identify stakeholders in this document.** Getting the document approved requires the identification of stakeholders and getting them on side prior to putting the document up for approval. Stakeholders could, and probably will, include the following.

- Board members. This will relate to both personal interest, and expenditure on behalf of shareholders.
- CEO (and indirectly the CEO's Spouse). They have to attend the associated events.
- Senior management, must be committed to the portfolio.

Summary

- **Sponsorship Strategy + Business/Marketing Plan for each sponsorship + Implementation + Evaluation = Demonstrated Return on Investment (a successful sponsorship).**

- **The policy and the strategy are utilised in the preparation of public sponsorship guidelines, assessment checklists.**

- **The policy and strategy also provide base material for all sponsorship plans and evaluations.**

- **Taking the time to formulate a sponsorship strategy with wide acceptance provides a climate of consent to the Sponsorship Manager.**

Chapter 15

Streamlining Assessment Procedures

The Need

The effectiveness of sponsorship programs or any mass communications medium is difficult to assess. There is certainly no shortage of sponsorship properties to choose from. All proposals lay claim to providing numerous benefits and delivering particular target audiences, and there is no doubt that some properties are cost effective and provide value for money. However many properties and promoters have no track record with handling sponsors and many overprice their properties.

Assessing sponsorships, replying to proposers, answering enquiries, taking follow up questions and keeping records and files of all requests is a time consuming activity and in a large company can take the full time services of at least one person. There are a number of ways of minimising the time taken on these activities, they include having a policy and sponsorship strategy with stated objectives for the sponsorship program, so you know what properties are likely to suit your firm. Providing the public with sponsorship guidelines eliminates the proposals that you just wouldn't take up any way as well as saving the time and money of the proposer.

The Assessment Process

Only larger companies have dedicated sponsorship staff. In many cases, sponsorship is handled by the Marketing Manager, the Corporate Affairs Manager or similar as an addition to their main position. Consequently, sponsorship proposals are often seen as an additional workload and not a priority.

They are not often handled in a timely manner, and need to catch the eye immediately upon being opened to get more than a cursory glance. Following are some fairly typical steps undertaken within large companies when handling unsolicited sponsorship proposals.

Step One

On receipt of the sponsorship proposal it is usually skimmed to see if there is any interest at all. Depending on the company and its resources, this process may take less than thirty seconds. Those properties that 'just don't fit' are immediately declined. Many companies these days are proactive about their sponsorship programs. In other words, they seek the properties that are most likely to achieve their objectives. This being the case, there is very little likelihood that an unsolicited proposal will "fit the bill".

Step Two

If the initial perusal evokes some interest the second stage involves reading the document in its entirety to assess whether this property is a possibility for sponsorship funding. If it proves not to be, which would happen in more than 95% of cases, it would also be declined.

Step Three

If there is still interest, you may need to do some research and see if the proposal can deliver everything it promises. This would typically, initially, include following up with past sponsors, checking industry sources and so on.

Step Four

Assuming the (seeker) organisation reference checks well, it is time to call the person/organisation offering you this wonderful opportunity and ask for a meeting to discuss the proposal. The first meeting is usually a fact-finding exercise, and should it culminate in continued interest, subsequent meetings should "tailor" the benefits package to suit your organisation, and ensure that all your expectations (and theirs) are covered in the contract.

Comparing Oranges with Apples

When receiving proposals and requests for sponsorship you will often need to compare sponsorships in different price brackets that target totally different demographic groups and offer varying benefits and costs. To effectively sift through the proposals received, you will need to know your organisation's marketing and communications objectives, and check to see if the target audience being delivered matches your desired demographic. (See Chapter 14 'The Sponsorship Strategy'.)

In assessing any sponsorship you will need to determine whether the property on offer is the most likely to cater for your organisation's unique needs:

- **Strategic Fit** - does the sponsorship property being offered match your company's sponsorship objectives and can this property deliver the required benefits or objectives cost effectively.

- **Strengths** - what are the property's strengths and what benefits does it deliver?

- **Weaknesses** - what are the property's weaknesses – and what effect would this have on the outcomes of the sponsorship program?

- **Opportunities** - what are the opportunities that this property presents. (For example, could it be used to influence policy makers, if that is what the company needs to do?)

- **Risks** - what risks exist and are they minimal? For example, is this an outdoor event that could be adversely affected (postponed, or even cancelled) by poor weather?

- **Uncontrollable Factors** - which items/situations are beyond the sponsor's control and are you comfortable with the situation.

- **Controllable Factors** - which factors are within the other party's control, and are you comfortable with the effect these factors could have on your organisation.

It is extremely unlikely that you would have time to assess, negotiate, draw up contracts and then plan for and run a successful sponsorship program if you received the proposal only six weeks prior to the event/season start etc.

Assessing sponsorships is often considered an art rather than a science, however companies use a number of tools to assist them in making their decisions.

Assessing Sponsorship Proposals

Sponsorship proposals should be assessed a minimum of four, and preferably six, months prior to an event. This enables you to consider the sponsorship and if you are interested it allows time to enter negotiations, sign the deal, prepare business plans to exploit the relationship and organise resources and budgets to implement the event.

It would be a very brave Sponsorship Manager who committed funds to an event set to begin in a fortnight. There are three reasons for this - a) There simply will not be enough time to evaluate the proposal and enter into negotiations, and b) you must wonder at the credibility of an event that has secured no sponsors only a fortnight before they require them to be on board and c) most importantly, you just would not have the time to plan and undertake the actions necessary (creative, advertising, promotions, etc.) to achieve your objectives.

Sponsorship proposals generally take anywhere from one to six weeks to be assessed and responded to depending, once again, on the resources of the company involved. It is common to be phoned by seekers asking if you have received and assessed their proposal - often twice before you even receive the proposal. To prevent this happening, respond to all requests as quickly as possible. After all, the majority of the proposals you receive will not be supported, so it should be relatively easy to respond to these with a standard letter within a few days.

Another successful way of averting time spent on unproductive telephone calls is to leave a message on your department's voicemail, giving the caller the option of leaving a short message either asking for follow up, or leaving their address in order to receive public guidelines. In leaving a message, you are saving the time required to field the initial call, and then having to ring back when you have located the proposal they are enquiring about.

If your public guidelines are as instructive as they should be, all necessary instructions relating to seeking sponsorship will be contained in the one document.

Be Proactive

Many companies who have chosen to be in the sponsorship game are proactive in finding properties that fit. They actively go and canvas potential properties looking for the right sponsorship. Occasionally, though, a property that will fit your particular needs will arrive via an unsolicited proposal, and for this reason it is worth going through the perusal process.

We believe that doing the research and analysing available properties is far more likely to lead to a well planned, well managed sponsorship program than taking on a property that has arrived via an unsolicited proposal.

The exception to this might be opportunities that arrive via. a credible Broker, who will have done his homework, and will know that he is offering your company an opportunity.

Telephone Contact

You will receive many telephone calls from seekers of sponsorship funding. If you do not have an assistant to field such calls, establish rules for handling them. We suggest that you state that it is company policy that any request for sponsorship/financial assistance/donation is made in writing. Mention that you would prefer this to be a short document, providing the following details:

1. Name of the organisation seeking sponsorship.
2. The nature of the event or property on offer.
3. The timing of the event (ie, a one day, one week, one season, three year term etc.) and dates.
4. How much the relationship is going to cost your company.
5. What benefits will accrue to your company from such a relationship.

Declining

It is always good policy to be as truthful as possible in responding to these unsolicited sponsorship requests. If it is because you have already committed your entire budget to one or more ongoing sponsorships, say so in the letter. If it is because the opportunity offered does not fit with your organisation's current strategy, you could advise them of this in the letter..

Reapplying

Some sponsorship seekers will telephone you after receiving a letter declining their request for assistance to find out if they can reapply some time in the future. Once again, be honest. If it is very unlikely that your company would sponsor this organisation, event or individual – say so. Save them the trouble of putting together another proposal, just to receive another rejection. Thank them for taking the time to present their opportunity to you, and display an understanding of the difficulty of their situation.

The assessment checklist takes into account all the factors listed above, you may wish to add some to suit your particular needs.

Assessment Checklist

In assessing any sponsorship you are determining whether the property is the most suitable for your company's needs. To do this requires assessment against the following criteria:

- **Strategic Fit** - Does the sponsorship property match your sponsorship objectives and can this property deliver the required benefits or objectives cost effectively?

- **Strengths** - What are the property's strengths and what benefits does it deliver?

- **Weaknesses** - What are the weaknesses - are they enough to kill the project?

- **Opportunities** - What are the opportunities that this property presents? (For example, could it be used to provide networking opportunities for management?)

- **Risks** - what risks exist and are they minimal?

- **Uncontrollable factors** - list those items that are beyond your control and determine whether you are comfortable with the situation.

Fit:

- [ ] Is the property consistent with your marketing and communication
- [ ] objectives? (Check Strategy.)
- [ ] Does the lifestyle of the event fit your core values, product, brand or brand positioning?
- [ ] Do audience demographics match those of the product(s) to be promoted?
- [ ] What size is the audience?
- [ ] Does the event's geographic reach match your product's requirements?
- [ ] Is the coverage national/state/regional or local?
- [ ] Does it fit with existing sponsorships - is there synergy?
- [ ] Is your business compatible with current or future sub-sponsors?
- [ ] Is the audience and the community interested in this activity? If not how can it be created?
- [ ] Does the community approve of this organisation?
- [ ] Does sponsorship timing fit brand strategy/seasonality?
- [ ] Does timing clash with other events?
- [ ] Can the sponsorship influence the target audience in terms of attitude and behaviour change?

General:

- ☐ Is category exclusivity guaranteed?
- ☐ Are naming rights available (preferably exclusive or dominant)?
- ☐ Are promotional rights available (use of name/symbol)?
- ☐ Is ceremonial involvement available?
- ☐ How many other sponsors are there and at what level?
- ☐ What is the likelihood of ambush/can it be minimised?
- ☐ Is the right of veto of other sponsors available?
- ☐ Is the event in a growth or decline cycle?
- ☐ Is the package tailored with the benefits required/or can the package be modified?
- ☐ Does it have long term potential and opportunity to grow the event?
- ☐ Can the benefits be delivered/ is there a future benefit?
- ☐ Does it enhance our brand/corporate image?
- ☐ Are you backing winners?
- ☐ Will it open doors to prospects, people of influence, decision makers and the media?
- ☐ Is there sufficient time to complete the planning processes prior to the event, season commencing? (Usually at least three months.)
- ☐ Can the event be utilised to deliver other organisational objectives? (i.e. trade, suppliers etc)
- ☐ Access to mailing list available?
- ☐ The capability of the venue to house substantial audience numbers?
- ☐ Does it require hands on involvement?
- ☐ Are all benefits itemised?

Sponsor seeker credibility and track record:

☐ Is the sponsor seeker responsible, able to work with sponsors (check with past and present sponsors), flexible, creative, professional, motivated to succeed?

☐ Is the sponsor seeker deemed as being a good ambassador to the brand?

☐ Does the organisation want a sponsor or is it simply desperate for funds?

☐ Will the sponsor seeker win in its competition?

☐ Does the sponsor seeker have the resources to run a sponsorship and look after your company's interests?

☐ Does the sponsor seeker have an event/organisation plan and objectives?

☐ Are their organisation's target audience demographics presented?

☐ Are evaluation procedures outlined?

☐ Is the event/activity budget detailed?

☐ Is the sponsor seeker morally and ethically sound?

☐ Are they financially viable and economically stable? (check with Commercial Dept)

☐ Check with a past or current sponsors regarding delivery of sponsorship benefits and reference check!

☐ Is the sponsor seeker authorised to represent the organisation?

☐ Does the organisation or representative actually use/recommend our products?

Costs:

☐ Is sponsorship the most cost effective means to achieve your objectives? (If not, consider advertising, direct marketing or sales promotions).

❑ Is the cost realistic in comparison to other similar events on the market?

❑ What are the below the line costs (see publicity checklist)?

❑ Are there any hidden costs? (staff travel, freight, etc)

❑ Will costs be justified by results?

❑ Cost of not sponsoring (will the competitor grab it)?

❑ Have the implications of GST been considered? (check with Commercial/S&F)

❑ Will they accept cash or contra or a combination of both? - Has contra freight been costed?

Awareness:

❑ Will it reach and favourably influence opinion leaders?

❑ What will our perceived association be with the sponsored property?

❑ Will the sponsorship broaden product awareness, and therefore stimulate sales?

❑ Is the community interested in this activity? (Check research.)

❑ Will it appeal to our customers? (Check research.)

Promotional Extensions:

❑ Can in store promotions be used?

❑ Can trade incentives be introduced?

❑ Can local promotions be created?

❑ Are compatible co-sponsors interested in cross promotions?

❑ Can advertising programs be created using the event or its personalities?

❑ Are there opportunities to create event merchandise?

❑ Are there opportunities for sampling?

❑ Are there display opportunities?

- ❑   Are there opportunities to get on-site concessions?
- ❑   Are there on pack opportunities?
- ❑   Direct sales opportunities?
- ❑   Can competitions / prizes be developed?

Signage:

- ❑   Will the signage receive media exposure?
- ❑   Apparel signage available?
- ❑   Is signage production, erection and costs included in the deal?
- ❑   Where is the signage located versus others?
- ❑   Duration of signage exposure?
- ❑   Who is responsible for maintenance of signage?
- ❑   Is a local government permit required?
- ❑   Are there restrictions on material composition or hanging of signage?
- ❑   Duelling Logos - what is the signage clutter like?

Hospitality:

- ❑   Is it available?
- ❑   Is it required?
- ❑   Is it included in price?
- ❑   Is the standard of client facilities acceptable? (Check!)

Media coverage:

- ❑   Will the media see the sponsorship or the event as newsworthy?
- ❑   Are there opportunities to get the brand or logo in all media stories?
- ❑   Is the event broadcast? Are there opportunities for advertising or on air promotions?
- ❑   Who is responsible for the media presence?

❏   Can we see the media, advertising and PR strategies?

❏   Do we need to develop our own media strategy?

Staff involvement:

❏   Are there opportunities to involve staff?

❏   How many staff are required, when and for how long?

❏   What are associated staff costs?

❏   Are staff costs contributed to ie parking etc?

❏   What skill levels must the staff possess?

❏   Is specialist training required?

❏   Will associates be motivated by this sponsorship?

Remember

1. **Shop around – it is always a buyer's market!**

2. **Say no quickly and yes slowly.**

3. **Make sure it "fits" and will achieve your objectives.**

Say NO QUICKLY, and say YES SLOWLY

By saying no quickly you eliminate a large number of time wasting follow up calls. Saying yes slowly gives you time to investigate the proposal and make sure it really fits and will work for your organisation. Don't make a rash decision because someone else might take up the opportunity, there just aren't that many buyers in the market place.

Remember every proposer is perhaps a client or potential client of your company, and as such it is important not to offend the proposer. Many companies have form letters that they send out stating that the proposer hasn't been successful in their application. Where these letters don't give a reason for declining the property you quite often find that proposers ring to find out why they were unsuccessful.

To counter follow up calls and show some courtesy to the proposer, we recommend having a number of form letters that state the true reason you aren't taking up their opportunity. This keeps the proposer happy and makes them feel like they have been looked after even though they were declined.

I suggest each form letter states why you haven't taken up their opportunity, for example:

No Resources Available

Dear Mr Long,

Thank you for your proposal detailing the opportunities available to us through sponsorship of the Australian Sports Festival.

Our Company prides itself on contributing to many sporting, arts, charity and community events and activities.

However, our sponsorship budget for the current financial year has been allocated, and there are currently no available resources to fund new sponsorship requests.

Regrettably, we are therefore unable to consider requests to support additional activity at this time.

Thank you again for taking the time to present this opportunity to us.

Yours sincerely

Can't Support all

Dear Mr Brown,

We have received your letter requesting support for the World Art Exhibition.

Your request has been carefully reviewed in consultation with other departments within the company.

As you can appreciate, we receive a large number of requests each week to support and be involved in worthy causes. Our company prides itself on contributing to many charity and community events and activities, but unfortunately we are not in a position to support all the requests that we receive.

It is therefore with regret that we must advise that we are unable to assist you on this occasion.

We wish you every success in your efforts for the World Art Exhibition.

Yours sincerely

Doesn't Fit Strategic Objectives

Dear Ms Smith,

Thank you for your proposal detailing the opportunities available to us through the sponsorship of the A-1 Touring Car Team.

Each proposal is assessed against a number of internal benchmarks including available resources, strategic brand fit, activity schedules and financial considerations.

We have carefully reviewed your proposal, and unfortunately it does not meet our strategic objectives or provide the wide scope of benefits we seek in being involved as a sponsor.

Given this, we therefore must decline your offer to sponsor the A-1 Touring Car Team.

Thank you again for taking the time to present this opportunity to us.

Yours sincerely

Individual Decline

Dear Mr Green,

Thank you for your letter of introduction.

Your list of achievements to date is certainly significant and it is evident that you have the skill and determination to achieve at a high level in your chosen field.

As you can appreciate, we receive a large number of requests to sponsor and to assist individuals in achieving their dreams and ambitions. Unfortunately we have limited resources and are unable to fulfil all the requests that we receive and, as a result, we have taken the approach to focus our support on events, activities and charities that benefit a wider community rather than an individual.

It is therefore with regret, that we are unable to offer you sponsorship.

I wish you every success in your pursuits.

Yours sincerely

Some proposers, when dealing with large companies like to cover all bases, or having no idea who to write to, use the shotgun tactic and write to everyone they can think of. It is very important to have a single person responding to all sponsorship request letters received company wide. If you do not handle your requests in this manner, you could have the situation where a multitude of reasons are sent out to the same seeker for not taking up their opportunity, or, even worse, some managers offering sponsorship, and others making excuses such as "there is no budget available".

Dear Ms Johnson,

I have received your requests for sponsorship, which were sent to Frank White, Dot Brown, Sibyl Marriot, and Daniel Black.

As mentioned in my letter to you dated 2nd September, it is still the case that our entire sponsorship budget is allocated to ongoing projects such as breast cancer research and children's sporting activities, and we are therefore unable to support your request at this time.

We would like to take this opportunity to wish you well with your future endeavours.

Yours faithfully,

The really persistent seeker will not accept no for an answer and will persevere by writing to multiple people within the organisation or climbing the ladder. In this case you may have to send out a letter that clearly states your position:

Dear Mr Costello,

Your letter to our Board Chairman, Barron Johnson, requesting that he reconsider my earlier decision not to support your request for sponsorship has been forwarded to me for response.

As advised to you previously, due to company policy, which precludes us from supporting this type of activity, we are unable to assist with your forthcoming attempt on the world earthworm eating record.

We would like to take this opportunity to wish you well in your endeavours.

Yours faithfully,

Summary

- Say yes slowly, and no quickly.

- Sponsorship properties must fit strategy

- Develop an appropriate check-list and use it every time you are considering a sponsorship acquisition

Chapter 16

Sponsorship Public Guidelines

The Need

Public Guidelines are an extremely useful tool to have in your armoury. They combat time wasted assessing sponsorships that just don't fit and wouldn't be considered. The guidelines provide a screening process that should eliminate receiving those requests for sponsorship that won't be considered. Guidelines also provide information to those organisations that do fit to enable them to structure their proposal to suit your businesses interests.

Public guidelines are available from a few of the larger companies and some associations and foundations. These guidelines are designed to give seekers of sponsorship detailed information on what the company will consider sponsoring, and what will not be sponsored by the company. They also offer assistance on how to apply for sponsorship. They list the information required to assess the proposal, detail when proposals should be submitted for consideration, and how they will be assessed.

Guidelines are often accessible via a company's website, and provide the facility for either downloading an application for sponsorship form, or even applying on-line.

Writing Guidelines

The public guidelines will be based on the Sponsorship Policy and the Sponsorship Strategy. They should include information on:

- What the company will sponsor

- What the company will not sponsor, ie, gambling, religious groups, conferences and international events – these will typically be listed in your **strategy** document.

- Assessment criteria used by the company to assess sponsorship properties. For example, must have media coverage, must be non profit organisation, etc.

- When to apply for funding if specific times for applications are required. For example, prior to commencement of the financial year.

- How long assessment will take before a reply is received. This may vary according to the amount of money being requested, to allow for board approvals etc.

- What is expected from sponsorship properties including: benefits, event management etc.

- What will be spent on purchasing properties. For example, local events maximum $5000, national events up to $100 000.

- Advise if there is a preferred proposal structure.

- List details required in order to complete the assessment. This could include financial details, details of co-sponsors, etc.

- List required methods of post evaluation to be undertaken and presented by sponsored organisation.

- An application form that is attached to the front of each proposal

Public Guidelines Example

The attached public sponsorship guidelines are an excellent example of a sponsor's guidelines.

SPONSORSHIP
PUBLIC
GUIDELINES

AUSTRALIA
POST

Introduction

Australia Post has long provided an essential communications service for all Australians. Its vast network delivers letters and parcels and provides value-added retail and financial services to people living in all parts of Australia. Servicing some eight million addresses every working day, Australia Post delivers one of the world's cheapest and most reliable postal services across one of the most challenging territories.

It is no surprise then, that Australia Post is among Australia's best known business corporations. Surveys show that it is also one of the nation's most well-thought-of service providers.

It has further developed this respect by carefully establishing closer community ties through support for community activities, including sponsorships of sporting organisations and the arts.

Australia Post continues to be a major supporter of Australia's elite athletes through its sponsorship of the Australian Olympic Team. It is also a foundation member of the Olympic Job Opportunities Program and the first corporation to employ Olympic Team members under this program.

These sponsorship activities at both national and local community levels reflect Australia Post's recognition that, as a major corporation it has a responsibility to make a positive contribution to the wider Australian community.

It is also mindful that, as a commercial enterprise, it must view each sponsorship proposal in terms of its potential to generate business for Australia Post.

Sponsorship will only be considered if it is the most cost effective means of achieving some or all of the company's marketing and communication objectives.

This document outlines all relevant items that should be considered in preparing an application for sponsorship from Australia Post.

What will be sponsored?

Australia Post will sponsor national, regional and local events, and activities and organisations which offer opportunities to market Australia Post's products and services or to communicate key messages and themes.

Australia Post's sponsorship program will seek to achieve a balance between community, environmental, sporting, educational, research and arts/cultural events and activities.

The following definitions may help distinguish between sponsorship and other similar activities.

Sponsorship is support for an individual, organisation, team, event or program in return for the right to use that individual, organisation, team, event or program to promote a corporation's name, image, products and services.

Generally, 'in-kind' services will not be provided

Sponsorship is not:

- A donation (in cash or kind) for which little or no commercial return is expected.
- Hospitality, which is defined as the provision of entertainment, food and beverages for existing and potential clients in expectation of commercial return. Where hospitality is included in a sponsorship package together with other benefits such as signage, acknowledgment on literature, etc., it is defined as part of that sponsorship.

Australia Post will give priority to sponsorships that recognise and uphold general community values and, in general, relate to:

- Direct business enhancement;
- Image improvement; and
- Community benefit.

Australia Post will not sponsor programs that:

- Support political or religious organisations;
- Denigrate, exclude or offend minority community groups;
- May be hazardous to the community;
- Create environmental hazards; and
- Uphold principles of respect that are different from those we apply to our own people.

Obligations expected in return for sponsorship

- Successful applicants will be required to enter into a formal sponsorship contract which details level of benefits agreed to, performance required, method of evaluation to be undertaken and payment terms.
- All benefits agreed to in contract must be delivered within the agreed period including ensuring all signs and logos are prominently displayed at all times.
- Support and promotion of Australia Post's activities.
- An evaluation of the project will be required, detailing all activities undertaken, exposure received by Australia Post and demographics of people affected by the activity.

Application Check List

The following information will be required by Australia Post to enable a thorough evaluation of your proposal for sponsorship:

- Concise description of the opportunity.
- History of your event or activity
- The geographic location, as well as local, State or national extensions
- Dates or times the sponsorship will be valid.
- Staffing of the event/organisation
- Estimated attendance if applicable
- Demographics - who watches or attends? Define your membership, public and audiences
- Brief background on the rights-holder, listing experience, mission statement and long term goals for your organisation or event
- What rights and benefits are being offered
- Opportunity/ies for client entertainment
- Exclusivity offered
- Signage opportunities
- Estimated value of all exposure including: television coverage, spot packages, radio, press, signage and back-up with statistics
- Potential for this sponsorship to grow Australia Post's sales
- How involvement with your organisation will help enhance Australia Post's image

Assessment of Application

- You will be advised of receipt of application by mail.
- Every applicant will be advised in writing of the outcome of their proposal.
- It should be noted that Australia Post receives many applications for sponsorship and is able to fund only a minority of those requests. Sponsorships will be selected on the basis of which are best able to promote Australia Post's products, services and / or image.

Submission of Applications

Sponsorship of activities that are contained within a single State should be forwarded to the State Communications Manager.

Sponsorships with an intrastate or national perspective should be forwarded to the National Sponsorship Manager for consideration.

Should you require further guidance and or assistance in completing your application for sponsorship contact the offices on the following page.

Sponsorship Application Form
Please attach to the front of your sponsorship proposal

Applicant's Name: _____

Organisation: _____

Address: _____

_____

Phone: _____ Fax _____

Event/activity: _____

Date/period of activity: _____

Summary of sponsorship opportunity: _____

_____

_____

_____

_____

Cost $ _____

For office use only:

File Number: _____ Date received ___/___/___

Tear out along perforation ↗

Sponsorship Acknowledgment
Please complete and attach to the front of your sponsorship proposal

Name: _____

Title: _____

Organisation: _____

Address: _____

_____

Suburb or town / postcode: _____

Your application for sponsorship to Australia Post has been received and is now being evaluated. A decision on your submission for sponsorship will be made as soon as possible and you will be notified of our decision by mail.

Please quote file number: _____ in any subsequent correspondence.

Tear out along perforation ⌝

Summary

- **Sponsorship guidelines are an excellent way of minimising time wasted assessing sponsorship properties that your company would not consider sponsoring.**

Part 5

Purchasing Sponsorships – Sponsors

Chapter 17

Sponsorship's Role in the Marketing Communications Mix

Sponsorships Are Hard Work!

Sponsorship should only be undertaken when it is the best method of achieving some of a company's strategic or tactical marketing and communications objectives. A sponsorship in isolation would rarely achieve all of a company's objectives, and an integrated approach throughout all marketing communications mediums is recommended.

History states that sponsorship is only effective as a marketing and communications medium where it is managed via a structured process. This process includes the policy, strategy, planning, leveraging and evaluation phases. (See Part 4 –" Streamlining Sponsors Processes".)

It would be a very rare sponsorship that delivered its full potential within, say, one year. Sponsorship success relies on awareness, and awareness only grows with reach and frequency, which occurs over time.

Reach = the number of people/consumers impacted by the sponsorship.

Frequency = the number of times those people are impacted.

Therefore short-term tactical sponsorships rarely deliver the desired outcomes for the sponsor. This is the reason why most sponsorships are signed up for a two or three year period, or longer, with an option to renew written into the contract.

The most important aspect of any sponsorship is the management of the relationship in order to gain the benefits contracted. Far too many times, we see sponsors who have purchased a sponsorship, and then sat back waiting for the sponsored organisation to deliver the benefits – and they probably will deliver the minimum contracted benefits.   However, if the seeker does not know what your objectives for undertaking the sponsorship are, it is impossible for them to deliver. It is also unlikely that they will have the budget or human resources to undertake huge leverage on your behalf – that is the sponsor's job!

And it must not be forgotten that the purchase price of a sponsorship is just the start.   In fact, you could liken it to purchasing a blank page in a newspaper on which to advertise. You then need to do something with it (the creative) – which will cost money, and require human resources to take to the next stage.

Donations

Sponsorships are often confused with donations. A donation is just that - a gift of product or cash with little or no expected return. Our definition of donation is 'free money' with no strings attached, and no return benefits or favours expected.

Those organisations seeking sponsorship that want cash to support their organisation's activities, but are not prepared to provide tangible benefits in exchange are not seeking a sponsorship. They are seeking a donation in order to fund programs, or perhaps even stay viable.

We cannot emphasise enough that sponsorship is not philanthropy (donating). Where a donation is provided, you may not ask for formal benefits to be delivered – if you did, this could not be called a donation - it would be a sponsorship.

Grants

A grant is generally provided by government or semi-government organisations.

It differs from sponsorship with the main difference being that the delivery of the item paid for by the grant (ie, scholarship, playground) delivers the required outcome for the grant giver, whereas sponsorship relies on the exploitation of the sponsored entity to provide a return to the sponsor. Grants are often given on one occasion only and are commonly given to assist in the development of a project, or purchase of an artwork or similar. Grant giving is generally of a non-commercial nature.

Event Promoter / Partner

Some companies have a preference for owning and running their own events and all related promotions either as a full or part owner (partner). The up side of this is that the company has total control, and is guaranteed exclusivity. They are also guaranteed delivery of all the benefits they require. The downside of such an arrangement is that the Company is exposed to all the risk, in terms of PR problems, insurance liability and so on.

Checklist - Is Sponsorship Right for Us?

To assist you to make the decision as to whether undertaking sponsorship is the right direction for your organisation, it may be worth working through the points below.

Answer each question, and if unsure go to relevant chapter in this book. If any of your responses are negative it may be worth rethinking the use of sponsorship. (A clean version of this checklist can be found in Appendix 5.)

1. **Are you being offered rights and benefits that you can use?**

   The only reason to pursue a sponsorship proposal is if it offers benefits that you require, and which cannot be purchased elsewhere. The organisation to be sponsored, and the benefits on offer must have some synergy with your organisation, and if you can achieve your marketing and communications objectives more cost effectively through an alternative medium such as conventional advertising, sales promotion or public relations, then sponsorship should not be undertaken.

2. Are Members / Target Audience Likely To Approve Of Commercial Sponsorship?

Commercial sponsorship can be been seen by some fans as 'selling out', although there is increasing awareness of the benefits of sponsorship within the general community. Most people are now aware that as government funding for a variety of organisations decreases, sponsorship is vital to the survival of many. However, for sponsorship to work for both parties it must have the support of members, staff, board and target audiences. The seeker must be able to demonstrate, either by track record, or by having undertaken a survey amongst members, that their supporters will accept a commercial sponsorship relationship, and that this will not threaten the relationship the organisation has with their fan base/members. For a sponsorship to be successful it must have broad support from every level within both organisations.

3. Are You Buying a "Hot" Property?

Remember - those sponsorships that are seen as "hot" properties will be in high demand, even during economic downturns. There will always be mediocre sponsorship properties on the market, and these will generally be picked up for a discount price – simply because they cannot deliver the audience that a "hot" property will. The bottom of the market will always be there, and will always be difficult to sell because it is hard to demonstrate value now, or in the future.

A hot property traditionally has a known point of difference. It usually has one or more of the following:

- Avid fans (remember - fans is an abbreviation for fanatics)
- High participation rates
- High reach and frequency (reach is the number of people affected, and frequency is how often they are affected)
- Significant sales returns
- Right timing
- High awareness of activity
- Extensive media/TV coverage of activity
- Regular occurrence

- Appeal to a younger age group, often with a high discretionary income.

4. Are You a Suitable Sponsor?

You need to be very careful that the sponsorship you are considering is suitable for your company. If, for example your company manufactures alcoholic beverages, you would find it difficult to gain acceptance for a sponsorship that impacted children or youth.

In short, you need to be sure that your sponsorship will not be viewed as a cynical marketing exercise by the public.

5. Do You Have The People to Manage / Run The Sponsorship?

Managing a sponsorship is, and should be, time consuming. You need to ensure that you have the people to plan, leverage and evaluate the sponsorship. **If you are unable to manage even one of these areas, the sponsorship will not succeed.**

6. Sponsorship's Role in the Marketing and Communications Mix

Marketing and Communications is utilised to provide:

- Exclusivity
- Point of difference
- Facilitate relationships and networking
- Imagery to be exploited
- Personalities
- Access to niche audiences
- Facilitate cause related marketing
- Facilitate experiential marketing
- Access to "hot property"

Summary

- Sponsorship needs to be selected wisely.

- Sponsorship is an expensive exercise in both time and money.

- Ensure the sponsored organisation's staff, membership and audience will be comfortable with you as a sponsor, and supportive of your objectives.

- In addition, be sure you have all the financial and human resources available to plan, leverage and evaluate.

Chapter 18

Guiding Principles for Purchasing Sponsorship

I would like to share a fascinating statistic with you. The average sponsorship lasts about the same length of time as the average marriage. Not so surprising really, when you consider that this is due mainly to the fact that sponsorships are based around human relationships.

The sponsorship relationship is between the sponsored organisation and the sponsoring company. The relationships are between the sponsored organisation's marketing manager and the sponsor's marketing manager, and the sponsored organisation's lifestyle and the sponsor's image or product.

Well-managed sponsorships are a very sophisticated form of relationship marketing. In the sponsorship relationship two parties join together to further their common goals. This occurs through the parties exploiting the sponsorship relationship or association, with the sponsor exploiting the benefits to maximise the return to their bottom line profit, and the sponsorship seeker exploiting the association through financial gain and gaining the kudos of associating with the sponsor's image and reputation.

Let's now turn our minds to the order in which personal relationships generally commence:

The Attraction

Initially one party is attracted to the other. Usually an organisation selling sponsorship is attracted to your (the sponsor's) money and image. It is increasingly common, however, with sponsors who have detailed policies and strategies to be pro-active in initiating the relationship.

The Approach

This phase is not dissimilar to the human relationship where one party has to make the bold move of introducing themselves to the other party.

Courting

Following a successful approach the parties get to know each other and the information exchange commences.

Proposal

This is the point where it is appropriate to present the proposal. Too often the proposal has been presented prematurely, when the sponsor does not have enough knowledge. It is commonly the case that successful proposals have been preceded by conversation, and knowledge exchange.

Engagement

If the response is "yes" or "maybe" there is verbal agreement to enter into a "marriage". (In reality, you now have a very short time to back out of this agreement.) After many meetings, dates are set, the contracts are drawn up and an announcement is made. The agreement has occurred.

Marriage

The marriage occurs, and for it to work the relationship has to be 'win win'. The old saying it takes 'two to make it work' applies to sponsorships as much as it does to human relationships.

Divorce

Sadly, marriages are breaking down regularly, and, not to trivialise divorce, probably for many of the same reasons as sponsorship relationships fail. The sponsorship breakdown, or divorce, can occur for a multitude of reasons, but the majority are due to either a breakdown in communications between the parties or a change of personnel or objectives by either side.

The majority of sponsorships are largely based on the human relationships that form between the two parties involved, and in fact most fail due to the departure of either the seeker's or sponsor's representative. Alternatively, the two parties stop "getting on" or sometimes because the sponsors objectives have been achieved, and there is nothing to be gained by extending the relationship.

The Golden Rules of Purchasing Sponsorships

Many mistakes have been made in the past with respect to sponsorship purchases. There have been countless millions of dollars wasted on sponsorships that have achieved very little, or even nothing at all, for the sponsor. This is, in ninety-five percent of cases, not the fault of the sponsored organisation. It is because too many sponsorships have been purchased before it has been established that they have synergy with the sponsor, and before it has been established whether or not this is the most effective medium to use in order to achieve objectives.

You must plan to succeed. Ad Hoc sponsorship purchase is a recipe for disaster. You must already have the sponsorship policy and strategy in place, and you must be sure of your leverage budget and that you have the human resources to manage any sponsorship purchased. So often this is not the case!

Rule One

Say no quickly, and yes slowly!

Decline all unsuitable sponsorships immediately. This will minimise follow-up from seekers, and will therefore free up time for you, and reduce your stress levels (saying no is never easy).

Never make a rash decision to purchase a sponsorship. All but the hot properties are difficult to sell, and it is unlikely to be "sold out from under you". You will have time to thoroughly investigate most opportunities, and negotiate a deal that suits your organisation.

Don't forget you must be able to make the sponsor's investment of time and money in your organisation justifiable in measurable returns to their company's bottom line.

Rule Two

Make Sure It Fits! It is imperative target audience's demographics, psychograhics and geographic fit matches that of your company or brand(s) to be promoted.

Rule Three

Prior to any decision to purchase, it should be established that the property fits with strategy, and is not duplicating the benefits already purchased with another sponsorship.

Rule Four

Make sure you are purchasing an appropriate package:

1. **The right benefits for the company.** Every company is in sponsorship for a slightly different reason and it is therefore quite acceptable to ask for a benefits package to be tailored to your specific needs. (See Chapter 20 – "Identifying Rights and Benefits".)

2. **The package should be priced realistically (at market value).** The old adage that any house will sell at the market price does not hold with sponsorship due to the constant over supply of sponsorship properties. Ensure that the property is priced competitively – this means that you will need to either shop around, or keep yourself appraised of the price of sponsorships in the market. It is possible that a property will be priced at market value, and your company still will not have the resources to both purchase and leverage it. (See Chapter 21 – "Determining Fair Market Price".)

3. **Positive Track Record.** A track record of delivering value for money will make it very much easier to justify the purchase and to plan for success.

4. **Don't Set Precedents**. It is very easy to be talked into taking out a "small" sponsorship of a local branch of a national body – say Neighbourhood Watch, or the Diabetes Foundation. To do this sets a very dangerous precedent, particularly if your company is a Government Business Enterprise, or a large multi-national publicly listed company.

You run the very real risk that every other branch that hears of your sponsorship of their sister branch will expect you to sponsor them – after all, you have set the precedent. It is never easy to say no, but it is a must in this case – otherwise you are leaving yourself wide open to claims that you are not equitable in your support of such organisations.

Reacting to a Request for Sponsorship

On receipt of a request for sponsorship, most companies will seek the answers to three questions:

1. **What am I being asked to sponsor** (event, organisation description). When and where does it happen?

2. **What benefits will my company receive** (list of possible tangible benefits)?

3. **How much this going to cost?**

Summary

The Golden Rules of Purchasing Sponsorships

- Say no quickly, and yes slowly.

- Make sure the price is right, and that your organisation can afford purchase and leverage costs.

- Make sure the right target audience is delivered.

- Ensure that this sponsorship fits with company strategy.

- Be sure the benefits will deliver your company's objectives.

- Make sure you have the human resources required to manage.

- Bottom Line: Unless this sponsorship is the most cost effective way of achieving your objectives, there is no justification to purchase.

Chapter 19

Identifying Potential Sponsorships

Selecting Sponsorship to Fit Strategy and Deliver Objectives

There are many different categories of sponsorship and depending on the objectives of your sponsorship program you may have a portfolio that includes sponsorships in only one category, more than one, or occasionally all categories (which would be more common in the case of large Government Business Enterprises and public companies such as postal and telecommunication companies).

The categories could include sport, arts, environment, education, expeditions, community events, cause related, charity sponsorships, individuals (sports people, performers etc.) and professional conferences.

Sport

The vast majority of sponsorship dollars are spent on sponsorship of sporting events, bodies, and individuals – both amateur and professional. Sport is able to provide: significant signage benefits, client entertainment, television broadcasts, media coverage, personality endorsements and huge viewing audiences. Sport has mass appeal and consequently gets the lion's share of the available sponsorship dollars.

Sports sponsorships include The Olympics, Commonwealth Games, Grand Prix, various codes of football, yachting, golf, tennis, basketball, amateur associations, motor racing, cricket, lawn bowls, darts, beach volley ball, and many more.

An area that has gained popularity within the sports sponsorship arena over the past few years is that of extreme sports, which particularly appeal to the younger generation.

The cost of purchasing sports sponsorship varies enormously depending on the size of the audience, the television coverage, popularity in terms of sponsors and how the property is being sold (ie, internally or via a broker). There is one sport or another happening year round. Sport offers a hugely diverse audience to sponsors in terms of fans, and of course participants

Sports offer vast potential to engage with particular demographic markets. (We say potential here, because, as always it depends on the resources put in to managing the sponsorship.) Sport provides a huge international audience via telecast in many instances (tennis, superbowl, soccer, cricket).

Sports sponsorships are relatively easy to evaluate and the benefits are generally substantial. It is just a matter of finding the sport with the right fit. Sport sponsorship at lower levels can prove to be a very cost effective manner of engaging with your target audience in a more personal manner than conventional advertising.

Sponsorship is generally available at the following levels:

- Federation or association
- State/area association
- Tournament or match
- Team or club
- Individual Athlete (although not generally in amateur ranks)

The Arts

The arts category includes, ballet, opera, theatre, museums, fine art (galleries and exhibitions), contemporary and classical music, and festivals.

The arts have, in the past, received significant government funding. The majority of private funding in the not too distant past was basically altruism undertaken by the CEO or on the Board's behalf and was basically little more than corporate philanthropy.

Sponsorship of the Arts will continue to increase as arts organisations continue to offer commercial and tangible benefits.

Accessing arts audiences is valuable to a high number of companies, as the audience comprises, largely, of decision makers and high income earners who are aged 35 years plus.

A large percentage of the big arts groups only give exclusivity to their naming rights or principal sponsor. There is every chance that sponsors below that level will not enjoy exclusivity.

You are unlikely to get significant signage opportunities in arts venues, and will often not receive signage rights in an auditorium/gallery with the exception of the major sponsor. There is a balance to be achieved in these circumstances – imposing signage is not often appropriate in the arts arena, however, there seems little reason why sponsors cannot have signage in lobby areas etc. It is a matter of negotiating arrangements that are suitable to both parties at the time of contract signing.

Segments of the arts community do not embrace commercial relationships. They feel that such arrangements are "not quite nice" and lower the tone. It can be difficult to get hold of artists for functions and quite often if they do arrive they don't (won't) mix with corporate guests. If these people have an understanding of what having a sponsor means to the organisation (ie – they can tour), they are, however, generally quite co-operative.

There is no doubt that Arts sponsorship provides high level client entertainment and networking, and often the best tickets are only available to sponsors – but it is worth checking. You may get just as much benefit from purchasing the tickets independently (and this of course applies to some sporting events as well).

Major Sponsors can expect:

- A full page ad in the program (check exclusivity)
- A message from your CEO
- Surtitle messages
- A single banner in the foyer, if agreed with building owners.
- Logo on relevant television and Press advertisement (logo will be smaller than principal sponsor)
- Drinks with the cast afterwards
- A limited number of premium tickets
- Access to some seats at a rehearsal
- Tours of the organisation

- Tours of the set
- Dinner for CEO and or Board members with sponsored organisation's board and other sponsor companies' CEO's.

Sponsorship is generally available at the following levels:

- Organisation or Governing Body
- Production
- Individual night/showing
- Individual artist
- Patronage sponsorship

Education

Sponsorship of education is an area that is growing. This encompasses such areas as computer studies, school sport, arts programs, through to tertiary institutions. Sponsorship of scholarships at schools, colleges and universities are becoming more common as companies with a vested interest, try to encourage the brightest students to take up a relevant discipline like science or engineering. And let's not forget that sponsorship of university sporting teams, Orientation Week, and similar, allow business to set up a relationship with some very attractive markets of the future.

There has however been controversy regarding sponsorship of educational sectors by some large companies. For example, parents are not amenable to companies that provide junk food having input into school curriculum's, nor for that matter having access to their children without parental supervision. It is very important that companies that undertake educational sponsorships are doing it for the right reasons (ie – benefits will accrue to BOTH parties) and that this is not seen to be a cynical marketing exercise. This is an area that could backfire very quickly and publicly, so it must be well thought out and executed to provide benefits.

Environment

Sometimes known as Green sponsorships, environmental sponsorships are very much in a growth phase. During the 70s and 80s we, as consumers, were relatively unaware of the damage we were inflicting on the environment. It took organisations such as Greenpeace, World Wildlife Fund for Nature, The Conservation Foundation, Landcare, Greening Australia and others to educate us via constant media coverage.

Companies that could be perceived to be damaging the environment in any way would be well advised to align themselves genuinely with one of these groups in order to negate any damage they are inflicting.

Never forget, however, that environmentalists are here to protect the environment!   Make sure that you have thoroughly researched your company's environmental record prior to becoming involved as a sponsor of an environmental group or organisation. If there is something to disclose, make sure that the disclosure is made in early discussions, and if you deem it necessary, have it noted in the contract. (Don't just ask management – it can be a good idea to check with operational staff "out in the field" or "at the coalface". Older staff members often have a lot of company history stored away in their heads.) They may remember that you have illegally stored PCB's or dumped chemicals. Don't just assume that your company hasn't indulged in such practices – dumping and environmental degradation was common and unfortunately accepted until quite recently.

It is very likely that any environmental organisation you approach offering support will either know your company history, or can find out very quickly. It is becoming increasingly evident that some radical environmentalists are singling out specific companies for negative attention because of their environmental policies, and dedicating websites to publicising their knowledge. This can have a detrimental effect on both company image and bottom line. In these days of triple bottom line reporting, it is very important, and in fact almost mandatory, for companies to have an environmental policy in place, which minimises any effect on the environment.

Environment Sells

It is very clear that consumers are increasingly willing to change brands based on environmental concerns and what a company stands for. People like to think that their purchase is contributing to the common good, rather than just to a money grab by an, often foreign, company.

Remember!

"Dark" greens, or the more radical groups of "Greenies" are unlikely to ever be happy with commercial deals. "Light" greens now receive bi-partisan and community support.

Numerous surveys indicate that the environment and its continued sustainability is high on the list of the majority of peoples' concerns.

Environmental sponsorship is generally available at the following levels:

- Organisation sponsorship
- On a project by project basis

Expeditions

Expeditions include climbing mountains such as Mount Everest; Dick Smith flying around the world solo in his helicopter; Richard Branson (attempting to) flying a hot air balloon across the Atlantic; searching for the elusive wreck with its gold bullion; walking to the South Pole, etc. In fact, the list is endless.

Expeditionists are usually very good at what they do. Expeditions are often not expensive to sponsor however, returns can be minimal, so it would be expected that the price would be low. Prior to agreeing to sponsor an expedition, you need to make sure that participants understand that your company is expecting commercial benefits to accrue from the relationship. You also need to assure yourself that they are capable, and have the resources to gain the coverage you require. (Take a little challenge here yourself – name us a *sponsor* of any expedition that has taken place anywhere.)

Often wherever the expedition is happening is out of range of mainstream communications equipment, however with smaller and more sophisticated satellite communications coming on stream these problems are fading. In fact, there have been recent expeditions where the participants have been in constant internet contact, and have also been able to provide live coverage of aspects of their adventure.

Expeditionists are generally passionate about what they do and will attempt the activity with or without sponsorship. Often what they really want is a benevolent donor to fund their ambitions, or a donation with no benefits expected or accruing to the donor.

Of more concern, expeditions are often fraught with danger, and therefore could bring negative publicity to the sponsor. However expeditions can, if planned and managed well, bring an enormous amount of exposure for very little cost. Once again, a good contract and sound planning needs to be in place.

Community Events

Sponsorship of community events is a recognised way of improving corporate image and demonstrating you are a part of that community and are giving something back to the community within which you operate.

Sponsorship of festivals such as the Chinese New Year and Spring Festival are common. Sponsorships are often of particular events or happenings at the festival. Local festivals have tightly defined geographic markets.

Community sponsorship is generally available at the following levels:

- Festival sponsorship
- A particular activity within the festival. For example a fireworks night or the animal nursery.

Professional Conferences

There are many professional conferences wanting sponsorship. They offer a very defined target audience and usually offer the opportunity to attach a logo, send a delegate free of charge and add material to the conference satchel.

Some pitfalls of sponsoring a professional conference are that they might have very few delegates, generate limited interest, little or no media and can be very costly. There is however the benefit that, for some companies, they are able to target a very specific segment of their audience. (For example, a pharmaceutical company sponsoring a conference where all delegates are Doctors.)

Many conferences request up to, for example, $10 000 for a major sponsorship. If there are 100 delegates this works out to a cost of $100 per impression. For that price you could personally take every delegate out to dinner, or buy a block of tickets at the tennis, or the ballet. You need to look very carefully at whether a conference sponsorship is the most cost effective way to reach your target. It may be worth investigating the possibility of buying trade stand space at the conference instead.

Cause Related & Charity Sponsorships
(These are not donations)

Cause related sponsorships need emotion, and must connect with the values of consumers, as well as having a close fit to work effectively. Cause related sponsorships require the sponsor to form a relationship with the cause or charity for the sponsorship to work and this requires employee and management commitment. The majority of charities are in the sponsorship business as a means of creating awareness and fundraising, with a number of charities promoting their own successful events.

Charity and cause related sponsorships are excellent for generating a positive corporate image and awareness and also corporate goodwill. Probably the best known would be Ronald MacDonald house in major cities. MacDonald's sponsors a number of houses for use of country families whose children are hospitalised in city hospitals. MacDonald's widely promote their sponsorship on tray mats and television.

It is essential that the charity and your company have good fit so that the sponsorship isn't seen as cynical exercise to buy goodwill. Research confirms that consumers will change their purchasing habits when confronted with a well thought out cause related marketing program, and that they do not have an objection to the company receiving benefit, as long as the benefits to the cause are obvious.

Summary

Identifying Potential Sponsorships

- Category and level sponsored depends on your objectives.

- Might sponsor in more than one category.

- Categories include:

  -Sports
  - Arts
  - Environment
  - Education
  - Expeditions
  - Cause Related/Charity (as opposed to donations)
  - Individuals
  - Professional conferences
  - Community Events and Festivals

Chapter 20

Identifying Rights and Benefits that will Deliver your Marketing and Communications Objectives

Whether proactively seeking a sponsorship, or assessing a sponsorship proposal, you must be able to ascertain the following before you make the purchase decision.

1. **The organisations composition.** The seeker must be able to clearly demonstrate who/what their organisation's membership and audiences are made up of in terms of demographic, psychographic, and geographic data.

   Demographics. Would usually include; age, education, ethnic back ground, family size, income, occupation, sex, and social class.

   Geographic information. Would indicate where the audience and membership resides by region or regions, in which state, nationally or internationally.

   Psychographic. This would give an overall indication of the group's lifestyles and personalities.

   Other information that you might require in order to make an informed judgement regarding sponsorship purchase might include:

   o Number of participants
   o Frequency and method of contact with the organisation seeking sponsorship
   o Attitudes to having a sponsor
   o Attitudes to the seeker organisation and its activities.

2. **General public perceptions.** They must be able to demonstrate that the general public perceive their organisations activities in a positive manner.

3. **Potential rights and benefits.** They must prove to you that the rights and benefits they can provide will result in either a positive commercial return, or improved public perception of their company's image.

4. **Synergy or "fit".** You must be able to see a natural flow on between the two organisations – in other words there must be a real synergy between the two organisations, or you at the very least must be able to realistically create that in the audience's minds. If there is no fit, it will be very much harder to create a program which will deliver objectives.

5. **Most cost effective medium**. It is a very good idea to satisfy yourself prior to signing up a sponsorship that it is the very best and most cost effective marketing and communications medium for achieving your company's objectives. There is nothing surer than the fact that you are, at some point, going to be asked the question, "what made you decide to purchase this sponsorship property". If you have done your homework, you will have all the answers, and will be able to justify the purchase. If not, you have left yourself in a very vulnerable position.

If the seeker organisation does not have the information that you require, or you cannot answer questions about value to your organisation, it is clear that some research is required.

The seekers part can easily be achieved via a simple questionnaire passed amongst the seeker organisation's audiences. Yours may require speaking to senior marketing people, or colleagues who have run successful sponsorship programs, or it may require spending a modest amount on getting an external consultancy to evaluate the proposal for you.

This should not be a costly exercise, and even if you don't purchase the sponsorship, the information you have gained will be valuable for you when you look at your next proposal, and valuable for the seeker when they next seek a sponsor.

Define Category

If you do make the decision to purchase, it is extremely important that your category is clearly defined to reflect your business. This will protect your sponsorship rights (against your competitors) and guarantee your point of difference.

List of Possible Benefits

Some, or all, of the following list of rights and benefits can be provided through sponsorship. Keep in mind that you are likely to be offered a long list of benefits, and may only need very few of them in order to achieve your objectives. In this case, you should ask to have a benefits package tailored to your specific needs, and if appropriate, seek a discount of the price sought.

Sales

A seeker organisation's guaranteed purchase of product can be a powerful incentive for a to become a sponsor, particularly if there are multiple providers of product in your category. Exclusive rights to supply to the organisation or event should be considered a core benefit. If you are in the food, beverage or merchandising businesses, ensure that catering or merchandising rights have not been sold off to a third party, which is often the case. If the property has sold the rights, they may not have the right to dictate exclusive supply rights.

Naming Rights

The value of naming rights can be questionable, particularly in the all too common scenario of media outlets not acknowledging the naming rights. You need to be creative about the name used. If the name used is the identifier of the event or venue rather than a prefix to the name the event or venue has always been known by, it is unlikely to be dropped. An example here would be "Uncle Toby's Iron Man". There are numerous Iron Man events around, however the identifier "Uncle Toby's" says that this is the elite event in Iron Man competition. To call it "The Iron Man" just would not work.

Exclusivity

The purchase of a significant point of difference is the ability to lock out your company's competitors from a high profile event. This is often a powerful marketing tool in its own right - it means that only your company's product will be used by the seeker's organisation and, hopefully, its members. Only your company will have the right to advertise in the organisation's publications, and your name and logo will be displayed on signage.

The level of exclusivity can vary substantially from total exclusivity (only one sponsor) to category exclusivity, for example, only beverage sponsor, or only bank sponsor.

Networking

Many sponsorship properties offer the ability to introduce your management to contacts who are important to your business. For example, potential clients or government and regulatory representatives who the seeker is able to introduce either formally or informally. There is no doubt that personal relationships are used to help companies succeed in business.

Merchandising Rights

A sponsor commonly gains the right to market product to the sponsored organisation's members and audience. This is a common category for, say, a beverage company to sponsor in a major sporting club. For example, you may offer Coca-Cola the right to be the only beverage in the beverage category to be sold at your venues and events. Please remember, such a benefit can only be sold by the rights holder. In many cases a venue has sold off the food and beverage dispensing rights to a third party, usually a large catering company. That company would therefore have the right to decide what food and beverage they were going to sell *unless* the venue owner had specifically reserved that right for future sponsors.

Media and Publicity

Are you likely to receive favourable media and publicity exposure for your corporate and/or brand and product identity?

If so how much? A seeker will preferably be able to quantify any claims of media coverage by producing articles and tapes that have been featured previously and include coverage of their current or past sponsors' products and identity. Any articles that feature the sponsored organisation, but do not feature their sponsor's image or identity are of no value whatsoever to a sponsor. Without awareness of the sponsors association, you have nothing.

Signage

Signage can be offered on an endless variety of items, ranging from members' apparel, stationary, venue signage, uniforms, vehicles, drink coasters, flags, tickets – in fact signage opportunities are limited only by imagination.

Advertising

Are there opportunities to tie this sponsorship in with your conventional advertising? This will not only promote the sponsored organisation or event but also reinforce the association between your company and the sponsored organisation. Do keep in mind that it can be a hard sell trying to persuade your advertising agency to encompass your sponsorship activity in their activities if they don't hold control of the sponsorship program. However, advertising agencies are now coming to recognise the potential of sponsorship in making a connection with the consumer while they (the consumer) are engaged in an activity of their own choosing.

There are often opportunities to gain exclusive advertising in the seeker's publications, through their mailing list or during regular media coverage? Do ensure the rights to their programs and publications have not been sold to a third party though. If this is the case, it may be difficult, or even impossible for them to guarantee exclusivity in the publication.

Sampling

Is there the opportunity for your company to demonstrate your product's attributes to the audience and members provided by this sponsorship? Product sampling or trial might be possible at events, meetings, annual dinners, open days, family days and so on.

Personality Availability

Are you able to get access to personalities, patrons, stars and success stories (ie, in the case of a charity, it may be a patient who has had a successful kidney transplant, or someone who has beaten a serious illness). These people could be utilised to advertise a product, endorse a company's activities, or make motivational speeches at a sales meeting. You must make sure that any such arrangements, including costs, are written into the contract, and that the use of the personality fits, and is not portrayed in a cynical manner.

Client Entertainment Facilities

Is this sponsorship giving you access to highly desirable client entertainment opportunities. Often sponsorship is the only way to get, for example, the best seats in the house, or hot laps in a car. Are you able to access dining facilities, offer refreshments at half time and provide VIP parking.

The seeker may be very familiar and comfortable with the facilities they are offering, but before you purchase the sponsorship, cast a jaundiced eye over them, and ensure that they don't need a 'spruce up' before they are of a suitable standard for business entertaining. In fact, it would be usual for you to be entertained there prior to signing up the deal.

Function Facilities

It is possible that the sponsored organisation has facilities that could be used by your company for meetings or conferences, thereby saving considerable venue costs and adding value to the overall package.

Ticketing

If you are a major sponsor you should expect, and receive, the best seats in the house for use in growing new client relationships and business networking.

A great way of gaining your staff's support of the sponsorship is to organise staff discount ticketing or membership with the sponsored organisation (remember – it is always easier to work within a climate of consent).

Publicly Identifying with the Sponsored Organisation

As you are purchasing the right to align your company with the sponsored organisation's image or lifestyle, you should take every opportunity to do that.

You can highlight the relationship by featuring your name/logo on the sponsored organisations advertising material, letterhead, uniforms, ground signage, foyer signage, and so on. You could also have them feature your name when their phones are answered (ie, "good morning, XYZ polo club").

As the sponsor, it may also be appropriate to exploit the organisation's image and identity in mainstream marketing and communications.

Endorsement

A very common benefit purchased with sponsorship is endorsement rights. In other words a star, or athlete, or high profile person will feature in your advertising endorsing your product. Do not assume that these rights are gained automatically with any sponsorship, however you need to cover this in the contract, once again stating your requirements, and covering off any related costs.

Endorsements can be extremely powerful sales drivers.

Typical Package

When you are presented with a package put together by an organisation seeking sponsorship funding, they will have packaged their benefits in such a way as to gain maximum advantage (ie – dollars) for their organisation. It is important that you seek to remodel the package to suit your company's needs and budget.

You will need to seek a certain amount of information in order to understand where you are likely to sit in the "pecking order" should your company become a sponsor.

You should know how many levels of sponsorship are on offer, how many sponsors there are within each level (existing and/or proposed), and how the seeker organisation has priced their packages (ie, on some sort of costed basis, or on "ability to pay" – which is unfortunately very common).

Any sponsorship that you are offered is likely to be packaged in one of the following manners:

Five Common Methods of Packaging Sponsorships

1. The Level Playing Field
2. The Hierarchical Package
3. The Sole Sponsorship
4. The Pyramid,
5. Ad Hoc, ie, each package provides different benefits to the sponsors and varying returns to the seeker.

Each of these is explained below.

Level Playing Field

The level playing field is probably the fairest method of dividing up benefits of all. The level playing field is used by the Olympic movement and it provides each sponsor with identical rights and benefits (use of the Olympic logo and mascot, and the right to associate with the team as a whole).

In each industry category there is only ever one sponsor. For example, one bank, one telecommunications company, one beverage company, one apparel sponsor and so on. It is very important to ensure that your category of sponsorship is clearly defined to ensure competitors cannot encroach on your exclusivity.

It should, however, be noted that on some occasions sponsors are charged significantly different amounts for the same benefits, and on some occasions they all pay equal amounts, depending on the seeker organisation. Payment levels sought may be based on competition within the category. If a number of potential sponsors in a single category are interested in the property, obviously the price goes up (we might add that this is not a common situation!). Also, to some extent, many sponsorship programs are priced on capacity to pay - the bigger the sponsor the more it is likely to cost.

When each sponsor is provided with 'a level playing field' it is then up to each of them to maximise their own returns. It is fascinating to see the varied ways different sponsors maximise those returns.

When all sponsors are 'created equal' differences in outcome are solely the result of the time, creativity and money invested.

Note: This type of package is usually only utilised at the top end of the market, for example, The Olympics, World Cup and other equally high profile events.

Hierarchical Package

This is probably the most common package of all. It is based on the amount paid - the more you pay the more you get. Let's take the example of an arts organisation such as a high profile ballet company. Normally the structure of sponsors would be as follows: one principal or title rights sponsor, two or three major sponsors, numerous minor sponsors and official suppliers.

- **Naming/Title Rights Sponsor.** Naming or title rights sponsor is the same as a principal rights sponsor and with the exception that a naming/title rights sponsor usually receives identical rights and benefits, with the addition of having the right to have their name added as a prefix to the organisation or event name. An organisation would not have both a naming rights sponsor and a principal sponsor. (A good example of this is the Volvo's sponsorship of the Round the World Yacht Race, The Volvo Challenge. Only one sponsorship can be sold at this level.)

- **Major Sponsor.** This is the level directly below the principal sponsor and in an arts organisation could either be a Production Sponsor (who has the rights to have their logo displayed with the principal sponsors every time a particular ballet is danced, ie, Swan lake) or a Tour Sponsor (who sponsors a particular tour where there will be a number of performances). Obviously there can be a number of sponsors at this level.

- **Sponsor.** Often used relating to the recognition of a low level sponsor. If you are invited to be a 'sponsor' ensure you are informed of how many levels of sponsors are above you.

- **Official Supplier.** This status provides the sponsor with the right to claim that your company is an official supplier to the organisation in return for providing free or discounted services and goods.

Alternatively, they may simply have the right to be the sole purveyor of goods in a particular category, for example the right to supply vitamins to the organisation.

The Pyramid

This is an interesting adaptation of the hierarchical method in that it is highly structured and inflexible and most importantly each level of sponsorship benefits and revenue adds up to one complete major package.

For example you would have one Principal sponsor who would receive a complete range of benefits for say $30,000. You would then have a certain number of major sponsors say three who would pay $10,000 each (total $30,000) who would equally divide exactly the same benefits the principal sponsor received. The minor sponsors, say six, would each pay $5,000 (total 6 x $5,000 = $30,000) and divide exactly the same benefits as the principal sponsor between them.

The pyramid method ensures fairness at every level.

Sole Sponsor

This is the most valuable sponsorship for any sponsor as they are assured that they will not be competing with other sponsors and that they have absolute exclusivity. An exclusive sponsorship will receive a premium due to its exclusivity.

If the Package Isn't Right

It is commonly the case that a sponsor will only want some of the benefits on offer, and it is quite appropriate to ask for a benefits package to be tailored to your company's needs. Of course it is unlikely that premium properties will accede to such a request.

Summary

- Know how many other sponsors there are/will be, and ensure that you are comfortable with where they will fit in.

- Carefully define your category.

- There are five methods of packaging sponsorships:

  - The Level Playing Field
  - The Hierarchical Package
  - The Sole Sponsorship

- The Pyramid, and

- Ad Hoc, where each provides different benefits to the sponsors and varying returns to the seeker.

- Negotiate a package that is going to achieve your objectives.

Chapter 21

Determining Fair Market Price

How Much is it Worth?

The important point to remember is that sponsorship is a commercial agreement, and in order for it to benefit both parties it must be "win win", (mutually rewarding). Even when considering a lower profile sponsorship, there is no point in negotiating the purchase price down so low that the organisation seeking sponsorship is making nothing out of the deal – obviously there won't be too much incentive for them to assist you in achieving your objectives. Their entire focus will be either on getting rid of you at the end of the term, or at the very least finding a way to make you pay market value for the benefits you have purchased. So remember, there is a real cost of having a sponsor, and obviously that cost must be covered in the sponsorship fee sought.

Ultimately, the value of the sponsorship to your company will be based on the return in terms of revenue generated or costs saved versus, say, the cost of a similar result through conventional advertising.

Therefore it is important that you can predict, with some accuracy, the likely outcomes of the sponsorship and the value to the company.

A combination of ROI and market value (ie, is there any competition for this sponsorship) should ultimately help set the purchase price of each property.

It is essential that you do your homework and accurately cost the benefits that you are being offered, in order to be able to establish whether the sponsorship on offer is cost efficient in comparison to other marketing and communications mediums. It may be that the property is priced realistically, but it is just more cost effective to utilise another marketing communications medium in order to achieve your objectives.

If the cost of a sponsorship is not immediately evident in the original proposal and you are still interested after the initial read, pick up the telephone and ask for that figure. It is becoming increasingly common for proposers to withhold that information in the hope of either getting you interested in becoming a sponsor before you know the price, or in being able to produce that information at the *end* of a meeting where they have personally had the opportunity to 'seduce' you with their charm and persuade you that you want/need to have a relationship with their organisation. It may be that you are simply wasting time assessing a sponsorship property that is beyond your company's budgetary means.

Guiding Rules for Valuing Sponsorships

If you want an idea of how a seeker might cost their property prior to offering it to you, please read Chapter 6, "Methods of Valuing Your Sponsorship".

Budget for Servicing

On receipt of the sponsorship cheque, more often than not the sponsored organisation's Board or management has already identified where those dollars are going to be used. Their calculations are commonly based on the full amount sought from the sponsor, and unfortunately do not take into account the actual expenditure that will have to be undertaken to service a sponsor. This amount regularly 'falls between the cracks', resulting in either a search for additional funds or you, the sponsor not receiving the benefits you have been promised.

It is important that Board members and accountants are aware that you, the sponsor, have purchased benefits from them, and that you expect those to be provided in a timely and professional manner. There will be a cost attached to having a sponsor, and they must be aware of that, and allocate the budget accordingly. It is worth covering this in the contract if there are indications in initial discussions that this might be a problem.

Additional Costs

In any business activity undertaken, there is always the danger of budget 'blow-outs', and sponsorship is one area where the dollars spent on below the line items can add up very quickly. In fact, it is not unusual for below the line items to cost as much or more than the original purchase price. It is essential that you budget for these items at the start, and not find yourself in the situation where you are struggling to find funds to pay for items which really are necessary in order to achieve your objectives.

The following is a list (not all encompassing) of items that can add additional costs to a sponsorship program – many sponsored organisations will undertake to pay for some of these. It really is extremely important that the 'owner' of these costs is detailed in contract documents.

- Signage production
- Signage erection
- Client entertainment, food and beverages, car parking etc
- Support creative/advertising
- Television production costs
- Apparel for competitors, officials, media etc
- Trophies and awards
- Evaluation research
- Media monitoring
- Sponsorship project management costs
- Public relations
- Trade and consumer promotions
- Staff time
- Merchandise
- Promotional items
- Travel
- Legal costs
- Sampling

Points to Note:

- If you, the sponsor, are prepared to spend significant sums of money promoting the sponsored organisation through a structured leverage program, this might result in a lowering of the price being sought.

- Make sure that the property you are about to purchase is priced at market value. Obviously a high profile hot property that is absolutely unique and has a very high number of fans will be worth more than a less popular property. There is a propensity for some properties to simply work out what they need in terms of budget to run their event, season or similar, and put that price on the sponsorship proposal. This is not necessarily market value, and it is often based on ability to pay. In other words a high profile, wealthy corporation will be asked to pay a lot more for the same property and benefits package than a smaller organisation with a more modest sponsorship budget.

- To calculate market value, compare the cost of similar properties in the market place. You can either check against other sponsorship properties in the portfolio, or ask a colleague in a similar position at another company whether they feel that what you are being asked to pay is a fair price.

- Compare the cost of the sponsorship to mainstream marketing costs. As sponsorship is a marketing and communications tool, once again, I stress that it is important to compare the cost of this sponsorship against the cost of either direct marketing or advertising. This calculation should be on a cost per person affected basis. The following simple calculation will determine the cost per person.

Sponsorship

Total cost # of sponsorship
÷ number of people effected*
= Cost per person

Don't forget the actual cost to your company for a sponsorship will be significantly more than the sponsorship fee. You will have to pay for all below the line costs such as signage, advertising and staff time to manage the property.

* Sponsored organisations members and live and TV audience.

Direct Marketing

The cost of a direct marketing campaign can be calculated as follows:

    Cost of postage
+   **production of material**
+   **cost of mail list**
X   **number of people targeted**
=   **cost per person**

Advertising Campaign

The cost of advertising can be calculated as follows:

    Cost of production
+   **Cost of airtime**
÷   **number of people in audience**
=   **cost per person**

The Dilemma of Contra

Contra (value or goods in kind) support is where a company's products or services are provided in lieu of, or as well as, cash for the payment of a sponsorship. Sometimes contra can suit both parties, however it is often problematic, and very hard to value.

Many companies do not offer contra due to difficulties relating to taxation and transfer pricing within a company. Quite often, particularly within large companies, the sponsorship budget or department does not have access to product unless they purchase it.

Get professional advice when agreeing to provide contra in lieu of cash, and be sure the organisation is going to store, deal with and distribute your product in an appropriate manner if they are going to handle it on your behalf.

Valuing Contra

It is often difficult to know how to value contra that you are giving in lieu of sponsorship dollars. Do you value the goods at retail price?

In other words what they would be sold for at retail - or do you value the goods at some other figure, perhaps your company's cost or wholesale price - and what happens if this cost changes throughout the period of the sponsorship agreement? Once again, this is an issue that must be addressed in the contract.

It may be appropriate to use the following formula when providing contra in lieu of cash.

Source	Valued at
Manufacturer	Manufacturers sale price
Wholesaler	Wholesale price
Retailer	Retail price

The Underwriter

In the case of events where there is a gate price, sponsorship is sometimes sought on the basis of the sponsor underwriting the set up costs and receiving a return from the profits made on the gate, which provides the potential for the sponsorship to either be cost neutral or even return a profit. There is, however, the risk that the event will flop – often because of inclement weather in the case of an outdoor event, or where an event has proven not to be as popular as forecast by the promoter. Potential sponsors would be wise to cover themselves for this eventuality, both in the contract, and via insurance cover!

Can I Have Some More?

We sometimes see the case where a seeker – even though they have your payment - has not gained enough sponsorship dollars to go ahead with their event.

They will then come back and ask you, the sponsor, for more.
This should alert you to the fact that perhaps they are facing financial difficulty, and that you may not be able to achieve your objectives if the event is downscaled for financial reasons.

This is why it is critically important that you undertake your due diligence out the outset, and establish that the finances of the organisation that you are about to sponsor are sound, and that they have the expertise to handle their own finances.

The Acid Test

A question you might ask yourself when purchasing a sponsorship is – "if this was my own money, would I be spending it in this manner".

Summary

- **Fair market price must be paid in order to gain that 'win win' situation**

- **Ensure sponsorship is the most cost effective marketing communications medium to achieve your objectives**

- **Ensure the leverage budget is covered.**

- **Undertake due diligence, and ensure that market value is being paid**

Chapter 22

Negotiating the Deal

It is pointless becoming involved in a sponsorship arrangement where the outcome isn't 'win win'. The best deals are where a good relationship is created and both parties benefit from the relationship. There is ample research to indicate that sponsorship benefits accrue and increase over an extended period – in other words, the longer you sign up for, the more recognition of the sponsorship you will receive. However, in saying that, you should only be re-signing a sponsorship contract if you feel that you got value for money, that the relationship was harmonious, and that you are likely to go on accruing those benefits.

Some Points To Remember in Negotiations

Following is some good advice from Tim Clarke, a Freelance Journalist who wrote a particularly useful article on negotiating for Discover magazine (Jan/Feb 2001).

> "When we think of negotiating, we assume one of two things will happen: either we'll win or we'll lose. But skilled negotiators don't see it that way – they know a successful negotiation is one where both sides feel like winners.
>
> Don't feel you have to win on every issue: score major victories but concede small points. Ask yourself "What can I give up that will please the other person without putting a major dent in what I want out of this?"
>
> Many people think that certain company policies and procedures are unchangeable, but the fact is that nothing is unchangeable and everything is negotiable."

Tim had some **handy hints to keep in mind when negotiating**, which are:

- A successful negotiation is one where both sides emerge feeling like winners.
- Never assume that just because something is written down on paper, it's therefore not negotiable.
- Before you sit down to negotiate, have three figures clearly in mind: the maximum you are prepared to pay, the minimum you are prepared to settle for, and the actual figure you are aiming to agree on.
- The person who controls the negotiation is usually the one who has set the guidelines for it.
- To succeed in negotiation, you need to be prepared. Avoid surprise negotiations.
- Gather all the facts that support your position.
- Learn as much as you can about your opponents before you sit down to negotiate.
- Keep your cool if you are on the defensive.
- Try to highlight the common goals and points of agreement.

We have a couple of our own to add:

- *Always* be honest.
- Be fair.
- Be realistic with what you are offering. Make sure the sponsored organisation is also going to benefit out of the relationship.

The Company Angle

The aim of the negotiations is to complete a favourable commercial agreement and in doing so obtain the right mix of benefits, value for money and minimise any competition or ambush by competitors.

Any proposal you receive is exactly that - a proposal, or a suggestion to do business and is only the starting point. Everything is negotiable.

Some benefits offered may not be of interest, others will be perceived as valuable and, possibly, you will require additional benefits that have not been offered at all.

Companies should enter negotiations with the view that if they don't get a package that is attractive and has the potential to achieve their objectives, they will go elsewhere, and as you know, there are many, many organisations out there seeking sponsorship support.

The relationship begins with the negotiations and if those negotiations don't result in both parties feeling satisfied with the outcome they should proceed no further. An unsatisfactory deal for either side is not a recipe for success.

Know Who You Are Negotiating With

There is absolutely no point in entering into negotiations with a person or persons who are not approved to negotiate and do not have the power to make decisions.   You do need to establish that the people you are negotiating with are authorised to negotiate on behalf of the organisation they purport to represent.

Payment of Fees

Most sponsorships have terms of payment set in the contract. It is quite usual that the first payment will be on signing with further payments happening at various milestones. These could include: after a specified period, or on commencement of the event/season. It is normal to have a payment near the end of the contract (which could well be performance driven). The timing of payments is often a negotiating platform worth considering. For example, you might offer to pay the entire fee at the commencement of the program in return for a reduction on the full purchase price.

Market Price

Make sure that the property that you are negotiating for is priced at market value prior to the commencement of negotiations.   (See Chapter 21 – "Determining Fair Market Price".)

It is very difficult to significantly lower the expectations that seekers have regarding the price of their property. It is therefore important that you set a price that you will not go beyond *prior* to entering negotiations. You must be prepared to stick to this figure, and walk away from the negotiations and the sponsorship opportunity if necessary.

Tax

Ensure that the final price is inclusive of any applicable taxes, such as GST, at the time of negotiations.

Listen

It is important during negotiations that you listen to what the other party is saying and that you commit to paper any proposal to expand or reduce the benefits so that these understandings are reflected in any resulting contract.

Third Party Approval (Good Guy - Bad Guy)

A ploy used successfully in negotiations is to have a third party, who is not present at the negotiations, holding the power to make the final decision regarding purchase. This allows for someone who is not affected by the emotion of being involved in the negotiations, to look at the amended proposal with a clear head. Often in the case of a very large company, this is not a ploy – the person who has the authority to sign does not do the negotiating.

Time is on the Sponsor's Side!

The closer you are to an event, the more power the potential sponsor holds in the negotiations. Without being unreasonable, if the event is imminent and remains un-sponsored, you really are in a powerful negotiating position! You may well be able to negotiate benefits that you would not have received if the negotiations had been undertaken some months prior.

Option for Renewal

Particularly in the case of a "hot property" a sponsor should consider adding an "option to renew" clause into the contract.

You will need to set the terms of the option. These might be:

- Renewal at same price, plus an allowance for CPI increase – ie 5%.

- First option for renewal – in other words this sponsorship will not be offered to any other sponsor until you have exercised your option (or advised that you will not be exercising that option.)

- Last option for renewal. This is not a common option, however is seen in the case of a "hot property" or in a sellers market, where the past sponsor wants to see who else is interested in the property prior to exercising his option.

Commonly if such a term is added it will also include a clause which ensures the sponsor advises many months prior to the end of the term if they are definitely not going to renew (6 – 12 months is reasonable).

Free Sponsorships

One method used by seeker of sponsorship who own the rights to a less than high profile event, team or new property is to offer the potential sponsor the first year's sponsorship at a discount, or even free of charge. This will enable you to get a taste of the benefits that can accrue. A similar method is the 'pay if you are happy' offer, where if preset benchmarks for delivery are achieved the sponsor pays for the deal at the end of the year. In either case, it is very important to go into this type of situation with honourable intentions, and to treat it as a commercial relationship, undertaking all the planning and leveraging that you would undertake with any other sponsorship.

Summary

Some points to remember in any negotiations are:

- Both parties must benefit from the sponsorship arrangement

- Know what you want to achieve out of the negotiations

- Know who you are negotiating with

- Say yes slowly – time is on your side

Part 6

Creating Successful Sponsorships®

A registered Trademark of The Sponsorship Unit® Pty Ltd.

Chapter 23

The Contract and its Implications

Please note: This book is not a substitute for professional legal advice. The services of a competent professional person should always be sought with respect to contracts.

Introduction

Because both parties require the same elements to be in place in order to create a successful sponsorship program, this part of the book is written for both seekers and sponsors, with the exception of the plan examples, which are written from each perspective – the seeker and the sponsor.

The Contract

You may be surprised to learn that, legally, a contract does not have to be in writing, with the exception of where copyright is assigned to a second party. A mere handshake and verbal agreement is, in the eyes of the law, a binding contract. However it is sensible to make sure any commercial agreement is in writing and clearly states the rights and benefits being assigned to the sponsor and details the payment terms. Lack of a written contract infinitely increases the chance of misunderstandings and thus the relationship turning sour. Another sound reason for committing the agreement to paper is that a change of personnel can mean the intent of an agreement is lost unless it is clearly detailed in documentation.

The contract basically states the intent of the agreement in plain English or in some cases "legalese" so the reader understands the intent of the sponsorship.

This is particularly important if the people who negotiate the contract move on, the new staff will be able to clearly understand the value of the property. Keep the agreement as simple as possible to eliminate any possible confusion. A contract is a legally enforceable arrangement between two or more parties.

Never assume you will get certain rights. If you require or expect particular rights to accrue to you, make sure they are clearly spelt out in the contract. The contract must be signed prior to expenditure being incurred.

The foundation to the success of any sponsorship is to make sure 'The Contract' is right for both parties.

A Successful Sponsorship Requires

        Fit
+ **Contract**
+ **Plan**
+ **Budget/Resources**
+ **Evaluation**
= **Successful Sponsorship**

Signing the contract can in fact be the first public acknowledgment of the new sponsorship relationship, and could well be used to promote the sponsor's activities.

The contract should become a working document, once signed. This will ensure that the sponsor remembers to claim contractual rights, and the seeker remembers to deliver them.

A point to note is that it is always the case that whichever party writes the contract invariably holds the upper hand and ends up controlling the negotiations.

Disclaimer

This book is not a substitute for professional legal advice. The services of a competent professional person should always be sought with respect to contracts.

Information to Include in a Simple Contract

The components of a sponsorship agreement will vary from sponsorship to sponsorship however any sponsorship contract, whether it be of the legal variety or a letter in plain English, should contain some or all of the points contained in the following list.

Note: This guide is not to be regarded as exhaustive. It is recommended legal advice be sought when preparing or agreeing to a sponsorship contract, however this information will provide a useful tool in preparing the contract agreement.

Contract Guide

Section One:

- **Parties to the agreement.** This section of the agreement should clearly name the parties involved in the sponsorship agreement, and could include the following:

- **The Sponsor.** The party providing cash or contra.

- **The Seeker/Property.** The party providing the sponsor with the rights and benefits agreed within the contract agreement.

- **Agents or Brokers.** Who have the right to sell the property and take a commission or receive payment.

- **Merchandisers.** Who have rights to produce licensed merchandise.

The Property

The exact nature of the property being sponsored, whether it is an organisation, event, team, venue or individual should be described, detailing any governing bodies and/or regulations that are to be complied with. If an:

- **Event.** Include any relevant points, such as required attendance of particular personalities or artists. Clearly describe the nature of the event, past attendance figures and the geographic boundaries of the event, and dates of occurrence.

- **Individual.** State minimum relevant events to be competed in and level of performance to be achieved by the individual if winning is important.

- **Organisation/Team.** State governing body, season dates, competition to be entered, and any other relevant dates.

Conditions Precedent

This clause would only be relevant if the sponsorship agreement is subject to conditions required by one of the parties. Conditions could include: a football team remaining graded in the highest level of competition, or the sponsored event occurring subject to a minimum level of funding being secured from other sponsors or government. If an individual, on being accepted to play in an orchestra, or reaching a certain performance level, for example, within the top ten in the country.

The Term

- **The Period.** This clause should state the length of the sponsorship agreement, for example, a three-year period. The period agreed will generally be governed by the nature of the property, and the date of commencement.

- **Option For Renewal.** Does the sponsor have first option to renew the contract? If so when does this have to be exercised by and under what terms and conditions and what formula to calculate any increase in price? The same terms plus CPI or different terms perhaps performance based. What period of time will the option be valid for?

- **The Season.** Detail when the property is active. For example, a football team's primary season of activity is during the winter months.

Section Two - Sponsorship Rights and Benefits

This section states the benefits that have been agreed to. Be specific - list everything, for example:

- 20 x A Reserve tickets for each match.

- One full page advertisement on back cover. (Include who is to cover production and related costs.)

- One four metre x three metre sign to be placed at rear of goal on ground perimeter fencing. All costs to be covered by sponsor.

Exclusivity

Detail the level of exclusivity being assigned. The relationship to other sponsors, the position in the sponsorship hierarchy, and the individual rights must be clearly described:

- **Naming/Title Rights.** This sponsor is the principal sponsor and has the right to have their company or product name included in the title of the sponsorship. e.g., the "DEF Company" event.

- **Sole.** This sponsor has the right to be the only sponsor of the property. This level of sponsor would normally have naming rights and absolute exclusivity in advertising promotion etc.

- **Principal**. This level of sponsor has the right of total category exclusivity with exclusive rights to advertising, promotion and supply of product to the property.

- **Major.** Usually there will only be one major sponsor, however, in large projects there could be a number of major sponsors with equal rights. Each major sponsor should, however, have the right of exclusivity by product or service category, ie, the only soft drink sponsor. Being a sponsor should provide exclusive category rights to advertising, promotion and supply of product to the property.

- **Minor.** All sponsors, even minor contributors, should have the right of exclusivity by category. For example the only soft drink sponsor. Being a sponsor should provide exclusive rights to advertising, promotion and supply of product to the property.

- **Official Supplier.** This is a lower level of sponsorship where the sponsor has few of the other rights, but has the right to be the sole purveyor of merchandise in a particular category, and the right to promote this fact.

Granting of Rights

This section describes licensed use of the property logo and/or trademarks and names, any conditions of use and any required approval processes, and whether any of the above are registered. This should also detail the use and approval for use of the sponsor's name and logos.

- **Official Event Logo.** This clause should detail the sponsor's rights to use the official event logo in advertising promotions and the like, and must detail any conditions of use, such as prior approval, size in relation to other logos, colour combinations etc. This clause should also detail if the logos are registered. This is particularly important where the trademarks may be copyright and registered. It is very important that the ownership of the logo is clearly detailed as it may become a generic logo with its own value. A good example of this is the famous gold on green boxing Kangaroo used by the victorious Americas Cup yacht.

- **Official Event Name.** This clause should detail the sponsor's rights to use the official event name in advertising promotions and must detail any conditions of use, such as prior approval, size in relation to other logos, colour combinations etc.

Advertising and Publicity

Describe the use of the sponsor's company logo on stationery, newsletters, signage, advertising, car stickers etc. Size of logo, colour, positioning, use of other sponsor logos, and the approval process that will be undertaken should also be detailed.

- **Television Rights.** The ownership of telecast and/or broadcast rights? Are these rights owned by the property owner, (ie, the sponsored organisation), the media outlet or the sponsor? Rules relating to the use of any resultant footage must be clearly spelt out. Does the sponsor have the right to use the footage in future advertising, if so are any fees payable and to whom? Will news cameras be permitted at the venue, if so do they have to acknowledge the correct naming rights? If the property is being televised is there a clause to protect the sponsor(s) from ambush through competitive advertising during the telecast?

- **Advertising Rights.** Describe all publications that advertising will be provided in, list publication dates, placement in the publication (ie bottom left hand page in front 1/4 of the book), deadlines for artwork, who pays for art production and what approval process will be used. Detail whether non sponsors can advertise in the publications and if so does the sponsor have category exclusivity to combat ambush.

- **Editorial Rights.** Detail acknowledgment of sponsor(s) that will be made in the media. For example, naming rights, logo on media backdrop, company hat to be worn by personalities during media interviews etc.

- **Media Monitoring.** Detail who has the responsibility for collecting all media related to the event. This is normally the sponsor's responsibility, but the seeker should also collect and forward copies to the sponsor whenever possible. (This shows an interest in the sponsor's needs, and an understanding of the value of media coverage.

- **Signage Rights.** This covers all details of signage; where, what, how many, how big, what is allowed, what is not allowed, etc. (Make sure, if you haven't done it already, that you check your local council regulations pertaining to signage.)

- **Where, What, When.** Detail exactly how many sites the sponsor is being provided with, where the sites are situated, the dimensions of the signs, the application material to be applied (ie paint, poster), who pays for manufacture and erection of the signs, whether the signage is permanent or temporary, is approval required to erect signs and if so what is the process? When is the signage to be erected and dismantled? Does the signage receive regular television or media coverage - if so how much?

- **Exclusivity.** Is the signage exclusive? Which other organisations can place signage at the venue? Are they all sponsors, if not exclusive size comparison to other sponsors signs, and where other sponsors signs are.

- **Additional Signage.** Can the sponsor purchase additional signage and if so, what is the cost? Can signage be placed on the grass, on tents, on food vans, drink machines, hats, clothing, banners, vehicles, etc?

Hospitality Rights

This clause should detail all relevant information pertaining to hospitality and ticketing.

- **Where, What, etc.** Where are the seats and how many are there? What is the standard of the facilities? Who is to pay for food and beverages? Are programs and car park passes provided, and if not, how much will they cost? Will there be extra tickets available, and if so at what standard and what cost? Are tickets available for staff, free or at a discount? If extra seats are required, detail contact details, and date that the tickets must be ordered by.

Personalities

- **Availability.** Are there rights for the sponsor to use personalities or individuals for such things as endorsements, sponsor functions, promotions or in their advertising? If so, are there any conditions? Is any payment required and if so what is the level of fees? (If personalities are being used for product endorsements see indemnity section to ensure the liability for product failure is not the responsibility of the personality promoting the product.)

- **Exclusivity.** Are your individuals/personalities allowed to accept individual sponsorship and if so can it be a conflicting sponsor? Are your individuals allowed to advertise or promote a non-sponsors product?

Merchandising

- **Merchandising**. Who owns the merchandise and licensing rights? How will profits be distributed? Is approval required for the use of the logo or name? Do specific suppliers have to be used by the sponsor? Are license or royalties payable and if so to whom and how much? Are merchandise items to be of a particular quality? What merchandise is allowed, who approves?

Section Three - Conditions

Payment

This section should clearly detail the terms of payment, including how and when that payment is to be received.

- **Payee.** Who is to be paid? (For example, does the money go directly to the property involved, or perhaps to their Broker?)

- **Payment Terms**. Detail here how much is to be paid, when the payments are to be made - it is also normal that the first payment will be on signing the contract, with further payments happening at various milestones (which could include after a specified period, or on commencement of the event). It is normal to have a payment near the end of the contract that could well be performance driven.

- **Contra.** This is the payment of some, or all, of the fee in products and/or services in lieu of cash. It is essential that the method for valuing contra is detailed in this section. For example, retail cost, wholesale or cost price. You will also need to detail clearly which party is liable to pay any taxes owing on product sale, delivery costs and time of delivery.

- **Late Payments.** If interest is going to be charged for late payment, the terms of penalties need to be outlined.

- **Use of Monies**. Any conditions of use agreed to for the sponsorship monies should be detailed here. For example, the sponsorship monies are to be used to fund a certain event, or certain research, or an athlete development program, and so on.

Termination

This clause should detail the grounds for termination, mediation and compensation.

- **Grounds for Termination.** Must be covered in the contract and they commonly include items such as: the organisation or sponsors insolvency; breach of contract by either party; either party bringing the other into disrepute (sponsorship of high profile individuals can be particularly dangerous); law change such as the banning of tobacco sponsorship; non performance of a team or athlete; if particular sportsman is not available, or the event is cancelled.

- **Mediation.** Detail here the process for dispute resolution. This could be for example, in writing with no public comment, and the use of an arbitrator to resolve the problem.

- **Compensation**. If either party has brought the relationship into disrepute are all payments to be refunded? If an event is cancelled are further payments required, or are the initial payments to be refunded.

- **Force Majeure**. The insertion of this clause covers events beyond the control of the contracted parties, for example, war, flood, earthquake, death of sponsored individual etc. If any of these occur the contract will be considered terminated without fault and liability by either party.

- **Product Withdrawal.** This should detail how long product can be on shelves bearing event logos, or your organisation's logo, and when should advertising be withdrawn following termination or completion of the contract.

- **No Publicity.** It is usual to have a non-publicity clause to cover the situation where the contract is terminated or not renewed.

Exit Strategy

If there is the possibility that either party is going to terminate the sponsorship agreement, particularly if this was unexpected, we recommend that an 'exit strategy' be determined prior to announcement of this decision to any one.

For example, we had a client who had been a long-term sponsor of a particular team. The sponsorship had been kind to them over the years, and they had a very good relationship with the team owner. If any objectives had not been achieved, it was the fault of the sponsor, who hadn't made any great attempt to exploit all the benefits available to them. They conducted a workshop to ascertain whether they would go ahead with this sponsorship and others, and planned for the next term of this sponsorship. When renewal time came around, they negotiated a new deal, talked about promotional items and requested new benefits. They made every indication that this sponsorship would be continued. However, on the very day that the sponsorship was due to be re-signed, they withdrew. This left the team in a very poor financial situation going into the next season (which was by this time imminent) and potentially the sponsor was going to receive some very bad publicity.

A far better tactic would have been to plan a withdrawal from the sponsorship many months in advance, which would have allowed time for the team to find another sponsor whilst still being sponsored. It would also have been helpful if the current sponsor had spoken to co-sponsors (most of whom they had brought on board in the first place), explained their situation – which was that their particular market was in turmoil, and they simply could not afford the expenditure at that time – and asked whether any of these could help out.

The whole thing was unplanned, poorly executed, and left the sponsor with a poor reputation, and giving the impression that they were in financial difficulties and the subject of much gossip.

Performance

It is common for a contract to contain prescribed levels of performance by the seeker.

- **Service Levels.** Service levels are included where a certain level of performance is required. This section details who is responsible for an event's success and details responsibility for preparation of reports and dates for delivery. This section also details what amount of advertising and promotion is to be committed to the advertising of the event and what the sponsor's rights are in relation to the management of an event, organisation or individual. It should also cover trader's rights, state which party is responsible for ensuring naming rights are observed etc.

- **The Ambush.** This details who will police the situation and who will mount legal action should an ambush take place. If non-sponsor promotions are allowed, this should be clearly stated in this section.

Warranties / Liability

- **Devaluation.** This is usually required when there is the possibility that a seeker may enter into an agreement that will adversely affect the value or standing of the event for the sponsor.

- **Insurance.** States who is responsible for public liability, insurance, wet weather insurance etc., and what level the cover should be.

- **Indemnities.** It is usual for both the sponsor and seeker to provide certain indemnities in areas such as public liability, product liability, product endorsement by seeker and indemnity against production or design faults

Confidentiality

- **Non disclosure.** It is usual for either (or both) parties to require confidentiality in relation to the terms of agreement and any disagreement.

General Clauses

- **Assignment.** This section clarifies whether the rights can be assigned to a third party through either selling or giving the rights to another company.

- **Entire Agreement.** States that all parts of the contract are contained within the contract document.

- **Right of Veto.** The right of the major sponsor to approve other potential sponsors is not uncommon. If this right is assigned it must be stated. Sponsors right of veto and the right to approve other sponsors and any grounds for rejection of a co-sponsor should be detailed here.

- **Governing Law.** This section details the governing law in relation to the contract. This is particularly important where the sponsor company operates in one state and sponsors an organisation in another state. The contract must clearly state under which laws the agreement is made.

Taxation

Taxation law is subject to quite frequent change and is a highly specialised area.

It is important to take the taxation aspects of any agreement into account prior to signing the contract, as various payments and time scales are subject to different taxation conditions. See your Accountant for more information.

The Bottom Line

Do all contracted parties understand what the contract means, and what the implications are?

Contract Checklist

The following checklist is designed to act as a quick check that all standard requirements relating to sponsorship agreements are included.

The components of a sponsorship agreement will vary from sponsorship to sponsorship, however any sponsorship contract, whether it be of the legal variety or a letter in plain English, should contain some or all of the points contained in this checklist.

Note: This checklist is not to be regarded as exhaustive and it is recommended legal advice be sought when preparing or agreeing to a sponsorship contract, however the checklist will provide a useful tool in preparing the contract agreement.

Contract Checklist

Parties

❑   Clearly state who the parties are that are involved in the sponsorship agreement.

❑   Name all sponsors of the event and their relationship (ie, major sponsor).

❑   Name any licensees and/or merchandisers and any royalties payable.

❑   Name any third parties (Brokers) that are part of the agreement.

Property

❑   Describe the exact nature of the property being sponsored and whether it is an organisation, event, team, venue or individual.

❑   Detail any governing bodies, regulations that are to be complied with.

❑   Details the owner or management of the organisation.

If an event

❑   Clearly describe the nature of the event.

❑   Detail required attendance of particular personalities or artists.

❑   State the geographic boundaries of the event.

❑   State dates of occurrence.

❑   State venue.

If an individual

❑   State relevant required event.

❑   Detail required performance level (if applicable).

Organisation or team.

❑   Include any details of state governing body.

❑   Detail season dates.

❑   Detail level of competition to be entered.

❑   Outline required level of performance if applicable.

The Term

❑   State the length of the sponsorship agreement, ie, for a three year period.

❑   State the date of commencement.

❑   Detail whether the sponsor has first option to renew the contract?

❑   If so, when does the option have to be exercised, and under what terms and conditions?

❑   What term will the option be for (an additional one year)?

Sponsorship Rights and Benefits

❑   Detail the level of exclusivity being assigned to the sponsor.

❑   Clearly describe relationship to other sponsors, their position in the sponsorship hierarchy, and their individual rights.

❑   Naming or title rights sponsor has the right to have their company or product name included in the title of the sponsorship.

❑   Does your 'sole' sponsor have the right to be the only sponsor of the property?

❑   Major sponsor usually there will only be one major sponsor however in large projects there could be a number of major sponsors with equal rights. Each major sponsor should have the right of exclusivity by product or service category.

❑   Minor sponsors should have the right of exclusivity by category ie, only soft drink sponsor, and does being a sponsor provide exclusive rights to advertising, promotion and supply of product to the property?

❑   Official Supplier is a lower level of sponsorship where the sponsor has few of the other rights but has the right to be the sole purveyor of merchandise in a particular category to the property (and the right to promote this fact)?

Granting of Rights

❑   Describe licensed use of the property logo and any conditions of use.

❑   Describe licensed use of trademarks and names and any conditions of use.

❑   Detail the use and approval for use of the sponsor's name and logos.

❑   Detail the sponsor's rights to use the official event logo in advertising promotions and detail any conditions of use, such as prior approval, size in relation to other logos, colour combinations etc.

❏　Detail the sponsor's rights to use the official event name in advertising, promotions and detail any conditions of use, such as prior approval, size in relation to other logos, colour combinations etc.

❏　Detail whether event logos are trademarks or copyright.

Advertising and Publicity

❏　Describe the use of the sponsor's company logos on event stationery, newsletters, signage, advertising, car stickers, size of logo colour, etc. Describe size of logo, positioning, relevance to other sponsor logos, and approval process that will be undertaken.

❏　Detail the ownership of telecast and/or broadcast rights. Advise whether they are owned by the property owner, the media outlet or the sponsor?

❏　Use of any resultant footage must be clearly spelt out. Does the sponsor have the right to use the footage in future advertising, if so are any fees payable and to whom?

❏　Will news cameras be permitted at the venue and if so do they have to acknowledge the correct naming rights?

❏　If the property is being televised is there a clause to protect the sponsor(s) from ambush through competitive advertising during the telecast?

❏　Describe all publications that advertising will be provided in. List publication dates, placement in the publication (ie, bottom left hand page in front half of book), deadlines for artwork, who pays for art production and what approval process will be used.

❏　Can non sponsors advertise in the publications and if so, does the sponsor have category exclusivity to combat ambush?

❑   Detail acknowledgment of sponsor(s) that will be made in the media (ie, naming rights), logo on media backdrop, company cap to be worn by personalities during media interviews, etc.

❑   Detail whose responsibility it is to collect all media related to the event.

Signage Rights

❑   Detail how many sites the sponsor is being provided with?
❑   Detail where the signage sites are situated?
❑   Detail the dimensions of the sites/signs?
❑   Specify the application material to be applied ie, paint, poster.
❑   Clarify who pays for manufacture and erection of the signs?
❑   Is the signage permanent or temporary?
❑   Mention whether approval (ie local authority) is required to erect signs and if so what is the approval process?
❑   Does the signage receive regular television or media coverage - if so how much?
❑   Is the signage exclusive? If not exclusive, detail size comparison to other sponsor's signs, where are other sponsor's signs?
❑   Which other organisations can place signage at the venue? Are they all sponsors? If not, do sponsors get better placement etc.?
❑   Can the sponsor purchase additional signage, and if so detail pricing?

Hospitality Rights

❑   Where are the seats (provide a seating plan, with the seats marked).
❑   Detail how many seats are available and at what standard.
❑   Clarify who pays for food and beverages.
❑   Are programs and car park passes provided. If not, detail cost

❑   Is there the ability to get extra tickets and if so at what standard and cost?

❑   Are tickets available for staff either free or at a discount.

Personalities

❑   Are there rights for the sponsor to use personalities or individuals for endorsements, sponsor functions, promotions or in advertising?

❑   Are there any conditions on the use of the personalities? Is payment required and if so what is the level of fees?

❑   Are individuals or personalities allowed to accept individual sponsorship? If so can it be a conflicting sponsor?

❑   Are individuals/personalities allowed to advertise or promote a non sponsors product?

Merchandising

❑   Who owns the merchandise and licensing rights - the sponsor or property owner or a third party?

❑   Detail how profits from merchandise and licensing rights will be distributed?

❑   Indicate whether approval is required for the use of the logo or name?

❑   Do specific suppliers have to be used by the sponsor, are license or royalties payable and if so to whom and how much?

❑   Are merchandise items to be of a particular quality?

❑   What merchandise is allowed, who approves?

Payment

❑   Who is to be paid?

❑   How much is to be paid?

❑   State when are payments to be made. It is normal that the first payment will be made on signing, with further payments happening at various intervals. It is not unusual to have a payment scheduled for near the end of the contract which could well be performance driven.

❑   Detail the payment of some or all of the fee in contra (products and services in lieu of cash).

❑   Detail the method for valuing contra. For example, retail cost, wholesale or cost price. Specify who will pay any taxes owing, delivery costs and time of delivery.

❑   Clarify whether interest is going to be charged for late payment, and if so the terms of penalties need to be outlined.

❑   Any conditions of use agreed to for the sponsorship monies should be detailed here.

Termination Grounds Can Include

❑   Either party bringing the other into disrepute (sponsorship of high profile individuals can be particularly dangerous in these days of outrageous behaviour and drug cheats.

❑   If a particular person is not available, or the event is cancelled.

❑   Non performance of a team or athlete.

❑   Either the sponsored organisation, or the sponsor, becoming insolvent.

❑   Breach of contract by either party.

Considerations upon Termination

❑ Detail the process for dispute resolution this could be in writing, no public comment, and the nomination of an arbitrator.

❑ If either party has brought the relationship into disrepute are all payments to be refunded?

❑ If event is cancelled are further payments required or are the initial payments to be refunded?

❑ Force Majeure. The insertion of this clause covers events beyond the control of the contracted parties. For example, war, flood, earthquake, death of sponsored individual etc. If any of these happen the contract would normally be considered terminated without fault and liability by either party.

❑ Product withdrawal - how much longer can product be on shelves bearing event logos and when should advertising be withdrawn following termination or completion of the contract.

❑ No publicity. It is usual to include a non publicity clause if the contract is terminated or not renewed.

❑ Sunset Clause. This states for how long imagery /logo /name/ association with the brand can go on being used after the contract has been terminated/discontinued. This often involves product which is already in-store.

Performance Requirements

❑ Guarantee of a certain level of performance in the prescribed competition (ie, must make the finals series).

❑ Detail who is responsible for the sponsorships success.

❑ Details of responsibility for preparation of reports and dates for delivery

❑   Amount of advertising and promotion support that is to be committed to the advertising of the event.

Ambush

❑   Detail who will police/monitor?

❑   Who will mount legal action in the event of ambush.

❑   Are non sponsor promotions allowed.

❑   State which party is responsible for ensuring naming rights are observed.

❑   Detail whether third party promotions, advertising, endorsements, etc. are allowed.

Warranty / Liability Clauses

❑   Guarantee seeker will not enter into any agreement that will adversely affect the value or standing of the event for the sponsor.

❑   Detail clearly who is responsible for organising public liability, insurance, wet weather insurance etc and what level is required?

❑   It is usual for both the sponsor and seeker to provide certain indemnities in areas which public liability, product liability, product endorsement by seeker and indemnity against production or design faults.

General Clauses

❑   State whether the rights can be assigned to a third party, through either selling or giving the rights to another company.

❑   Entire agreement. State that all parts of the contract are contained within the contract document.

❑   Right of veto. The right of the major sponsor to approve other potential sponsors is not uncommon. If this right is assigned it must be stated in the contract.

❑   State the governing law. This is particularly important where the sponsor company operates in one state and sponsors an organisation in another state. The contract must clearly state   under   which laws the agreement is made.

Please note: This book is not a substitute for professional legal advice. The services of a competent professional person should always be sought with respect to contracts.

Summary

- **The foundation to the success of any sponsorship is to make sure The Contract is right for both parties.**

- **Never assume a right or benefit is agreed to until it is in the contract.**

- **A good contract rarely has to be checked. A bad one is regularly revisited.**

- **Poorly prepared contracts are a huge factor in the failure of sponsorships, due to the expectations of one or both parties not being realised.**

- **When dealing with Copyright, Trademarks, Merchandisers etc., use the services of a Solicitor to make sure your rights are protected.**

- **Be aware of tax issues and seek professional advice.**

Chapter 24

Creating the Sponsorship Plan

Planning

There are many sponsorships where all sponsors are created equal. Sponsors all purchase identical benefits and opportunities, however, the results achieved by different sponsors vary enormously. The sponsors that complete the planning, and then implement their activities in a structured manner, in accordance to that plan, achieve many more times the return on investment than those who purchase the potential and waste it.

Planning provides a structured process where a document, the road map to a successful sponsorship, is produced. The final document will provide a detailed, fully costed, implementation plan, which will enable the manager to bring the sponsorship in on budget, having achieved or exceeded all pre-set marketing and communication objectives.

Return on sponsorship investment is directly related to the creativity and resources put into managing the sponsorship! The purchase of a sponsorship property is little more than the purchase of intangible latent potential. It is impossible to achieve a successful, cost effective sponsorship that delivers all objectives without going through the pre-planning phase. Strategically planned sponsorships minimise wasted expense because they only include those activities which will deliver the sponsor's objectives cost effectively.

History proves that a return on sponsorship investment must be planned in order to be delivered.

The sponsorship plan should also detail what management is required in terms of resources, budget and promotional programs. Writing the sponsorship plan is a creative time, and sets the sponsorship on the road to success.

It is the time when you create viable events and/or promotions that will ensure that objectives are achieved. Once the plan is in place, you can get on with the fun part of your job - implementing the plan! If you are able to achieve all that is set out in your plan, you will have a successful sponsorship on your hands (assuming that you have adhered to the plan, and no issues outside of your control mar the event).

Predicting and Measuring the Impact of a Sponsorship

The ability to accurately predict the outcome of a sponsorship program will ensure that sponsors have a successful sponsorship on their hands. To make this prediction, you will need:

- A structured selection process (selecting sponsorships that will deliver your marketing and communications objectives).

- To write sponsorship business plans which detail quantifiable objectives to be achieved through the sponsorship, and the actions required to deliver those objectives.

- To introduce a continuous review process. This will ensure that the sponsorship is on track, and to enable adjustments that will avoid a failure at the end of the term.

- A formal post-evaluation of each sponsorship to ensure all planned objectives were achieved.

Sponsorship Business Plans Must

- Set sales or volume targets to be directly achieved by the sponsorship program.
- Define corporate and brand objectives to be achieved by the sponsorship program.
- Contain a detailed timeline.
- Identify promotional extensions and their cost and value.
- Accurately predict the program's below the line costs.
- Detail the person hours required and their cost.
- Detail the review and post evaluation methods to be undertaken.
- Details responsibilities.

A Guide to Writing the Plan

The sponsorship business plan is a bit like a street map. It identifies opportunities, areas for caution and offers a number of routes for getting to the destination or outcome of a successful sponsorship.

The length of the plan would depend on the size and number of back up promotions and promotional extensions. A typical Olympic plan would be a document that might be as lengthy as 70 pages (any more could become unmanageable), whereas a plan for a small arts sponsorship may only contain one or two pages.

Generally a sponsorship plan will include the following:

- **Introduction.** The introduction should include brief details of the aims and objectives of the plan. It should briefly detail the focus, direction and activities that will be undertaken to achieve your stated objectives and those of your sponsors.

- **Situation Analysis.** The Situation analysis will provide a point of reference from which to operate. It details the environment in which your company operates, and the history of the sponsorship activity.

- **Objectives.** Objectives must be specific, tangible, realistic and measurable, without knowing and identifying these objectives it is impossible to implement a sponsorship support program. It is like the old story of the chicken and the egg. Don't get involved in sponsorships or managing them if you don't know what your objectives are. If there are no objectives to be achieved, you shouldn't be involved. It is impossible to measure the success of your sponsorship program without pre-set objectives!

  In setting your objectives ensure you are able to accurately predict the results you are likely to achieve. Take into account the economic environment, the size of the market, your targeting, the staff you have available to accomplish the sponsorships objectives, the time available and of course the below the line or support dollars you have to spend.

  Objectives must be realistic quantifiable and deliverable. For instance one of my staff listed as an objective 90% public awareness of our sponsorship of a sporting event.

Considering the highest recognition was, at that time, about 58%, I had to question the sense in aiming for a 90 % awareness factor when there is every likelihood that 30% of the population will never recognise you exist – to aim this high is to set yourself up for failure. Be realistic.

- **Target Audiences**. This section details who will be affected by this plan both internally and externally. The target audiences would probably include the following audiences: staff and their families, management, shareholders, regulators, customers, potential customers, dealers, suppliers, the public, television audiences, event audiences, co sponsors, the competition etc

- **Action List/Timeline/Accountability.** The action list details all events, launches and meetings with a date against every item. It should also nominate a person or persons who will be accountable for ensuring the listed action takes place effectively and on time.

- **Budget Finance and HR**. No matter how small your sponsorship, you are almost certainly going to have to outlay some money to service your sponsors, so budget for all items. Calculate all the below the line costs of managing the sponsorship. The budget should also include the person hours required to complete each activity.

- **Evaluation.** Detail here how and when you will measure if the result required of the program (and detailed in your plan) was successful.

Objective Setting

Objective setting is one of the most difficult skills to master. The objectives you set must be measurable, therefore they logically must have a number (or value) associated with them. They must also be achievable, so you are going to need to be experienced to know what is achievable, and what is not. Some typical objectives follow:

- 60% unprompted awareness of the sponsor within the organisation's target audience within one year.
- 25 news stories featuring sponsor in free media within one year.

- 80% of the target audience to have a positive image of the sponsor by the end of contracted term.
- 60% of target audience to have a propensity to choose a sponsor's product over a non-sponsors product by end of contracted term.
- 70% of those aware of the sponsorship to be able to name the sponsors product and/or key messages by end of contracted term.
- 14% incremental sales growth attributable to the sponsorship within one year.

Checklist of Costs

A major sponsorship program may include some, or all, of the following costs.

- ❑ Legal fees.
- ❑ Support advertising: air time, space and production.
- ❑ Signage manufacture, both fixed and temporary, erection and maintenance, apparel, vehicle, media backdrops.
- ❑ Promotional material: Hats, t-shirts, key rings, point of sale material.
- ❑ Prize money, trophies.
- ❑ Appearance fees.
- ❑ Travel.
- ❑ Media support: photographers, journalists, media releases, media training, media gear.
- ❑ Consultants (project management).
- ❑ Television broadcast.
- ❑ Client entertainment: invitations, food and beverages.
- ❑ Evaluation fee.
- ❑ Staff costs (wages, over time, travel and accommodation).

Human resource budgeting is a necessary component of the overall budget and this requires the allocation of person hours to each activity being undertaken.

You may find you simply do not have the permanent staff or volunteers to complete the activities, and if this is the case you will need to either to budget for outside consultants to do the job, or drop some of the planned activities.

Sponsorship Plan

An example of a plan for seekers is detailed below and one for sponsors immediately follows.

(example)
for Seekers

Implementation Plan of Fast Fuel's sponsorship of Gazelle's Racing Car Motor Racing Season

Executive Summary

This plan details how all the agreed benefits will be delivered, when reports will be sent to the sponsor and details the ways in which the sponsor will be serviced.

Situational Analysis

Fast Fuel have agreed to continue sponsoring John Gazelle's racing car for a further three years. Following an end of season meeting Fast Fuel indicated they had received most of the benefits, however they would like to organise dealer incentive programs and they would like to see John win more often and receive more exposure of their logo.

The season commences mid-February and there is one race on the second Saturday of every month until the end of October.

It was agreed that during the forthcoming season, Gazelle Racing's Assistant Manager will become the liaison person between the team and the sponsor.

The relationship has been quite satisfactory, however could be further enhanced. Getting Fast Fuel's Dealers on-side appears to be a key to having the sponsorship renewed the season after next, as these people as Franchisees do have a say in the allocation of marketing budget.

Objectives

1. To win 4 out of the 7 races to ensure adequate exposure for our sponsor, Fast Fuel.

2. To contact every Fast Fuel Dealer and offer to have one of the team's cars displayed in their outlet.

3. To entertain every Fast Fuel Dealer at a race meeting and offer them a "hotlap" of the circuit.

4. Update all logos and position Fast Fuel Logos to receive maximum media coverage.

5. Keep Fast Fuel informed of all relevant information including race results, media coverage and Dealers entertained.

6. Talk to the media and grow relationships, create angles the media will report (we aim to have 10 news reports per year mentioning the sponsor).

Target Audiences

1. The Media in relevant geographic areas, particularly the sporting press, and their audiences.

2. All Fast Fuel Dealers.

3. The sponsor

4. The team

5. The race going public

Action list/Timeline/Accountability

Feb 1	Change logos	Simon
Feb 1	Invite all dealers to local race meeting, follow up fortnight before each meeting offering car to all dealers for site display.	Sharon
Feb 5	Sponsor to inspect logos	Sharon
Feb 9	Media Launch	Team
Feb 10	Race meeting Entertain dealers and organise lap in car	Team Sharon
Feb 12	Send news clips and report to dealer and sponsor	John
March 10	Race meeting Entertain dealers and organise' hot' lap in car	Team Sharon
March 12	Send news clips and report to dealer and sponsor	John

Oct 31   Prepare sponsor report   Sharon

Nov 4   Deliver Report   John

Budget

Postage	$ 120
Signage changes	$ 1800
Media entertainment	$ 2000
media gifts	$ 1400
Telephone calls to dealers	$ 135
Printing invitations	$ 200
Wages Host for dealers	$ 3800
Event tickets for dealers	$ 4600
Compile final report	$ 600
Total	**$14655**

Evaluation - Success will be achieved when we have:

1. Won 4 races.

2. Displayed team car in 50% of Fast Fuel outlets.

3. Entertained 80% of all Fast Fuel Dealers at a race meeting and take them for a 'hot lap' of the circuit.

4. Updated all logos to exceed sponsors expectations.

5. Provided monthly Reports on all activities to sponsor

6. Obtained 10 news reports per year mentioning the sponsor.

Sponsorship Plan

Following is an example of a plan for sponsors.

(Example)
for Sponsors
Sponsorship of XYZ

Introduction

This plan outlines how (insert company name) will use its Sponsorship of (insert seeker) and their associated programs and events to promote specifically our new product, (insert product/brand).

The objectives and activities listed in this plan will form the basis of a review of (insert seeker name) performance in servicing it's Sponsor, and measure the success of (insert project managers name) project management of the Sponsorship.

Situation Analysis

Detail sponsors business, and all details relating to the environment the company operates within that may be relevant to the sponsorship.

Detail seekers property and its relationship to the target group and all relevant information about the environment the organisation operates within.

The property provides the following specific benefits to *(insert sponsors name):*

1.   (list all benefits from contract).

Objectives

The following objectives if achieved will ensure this property is a success:

1.   List each objective (it must be quantifiable): who is responsible for it being successfully achieved and by what date.

For example:

2. Generate regular publicity to the product's target market naming the Sponsor of (insert property name).

- Regional Newspapers   60 articles minimum   C Bentley

- Suburban Newspapers   50 articles minimum   C Bentley

- Metropolitan Newspapers   10 articles minimum   C Bentley

- XYZ's magazine   10 articles minimum   S Brown

3. To introduce the *(product A)* to school age children through *(insert property name)* activities.

    6000 school children by 21/11/04   S Brown

Target Audiences

Internally

- Staff
- Sales people
- Senior management

Externally

- XYZ Association and Clubs, administrative staff
- Association members and competitors
- The Media
- (Brand A's) customers
- Retailers
- Women 18 to 39
- School Children
- General Public
- Vendors

Key Messages

The following Key Messages promoting *(insert Sponsors brands)* need to be transmitted through the Sponsorship:

- *(brand name)* is now available.
- *(brand names)* attributes, It tastes great, highest in calcium and low fat.

Tactics

The strategy for ensuring the success of this Sponsorship is:

- To work with *(insert seekers name)* and effectively make use of all events in their calendar.

- To gain as much media exposure as possible, to constantly reinforce to *(brand a's)* target audiences the value of this Sponsorship to the community.

- To work with *(insert seekers name)* to create extra opportunities for *(brand a's)* to gain exposure and reach target audiences.

- Sell the benefits of the Sponsorship to Association and club members to ensure they become advocates of the brand

- Introduce a sampling program to ensure all members know the great taste of *(brand a)*.

Implementation

The actions and activities needed to achieve each objective are listed below each objective.

1. **Generate regular publicity to the product's target market naming the Sponsor of** *(insert property name)*.

   - Regional Newspapers   60 articles minimum   C Bentley

   - Suburban Newspapers   50 articles minimum   C Bentley

   - Metropolitan Newspapers   10 articles minimum   C Bentley

   - XYZ's magazine   10 articles minimum   S Brown

Actions

   1. Select media spokes people a current player and a past older player who has credibility to talk on women's shows and radio.

      by 14/03/95   S Brown

   2. Train Media Spokes people.

      by 28/03/95   S Brown

3. Create regional media press kit, with a newsworthy angle.

   by 14/03/95   S Brown

4. Create a range of media apparel, including shirt and hat: This gear is to be worn at all media functions and interviews by members of XYZ association.

   by 28/03/94   S Brown

5. Produce signage required to ensure adequate coverage including:

   > permanent signage
   > portable X 5 sets
   > media apparel
   > apparel signage
   > umpire uniforms
   > pole signage
   > by 07/03/95   K Johnston

6. Write editorial and circulate research for publication in regional and suburban newspapers.

   ongoing 6 articles per year   S Brown

Timeline

Date	Activity	Responsibility
22/02/02	Identify person for ensuring players wear Sponsor gear	K JOHNS
22/02/02	Identify person responsible for transport and erection of signage.	K JOHNS
01/03/02	Review Meeting	K JOHNS/ S BROWN
04/03/02	Association members advised of the Sponsorship, and all details	K JOHNS
07/03/02	Produce signage required to ensure adequate coverage including: permanent signage portable X 5 sets media apparel apparel signage umpire uniforms pole signage	S BROWN
07/03/02	Sampling program at major competitions and venues	S BROWN /K JOHNS

14/03/02	Product signage provided to canteens and retail venues	S BROWN
14/03/02	Advertisement created	S BROWN
14/03/02	Use one page of editorial for advertisement in each edition.	S BROWN
14/03/02	Select media spokes people	K JOHNS /S BROWN
28/03/02	Create a range of Media Apparel	S BROWN
28/03/02	Organise regional Media Launches	K JOHNS /S BROWN

Evaluation Methods

The following evaluation methods will be used to determine each of the following objectives were achieved.

Evaluation Method 1

1. **To make available for purchase brand A's product range (as listed in the contract), in every venue in which the sport is played:**

    - Clubs   100% by 07/03/02   S Brown
    - Venues   100% by 07/03/02   S Brown

Evaluation Method 2

    - Compare sales data with XYZ Associations venue and competition list.
    - Measure actual sales revenue

2. **Generate regular publicity to the product's target market naming the Sponsor of (insert property name).**

    - Regional Newspapers   60 articles minimum   C Bentley
    - Suburban Newspapers   50 articles minimum   C Bentley
    - Metropolitan Newspapers   10 articles minimum   C Bentley
    - XYZ's magazine   10 articles minimum   S Brown

Evaluation Method 3

    - Count the articles that mention the naming rights, that contain key messages listed in this plan, logos, incorporated in photos against total articles received by netball.

    - Calculate media coverage and compare to competitive advertising.

Budget	$	Man Hours
Launch of Sponsorship		
Selection of media spokes people	Nil	8
Media Apparel, including shirt and hat X 30:	3000	8
Signage		
Apparel	8000	1
Maintenance and replacement	2000	4
Permanent signage	10000	8
Portable X 5 sets	4000	4
Umpire uniforms	600	2
Pole signage	400	3
Communications and Media Program		
Media Training	1500	3
Direct mailings X 4 (writing)	Nil	18
Editorial X 4 (writing)	Nil	12
Players fund for promoting sponsor	5000	2
Editorial for papers X 6 (writing)	Nil	18
Staff Bulletin (writing)	Nil	1
Identify active staff netballers	Nil	1
Staff stories X 4 (writing)	Nil	16
Merchandising program		
Licensed merchandise	2000	8
Sampling program (netball)		
Product 25000 by 30 cents	7500	2
Samplers 50 hours X $30	1500	4
Advertising		
Production	2000	5
Purchase (external)	20000	2
Bumper stickers	7500	4
Retail Program		
In Store Competition	5000	8
On pack cross promotion	2000	40
Sampling	5000	6
Administration		
Review meetings X 10	Nil	10
Approval of material with brand	Nil	5
Formal Evaluation and review	4500	2
Omnibus survey X 2 questions	1800	2
TOTAL	**138300**	**H 235**

Sponsor Plan Template (example)

(A clean copy of this document can be found in Appendix 6, and also on the accompanying computer disc as a template named Sponsor Plan.)

Sponsor Plan for _____

Introduction

Briefly detail the focus, direction and activities that will be undertaken to achieve your stated objectives and those of your sponsors.

_____

_____

Situational Analysis

Provides a point of reference from which to operate, it details the environment in which your event operates, the sponsors and the status of their contracts, ie, when they are up for renewal, the organisations history, sponsors and target audiences.

_____

_____

Objectives

Sponsors objectives must be specific, tangible, realistic and measurable.

_____

_____

Action list/timeline/accountability

Details all events, launches and meetings and must have a date against every item and the name of the person who will be accountable for ensuring the listed action takes place effectively and on time.

Date	Action	Responsibility

Sponsorship Cost Sheet

List all items that will incur either financial expenditure or person hours (this list is not necessarily comprehensive. You will need to check your plan to ensure all activities are allowed for).

Item and quantity	Real Costs
Tickets	
Hospitality food and beverages	
VIP parking passes	
Event programs	
Additional printing	
Signage production	
Signage erection	
Support advertising	
Apparel for competitors, officials, media etc featuring sponsor	
Evaluation research	
Media monitoring	
Fax's and phone calls	
Public relations support	
Legal costs contract preparation	
Travel	
Transport/freight costs	
Sampling programs/casual staff	
Cost of selling (for seekers) sponsorship staff time and expenses based on ?? hours at $10 per hour X 1.9 for real cost of salary	
Cost of managing sponsorship in staff time based on ?? hours over the season $10 X 1.9 for real cost of staff member	
Total Costs	$

Evaluation Method

Detail here how you will measure if the result of this plan was a success.

Summary

- Writing the sponsorship plan is a creative time, and can prove to be incredibly rewarding. It is the time when you create viable events and/or promotions that will help you and your sponsor(s) achieve all stated objectives.

- Presentation of the final plan should demonstrate that the program will be a success and achieve its objectives. Now you can get on with the fun part of your job - implementing the plan!

- If you are able to achieve all that is set out in your plan, you will have a successful sponsorship on your hands, barring unforeseen events.

- Objectives must be achievable and measurable.

Chapter 25

Sponsorship Management

Once you have a signed sponsorship contract, it is in the interests of all parties to ensure that every single benefit promised, and contracted, is delivered. From the seekers perspective, this will help at the end of the contract period when you want the sponsor to resign, and from the Sponsor's perspective, you should have achieved all your pre-set objectives, which will justify your activities to your manager!

Sponsor Servicing

What is sponsor servicing? Well, in short it is all the things the seeker needs to do to ensure their sponsor remains happy. It is everything from the two way communication (the relationship), right through to making sure your sponsor's signage is kept clean, in good repair, and is strategically placed at all appropriate times. The secret to effective sponsor servicing is to adopt a 'can do' attitude and look for opportunities to extend your sponsor's return on investment. Conversely, the sponsor should be looking for this attitude from the organisation they have sponsored.

To effectively service your sponsor you will need to know what the sponsor expects from the relationship and what they will be undertaking to manage their sponsorship. Normally on signing a sponsorship deal, a company will put together a sponsorship plan that will detail how they are going to exploit the benefits they have purchased. This will identify budgets, promotional tools to assist them, create advertisements and promotional materials to back up their sponsorship. In the ideal situation, the planning process should be a collaborative effort between sponsor and seeker – then there can be no misunderstandings as to what the sponsor needs to achieve.

If, when you put the deal together, you were realistic and honest about your organisation's capabilities, and didn't oversell the benefits, you will find sponsor servicing "a breeze" and very rewarding. You will be able to over deliver (exceed the sponsor's expectations) thereby ensuring you have a happy sponsor who is getting value for money.

The Seeker's Obligations

- To deliver all the benefits promised and outlined in the contract **without being prompted by the sponsor.**
- To be genuinely committed to the sponsorship.
- To service the sponsor to the best of your ability.
- To protect your sponsor's rights.
- To promote your sponsor at every opportunity.
- **Always acknowledge** your sponsor.
- Introduce ideas and promotions to assist the sponsor to meet and exceed their objectives.
- Control your members and ensure they look after the sponsors rights.
- Keep your sponsor fully informed of all relevant happenings in your organisation.
- Warn the sponsor **in advance** of any potential unpleasant publicity.

The Sponsor's Obligations

- To provide the payment in cash (or contra) as agreed and in a timely manner. (To assist them to do this, the seeker should send an invoice giving plenty of time to get it through the accounts process. It is perfectly acceptable for the seeker to follow up if this payment is late – you do have a legally binding contract regarding this payment.)
- To be genuinely committed to the sponsorship.
- To look after the seekers interests wherever possible.
- To commit below the line funds to ensure the sponsorship is a success.

Single Contact Point

One person representing each organisation must become the sole contact for the other. This person must be able to strike up a relationship with the others representative and have enough power to get things fixed if there is a problem. They must be easy to contact.

Know Your Sponsor

The seeker should be made familiar with the sponsor's company. They should become familiar with senior management, company hierarchy and the company's business. Most importantly, we would recommend providing a copy of those segments of the sponsorship business plan that are relevant to both parties, so each of you know exactly what the sponsor hopes to get out of the relationship. Without this knowledge it is very difficult to for the seeker to service the sponsor's expectations.

In short make sure the lines of communication are open and regular. Keep each other informed of anything that is happening that is either relevant or interesting to them, and make them feel either part of your organisation.

Seekers Must Sell the Value of Sponsorship to Their Members and Reinforce It

It is very important, prior to the signing of any sponsorship, to make the sponsored organisation's members aware of the impending sponsorship, the reasons why you are seeking or accepting sponsorship, and the ensuing benefits to your organisation.

Your members must be prepared to publicly support the sponsorship and not criticise it. Invariably if there is criticism you can bet the sponsor's representative will get to hear of it one way or another.

Privacy laws vary from country to country, however, it is always wise to seek the permission of your members prior to handing their details over to the sponsor – they may feel that doing so without permission is a violation of your relationship.

Seekers Should Control Their Members

If an organisation is team based or has many members you must ensure they understand the legalities of sponsorship. They should be kept informed of what is in the contract and be advised that they should not ambush the sponsor and disadvantage general membership by undertaking personal endorsements and/or sponsorship agreements.

One major swimming association lost a sponsorship that was worth over a million dollars because the body sponsored had no control over its individual athletes. Effectively it was cheaper for their ex-sponsor to go and sponsor the cream of the swimmers individually, for a fraction of the cost. This problem was resolved prior to the next sponsor of swimming signing their contract!

We also remember a high profile basketball team that our organisation sponsored, and who, just prior to the end of the contract (and re-signing time) were going through a bad losing streak. Then to top off a bad run, a photo was published of one of their high profile players endorsing our opposition's service. What was worse was that this photo was taken prior to the original sponsorship being signed and the team hadn't asked the opposition for payment for the player's services. So they devalued a sponsorship overnight. Needless to say, our organisation did not re-sign, and the team was still struggling, some months later, to find a new sponsor.

Prior Warning on Controversy

If a profile member of a sponsored organisation is about to receive adverse publicity, ensure the sponsor knows before the media does! Most organisations do not like surprises of the negative kind – and this goes both ways – remember that the seeker's organisation has allowed the sponsor to associate with their name and image, so if something is going wrong let the other party know, and tell them how you intend to fix the problem. (If you don't know what to do, perhaps professional PR advice will provide the answer.) Always keep your partner up to date with all happenings. If you know your organisation is about to change management, lose a star or declare itself in liquidation give your sponsorship partner advance warning - they have the right to know.

Personality Behaviour

A sponsor buys the right to use the images of the personalities in the sponsored organisations 'stable', so they have a right to expect that those personalities are not about to appear in the media for taking drugs, drink driving, violence, or other unacceptable behaviour. It is a gamble for the sponsor.

A very successful soft drink manufacturer severed their relationship fairly quickly after unsavoury allegations were published about a very high profile personality in the press – however, even after all these years, the two names are sometimes still linked. It is up the seeker to ensure that members and personalities don't cause the sponsor embarrassment through the sponsorship association.

Make sure your personalities are aware of the benefits to them of having a sponsor, and that they are prepared to recognise the sponsor and welcome them into your environment.

Personality Availability

Ensure personalities (team members, performers, singers etc.) are available to the sponsor for client entertainment opportunities, staff motivation purposes and similar. Make sure personalities know the sponsor, greet them whenever possible, and welcome them into your environment. Every so often it may be prudent for the seeker organisation to remind their people of the benefits of having a sponsor.

If a personality is out of action, organise for them to visit the sponsor's box or table to meet their clients and perhaps explain the finer points of the performance, game or organisation, and sign some autographs. This is an easy thing to do, and always scores points!

Win at All Costs

Companies like to sponsor and associate with winners, not losers. This poses a problem! There can be only one winner in any competition or category, so if you can't win, make sure you generate media coverage through the use of characters, staging an incident - a dramatic example (although unrealistic) would be to crash the car in front of the camera. If you are a winner everyone loves you, and it really assists in justifying your sponsor's investment. This applies to organisations as well as seekers. Be the best at what you do, and let people know how good you are! Let your sponsor(s) share in your glory; it makes them feel good. Perhaps provide the company with a trophy to put on display in their foyer, include their representative in group photos, and so on.

Sponsor Acknowledgment

In **every media story** the sponsor should expect acknowledgment. A sponsor has the right to be acknowledged and expects to be. Sponsors should be acknowledged at all public functions whether it be over the PA at a football game or at the annual general meeting. Remember, lack of acknowledgment is (or should be) a major problem for sponsors. It is, at best, lack of courtesy and, at worst, breach of contract! The following communications mediums offer the opportunity for sponsor acknowledgment through editorial, advertising or verbal acknowledgment:

- Annual Report
- Newsletter
- PA
- Club House
- Xmas Cards
- Media Stories
- Telephone

Always Acknowledge Naming / Title Rights

If a seeker has sold naming rights to their organisation, they have received a premium for the sponsorship. **It is the seeker's obligation from that day on to acknowledge those naming rights in everything they say and do**. It is also the seeker's responsibility to ensure that the media are aware of and adhere to the naming rights. This could require designing a logo and providing that logo to all media outlets with instructions for use, reminding all journalists of the value of naming rights. This is regardless of whether it is naming rights of a team, a building, a club or an organisation.

Answer the Phone With Sponsor Acknowledgment

Principal or naming rights sponsors should be acknowledged at every opportunity. This includes using the sponsor's naming rights when answering the phone. If the correct title is The GMH Goers, answer the phone "GMH Goers", not "the Goers". This is a benefit that costs nothing and shows that the seeker values their principle sponsor. Most telephone systems have the facility to put people on hold. Don't use the radio.

Create some messages (with your sponsor's input of course) extolling the value of your sponsor or use existing advertisements the sponsor may have. Again, this is another free benefit you can offer.

Community Service Announcements (CSA's)

Community organisations may be able to get free air-time on radio or television, or free space for print ads in your local newspaper. If this is the case, use the space to promote your activities and the sponsor's commitment. Community Service Announcements for television, radio and community billboards in newspapers all offer the opportunity to get the sponsor and your organisation or events awareness increased.   Sponsors may be interested in financing the Community Service Announcement in return for advertising placement. CSA's are transmitted free of charge, generally in difficult to sell slots. They commonly go to air during the Christmas period and in early January. They also get played during the morning and midnight to dawn time slots. CSA's can assist in improving a sponsor's image and increasing awareness for them. It is worth checking with your local TV and radio stations to see if there is a possibility of doing this.

The Launch

The launch of the sponsorship will almost certainly be the first acknowledgment of the sponsorship. Launches take many shapes, ranging from a private meeting to hand over the cheque through to large media events. The launch of a major sponsorship has the potential to be extremely newsworthy and may be picked up by all media. Local launches should be designed to attract local media and even though no media may show up, privately commissioned photos and a press release sent to the local paper often results in a good story being published.

Media Monitoring

Whenever any member of the sponsored organisation, have completed a media interview, they should always provide a copy of the tape or the clipping to the sponsor. Many larger companies do retain media monitoring services, however the seeker sending such material shows they are interested in their sponsor and alert to the benefits they are receiving.

Fund Raising Mentality

Avoid the "fund raising" mentality. Unfortunately for seekers, if you have undersold, the seeker will have to live with that until re-negotiation time. **Once the seeker has signed the deal don't keep going back for more!**

Individual Sponsorships

If personalities, or teams within the sponsored organisation, have individual sponsorship agreements, it is very important to ensure contractually that they do not conflict with the sponsor organisation.

Signing a New Sponsor

Prior to a seeker organisation signing a new sponsor, they should advise all of their current sponsors. Current sponsors may want to take up the additional sponsorship or know of another company that may be interested. Give existing sponsors the opportunity to address any concerns they may have over the signing of a particular sponsor. In fact, many major sponsors now include reasonable right of veto over new sponsors as a clause in the contract.

Always Wear Sponsor Gear

Regardless of what the contract says, sponsors gear should be worn for all media interviews. Ensure any background signage features your sponsor(s).

Principal Sponsor on Everything

The principal sponsor has a right to be on everything! Their interests should be looked after absolutely! Their flag should be run up the flag pole, their logo should be featured on letterhead, sweaters, caps, in front reception, on newsletters, on carry bags. They should be allowed to place samples of promotional material on the table at fundraising dinners, etc. etc.

Merchandising

Merchandise provides association by having the corporate and the sponsored organisation's logos tied together on the merchandise or the logo on the sponsor's product. It also creates awareness of the association and the opportunity to create premium products, which might either create a new market or the opportunity for a premium price to be charged for the product. If merchandise is created it is worth using the merchandise uniform in advertising rather than the official uniform. This allows for reinforcement of the sponsor's association with the team.

There are a number of legal matters to consider prior to entering into any merchandise program. Be aware of the licence fee or, rightly, it may be payable on every item manufactured or every item sold. The licence fee could either be a single fee, a royalty, or a percentage of the retail price of each item sold or manufactured.

Merchandising gets more complicated where the rights have been assigned to a third party, and the seeker therefore does not control the rights to the logo or emblem. Commonly in this situation, the governing body controls the rights and trademarks and governs the rules of their use.

Be Professional

An organisation may be largely run by volunteers, however that is no excuse for them to act like amateurs. Businesses that sponsor, expect, and have a right to deal with professional behaviour, whether an organisation is run by full time paid professionals or unpaid amateurs.

Support Sponsors Related Programs

Sponsors should be assisted with spin off programs from the main sponsorship wherever possible. If it is possible to provide extra benefits without watering down or creating a Trojan horse ambush, those benefits should be provided.

Publicity Checklist

The publicity checklist details all likely expenditure items required to be produced or paid for by the business to ensure the sponsorship runs successfully. These additional costs add significantly to the overall price of the sponsorship and should be considered when assessing the sponsorship. In some cases many of these items are included in the purchase price of the sponsorship. (Master copy of this checklist can be found in Appendix 6.)

Signage

Production	$
Erection/dismantling	$
Permits	$
Storage	$
Cleaning	$
Repairs	$
Person hours	$
(estimated hours X hourly rate)	
Sub Total	$

Advertising

Production	$
Placement external	$
Event materials	$
Person hours	$
(hours X hourly rate)	
Sub Total	$

Personalities

Payment	$
Expenses	$
Person hours	$
hours X hourly rate	
Sub Total	$

Event Management

Event Manager ... ... $
Person hours ... ... $
(hours X hourly rate)

Sub Total ... ... $

Media Management/PR

Media consultant ... ... $
Person hours ... ... $
(hours X hourly rate)

Sub Total ... ... $

Hospitality

Invitations ... ... $
Additional Ticketing ... ... $
Food and beverages ... ... $
Follow up gifts ... ... $
Cab dockets ... ... $
Host time ... ... $
(usually 30 hours minimum) X hourly rate

Sub Total ... ... $

Negotiation/Contract

Negotiation time ... ... $
(usually 10 hours minimum) X hourly rate
Negotiation expenses ... ... $
Legal Costs ... ... $

Sub Total ... ... $

Post Evaluation

Media Monitoring   ...   . $
Media analysis   ...   . $
Research (target audience attitudes)   ...   ... $
Sales analysis ...   . $
Hospitality surveys   ...   . $
Person hours   ...   . $
hours X hourly rate

Sub Total   ...   . $

Merchandise/Promotional material

Design   ...   . $
Licence fees   ...   . $
Stock   ...   . $
Person hours   ...   . $
hours X hourly rate

Sub Total   ...   . $

Employee Relations

Staff communications ...   . $
Staff tickets/discounts ...   . $
Person hours   ...   . $
hours X hourly rate

Sub Total   ...   . $

Group Total ...   . $
Sponsorship Fee   ...   . $
Total Cost of Sponsorship   ...   . $

In conclusion:

Effective sponsorship management relies on both parties working together within a planned framework.

Summary

- The sponsor should be serviced from day one.
- The sponsor should be involved in as many activities as possible.
- The sponsored organisation should assist the sponsor to manage his sponsorship to get the most out of the property.
- The sponsor should always be acknowledged.
- The sponsor should always be thanked.
- Both parties should measure their success
- Make sure your property is a raging success, everyone likes winners - especially the sponsor.
- Be flexible. Where ever possible offer additional benefits.
- Ensure naming rights are acknowledged by media.
- Undertake cross promotions between sponsors
- If necessary, teach sponsors about the value of sponsorship and how to use it
- Respond quickly to each others requests and endeavour to accommodate them.
- Once again - under sell and over deliver.
- Keep each other informed.
- Have one key contact in each organisation, with a back-up in case someone moves on.

Chapter 26

Strategic Signage and Logo Placement

Signage

Signage is any logo or message on a surface. If no surface exists create one and suspend it. Marketing Managers must, on the whole, believe that signage works for them - because it is everywhere, and there is an ongoing push to find more creative surfaces on which to place signage. The secret is to get your sponsor's signage noticed, either consciously or subliminally. Signage is generally expensive in terms of both the purchase of space and the manufacture of signage and it therefore needs to return benefit to the advertiser to make it cost effective.

For signage to be effective ensure you keep the message short and apply the right message to the sign. Putting your sponsor's company logo or word mark on a sign may raise the awareness and profile of the company, but it doesn't promote your sponsor's brands, nor does it sell the attributes of the product, nor does it direct the reader to do or feel something. So consider carefully whether you should be using the company logo, promoting their brand, or whether the sign should contain a call to action such as "drink more water".

Use of Sponsor's Logo

Company and brand logos are extremely valuable and must not be used without the relevant permission. Most companies have specific guidelines for the standard use of their brands, whether it be on advertising or sponsorship related material. These guidelines include the use of correct fonts (shape and size of words) and logo shape and size. Never change the size of the logo in relation to the word mark, nor change its orientation, positioning, colours or the information it imparts. Most – *but not all* - logos have the option for use in black and white if necessary. Many companies also have rules on the amount of white space allowed around their logo.

These will generally be stated in their corporate identity guidelines. Do check, as the majority of companies have invested large amounts of money into developing and building their brand, and they are understandably sensitive about how that brand is portrayed.

'Duelling Logos'

Nothing looks worse than "duelling logos", or "clutter-boards". This is the industry term for the situation where you have a page or a board full of sponsor logos. Clutter is a big problem at any event or anywhere where signage is featured. Often there is so much signage in a particular venue, or on a particular page, that it is difficult to differentiate one company's logo from that of another company. Obviously, this type of clutter renders the signage or advertising far less effective, and therefore the returns will be negligible. It should not excite sponsor(s) to be featured in this manner!

If possible, sponsors should be acknowledged on separate pages, for example on a page next to the advertising for the event they are associated with, or on separate boards.

Signage Placement

When you are considering signage locations, always physically check the location and check previous television coverage, if applicable, to see if that particular sign was ever covered. It is possible that you will find that it has been largely anonymous, due to camera placement or angle.

Signage Erection

In taking out a sponsorship it is extremely important to clarify at the contract negotiations who is responsible for paying for the manufacture of signs. It is also important to clarify who is responsible for erecting, maintaining and dismantling signage.

If an annual or travelling event is involved, it is important to clarify who will be packing, paying for transit and insuring the signage.

Types of Signage

- **Aerial Signage.** (eg, helicopter towing a flag) As mentioned, it can be difficult to stand out from the clutter. One way of achieving recognition is through aerial signage. Aerial signage works well where you have a captive audience (an audience who will be in an open venue for a certain amount of time, such as at a football match). It can be extremely expensive or very cheap and it may only last for a very short duration. Be aware that this type of signage is subject to the prevailing weather conditions.

- **Flags.** Flags can be a cheap way of getting your logo in front of a crowd. Their movement normally attracts attention, so if there is no wind there will be no movement, which leaves the logo or message obscured. Flags come in various sizes, the standard being 6 foot by 3 foot, which is quite big enough to attract attention. Flagpoles are easy to erect and can be hired from most hire companies for a moderate charge. They can either be dug into the ground with a post hole digger or flag stands can be used but may be dangerous in high winds.

- **Sky Writing.** Sky writing is effective on a still, clear sunny day, when the message written contains very few letters. An acrobatic aircraft producing smoke and literally spelling out the message generates the writing. When conditions are perfect, skywriting has the potential to be seen by very large numbers of people. One problem is that it may be difficult to gain air traffic control clearance at the optimum time to spell out your message, particularly at an inner city venue.

- **Solid or Inflatable Product.** Large products, whether they be of the solid type, generally made out of plastic or steel, or inflatables, which are filled either with helium or cold air, are expensive items to manufacture. They can be internally lit at night, which is very effective. There are many benefits in using these types of signage. The message can be as creative and colourful as your imagination, and they therefore attract a lot of attention and get your message across easily. Research indicates that this type of signage is most effective in the short period of time after it is introduced, and then awareness drops off. These products can be used multiple times, however as they tend to be deflated or packed up on the ground, regular cleaning and maintenance is critical between uses. Both type of signage can be unstable in high winds, so tethering must be checked regularly.

- **Tethered Balloons.** Tethered balloons are generally up to 30 feet in length and are oval shaped. They can feature either permanent or temporary signage on their sides which is highly visible. They can be unstable in anything higher than a light breeze, and require something fairly substantial as an anchor. The anchor should be in a secure position, otherwise tether ropes can be interfered with.

- **Hot Air Balloons.** One of the largest signage mediums available is the hot air balloon. They also have their problems. Commonly they are in the air at dawn and dusk, and are dependent on prevailing weather conditions. Obviously, for this type of signage to be effective, clear, reasonably still weather is required.

- **Parachutes/Skydivers.** Skydivers can gain high exposure at large audience events. This is an exciting medium, which is sure to gain the attention of people waiting for the main event to commence, or during half time. Before booking parachute displays, you will have to check with venue management to ensure that they allow skydivers to land. Some venues do not allow Skydivers for safety reasons. (Often a past experience that has been less than optimal!)

- **Parachute Flags.** These are the latest addition to skydiving displays. Due to the requirement for a heavy weight in order for the flag to open and be displayed correctly, skill is definitely required to jump with one of these flags. There are skydiver's in all main centres who are now quite experienced at jumping with flags. Check with a reputable skydiving centre.

- **Street Banners.** Many local authorities and events have equipment on power and light poles to enable street banners to be secured. These are made of heavy duty vinyl which can stand up to reasonably high winds, however, they need to be kept taut to be effective. Permits are generally required to erect this type of signage – check with the relevant local authority.

  Another type of street banner or flag is the type that hangs parallel to a lamp-post, and is made of a polyester type fabric. They commonly hang from each, or every second lamp-post, in a main street, and are a colourful and festive way to get your message across.

- **Vinyl.** The trusty old vinyl banner strung up between two trees certainly still has its place, however the banners are rarely taut and as they stretch they look untidy. If you are using banners that will be seen on Television a satisfactory result is achieved by fitting the signage to a frame.

- **Night Signage.** Night signage includes a variety of options including, lasers, fireworks, projectors search lights and light looms. Night signage requires a large captive audience to justify the expenditure required.

- **Lasers.** The effect of Lasers has improved over the years. There are some very experienced operators around, and this can be a very effective signage medium. It is definitely a job for the professionals!

- **Projectors.** Projectors, both still and moving, are available and reasonably effective for projection on the side of buildings etc. There are projectors that can project video images in excess of 20 metres wide – however, once again, a job for the professionals.

- **Fireworks.** Pyrotechnics still attract old and young alike and they can be fashioned to provide logos and word marks. There are however restrictions that vary from state to state depending on the season. Obviously a check with local authorities is in order before staging a fireworks display.

- **Light Looms.** Light looms as well as being fitted to air ships have also been successfully fitted to both fixed wing aircraft and helicopters. The signage consists of thousands of bulbs on a loom that is either fitted to the bottom of the wings on a fixed wing aircraft or to the skids of a helicopter. They effectively scroll messages that are easily visible.

- **Apparel Signage.** Signage on human competitors has become prolific in recent years. It is a great way of getting your logo covered and creating awareness, however, the media when interviewing or taking non-action photos try their best to eliminate signage.

  The best way to get around the media's aversion to giving free publicity to sponsors is to place your apparel signage appropriately. A round necked t-shirt with the logo and word mark printed on the collar or a cap are very effective. The media will crop photos to just below the neck, however usually not beyond that.

Often interviewers will request a personality to remove a cap with a sponsor's logo or message on it. Your personalities should be advised to decline the request.

- **Shirts, Singlets, etc.** Upper torso wear has the advantage that is rarely removed and can present a number of areas for signage, The best sort of garment is the crew neck T- shirt because it is almost impossible to crop out the collar.

- **Mobile Signs:** Anything that moves can be pressed into service as a mobile sign. This includes buses, taxis, delivery fleets, semi trailers, trailers and so on. There are purpose built signs available for rent if you don't have the luxury of a fleet of vehicles.

- **Building Wraps:** During the Sydney Olympics, one of the larger international sponsors actually "wrapped" a high profile building with an image depicting a well known/popular athlete using the sponsors brand. This was a variation on the outdoor billboard, and was highly effective – being visible to all pedestrians and motorists who passed the site. It also received a great deal of media coverage.

Recommended apparel signage for media coverage

- **Collar**. Logo and word mark for close up interviews television or press.

- **Back**. Large logo for action shots from a distance. Close ups of someone's back are rarely taken, but they will appear as incidental signage in an action shot.

- **Front**. Large logo for distance action shots.

- **Sleeves**. Offer the option of further signage but don't over do it.

- **Colour.** Will no doubt be dictated by the corporate and event colours, however, white as background washes out other logos and 'flares' on television. Wherever possible, have a dark background with light or white logos. Try and maximise the contrast, bearing in mind newspapers are mainly printed in black and white.

If you want the shirt to be worn and the association to grow it is appropriate to provide a high quality second shirt for the non-media environment that people would be proud to wear. This shirt should be a polo style shirt with a single logo on the left breast no bigger than 4cm X 4cm. This could not be seen as overkill, or overly commercial. If your apparel is to be worn during cold conditions it may be worth producing a quality windcheater or polar fleece for media use featuring, once again, logos on the collar.

- **Specialist Sports.** Placing signage on specialist sportsmen such as speed skaters and cyclists may require different positioning. The best way to decide where to position the signage and how big to make it is to view videotapes of the sport in progress, noting which parts of the body are featured predominantly.

- **Event Signage.** Event signage is featured on almost every surface imaginable - placement, it seems, is only limited by your imagination and creativity. The strategic use of signage will increase with technology, and in the not too distant future the keepers of ground signage will probably be offering signs that will move with the play.

- **Scoreboards.** The advent of outdoor electronic scoreboards has allowed replays to be played to the crowd and commercials to be played to those attending these events.

- **Tri-signs.** The introduction of motorised tri signs has tripled the amount of signage space at grounds but reduces exposure by two thirds. The theory is that because the signage is moving, it constantly attracts attention, and is therefore more effective than static signage. The jury is still out on this one!

- **Balloons.** Helium filled rubber balloons are a most effective means of signing a street parade or a motorcade to ensure coverage of your logo in the media. The first major use of balloons to gain television coverage was in the 1992 Olympic Welcome Home Parades. Every car carried two or three athletes. Each was signed with a sun visor style sticker on the windscreen and three or four heavily logoed balloons tied to the rear bumper bar. The balloons were positioned at head height and the result was that every media story visually described the sponsor. Without this signage the sponsor would have barely received mention.

There are balloon specialists in every major city who will inflate and attach the balloons at the appropriate time.

- **Stickers.** Application of temporary vinyl stickers can be a very cheap and effective way of signing a street parade, building, etc. The application of these stickers can be problematic depending on temperature, so make sure you get specific application instructions from the manufacturer.

- **Turf Signage.** This is the groundsman's nightmare! The grass is physically painted with the appropriate logo and then after the game it is mowed off. Typically these signs gain good press coverage in both print and television. Interestingly I have yet to see turf signage on the fairways of major golf tournaments - as a sponsor I would demand it as I believe you would get as much coverage from a turf sign as you would from the current Tee and Green signage.

- **Ice signs.** You can even have very effective signage on ice. A hole is cut into the surface of the ice, the sign is then painted at the lower level of the ice rink by a sign writer, and the hole is then filled up with water and re-frozen, thereby creating a sign which is very effective for an extended period.

- **Mobile Signs.** Anything that moves can be pressed into service as a mobile sign. This can include buses, trucks, taxis, the delivery fleet and so on. The attractive aspect of this signage is that if you are the owner of the medium it is free. Purpose built trailer and truck back signs are available for rent if you don't have the free use of a vehicle fleet.

- **Non Signage.** Non signage is signage masquerading as other items. (See chapter 30- 'Ambush Defence Planning and Rear Guard Actions'.) These items could include event clocks, drink machines, food/beverage coolers, fast food trailers, food and beverage packaging etc, etc.

- **Tents.** The use of marquees and tents at events offer great signage opportunities. Some companies keep well signed tents and marquees that they will either loan or hire out to community groups for use at events.

- **Roof Top Signage.** Any televised event that includes a component of coverage shot from a helicopter, such as motor racing, offers the opportunity for effective roof top signage.

- **Bunting.** An old, relatively cost effective, and noisy favourite of car yards, bunting offers signage opportunities and is regularly pressed into service as a makeshift barrier. A word of warning here - dirty, damaged or tatty bunting is an absolute eye sore, so it should be checked after every event, and discarded if it is not in perfect condition.

- **Media Signage.** The art of positioning signage for the media is one of preparation and trying various camera angles and company logo sizes with a person sitting in the hot seat to see what works best. The only signage opportunities in a media room are the back drop, apparel signage and possibly a lectern if one is utilised.

- **The Backdrop.** The media backdrop can provide significant signage opportunities if the logos are the right size and positioned correctly. There are two options - one is to have one large sign. The second and most desirable option is to have your media backdrop covered in numerous small logos.

- The inherent problem with backdrops is that people sit or stand in front of them, therefore if you have large logos it is likely that the person or people talking to the media will either totally or partially obscure your logo. Therefore, as mentioned, the best option is to have a flat surface covered with multiple logos approximately 16cm long. Obviously some of the logos will be totally or partially obscured, but because of sheer numbers you can be guaranteed that some will be featured in full.

- **Lectern Banners.** These work quite well in long or wide shots but are not of much value in the close up where the only part of the lectern that will be seen, if any, is the top edge. If using a lectern banner or media backdrop make sure it has been pressed prior to use.

- **Television Signage.** Placement of signage for television requires some planning. Signs that receive good exposure cost more, and the temptation might be to choose cheaper signage in the hope that it too will receive coverage. You should be aware, however, that there is some signage in every stadium that is unlikely to ever receive television coverage.

The best method of planning signage placement is to watch some previous coverage of the venue, taking particular note of which signage receives the best coverage.

- **Clean Signage.** Once signage is placed, it is often left in place for long periods of time without any maintenance. It may become dirty, faded, damaged or untidy. The contract should detail whose responsibility it is to maintain signage.

- **Use Of Logos In Signage.** Company and brand logos are extremely valuable. The majority of companies have specific guidelines for the standard use of their brands and logos and to protect both parties, they should not be used without the relevant permission. These guidelines can include the use of correct fonts (shape and size of words) and logo shape and size. Many companies have corporate identity guidelines which specify the rules for use of logos and brands, the amount of white space allowed around their logo and so on.

- **Company Logo Sizing.** When it comes to acknowledging differing levels of sponsors it is important to make the size and position of logo use relevant to the significance of the sponsor. If you are in this situation, it is a good idea to clarify these issues in the contract, and then there will be no misunderstandings or disappointments.

- **Copy Approval.** All advertising and/or press release material, or any item the public will see with a sponsors logo must be approved by the sponsor. Make sure you allow enough time for the appropriate manager to approve and make any necessary amendments. The sponsor is the owner of their company logo and it should not ever be used without their approval. (Make sure you get the sponsor to sign an approval form to avoid disputes.) The same rules should apply to use of your organisation, event or team name - you also have the right to approve all advertising and promotional items that use your logos.

Summary

- Signage and the use of company logos is one of the most important vehicles for generating awareness of the sponsor's relationship with your organisation, and therefore must be well executed, to the satisfaction of both parties.

- Signage mediums are only limited by your creativity and funds - practically any surface can be used to place signage on.

- Make sure the signage is well maintained at all times - don't just place it and then forget about it.

- Ensure that details of which party is responsible for manufacture, erection, maintenance and transport of signage is noted in the contract.

Chapter 27

Promotional Extensions and Innovation

Sponsorships have been used very effectively as incentives to the trade (retailers or wholesalers) to purchase more product, provide better shelf space, and generate customer loyalty. Successful sponsorships generally involve the use of a variety of marketing tools, which include advertising, direct marketing, publicity, events and promotions.

This chapter looks at the menu of promotional tools that have been effectively used by sponsors to leverage sponsorships. They include activities such as the strategic use of hospitality, cross promotions, creating add on events and sales promotions.

Competitions

Competitions often prove to be a cost-effective means for sponsors to promote product and brand awareness through sponsorship. The seeker can assist the sponsor, for very little extra money, by offering them premium items such as, for example, ten season tickets to all football fixtures, which they in turn can use as competition prizes or incentives.

Cross Promotions

A cross promotion is where two or more sponsors group together and create a promotion themed around the sponsored organisation or directed to its members which mutually benefits all parties involved.

The Olympic Committee is particularly good at fostering cross promotions through the Olympic Family, which is a loose term for its sponsors collectively. Through functions and meetings the Olympic Committee introduces sponsors, ensuring they know each other and each other's objectives for being sponsors of the Olympic movement.

This creates good personal relationships between the sponsor's representatives and a sense of bonding. As a result numerous Olympic cross promotions are undertaken which benefit the sponsors involved as well as the Olympic movement. The cross promotions generally cost the seeker little or nothing, other than the provision of personalities and ideas.

The secret to a successful cross promotion is to match the resources that one sponsor can offer another so that they both further their business objectives for very little outlay. Cross promotions can be so successful that occasionally they will return more benefits than the core sponsorship, which guarantees very happy sponsors.

How to Create Cross Promotions

Think creatively! Work with co-sponsors who have the same or similar markets and then mix and match their products. Include a redemption offer or a competition and you are 'off and running'! Cross promotions generally cost the sponsored organisation no cash, just some organisation, and perhaps the use of personalities (for endorsement) or ticketing. Sponsors generally put up the cash, product and advertising to get the promotion working.

Client Entertainment

It is often the case that the best tickets or packages to an event are only available to sponsors. This is so with the Olympic Games, the Ballet, Opera and various sports. If you have the ability to offer these types of packages as benefits, they can be used by a sponsor as an incentive to their customers to increase sales space and/or incremental movement of product.

An extremely well executed entertainment incentive scheme was a promotion where a tool manufacturing firm offered retailers a free trip to the Olympic Games if they met vastly increased sales targets. The manufacturing company's turnover increased in excess of 35% over the period of the promotion, which exceeded their wildest expectations. This shows the value of offering this type of package, particularly to an event that is difficult and expensive for the average person to access.

Character Creations

It may be appropriate to create a character to help promote the sponsorship and the sponsor's brand. Undoubtedly Ronald MacDonald has been invaluable for MacDonald's, as children are able to relate to the character and feel comfortable with him.

Awards

The use of awards provided and presented by the sponsor is a great way of generating positive awareness within an organisation. Sponsoring an award such as 'most improved' can also help the sponsor by generating goodwill within your membership. The award can be seen as something that the sponsor is giving back to members and this can help to remove the cynicism that is sometimes associated with commercial sponsorship.

Creating Events - The Need

The purchase of a sponsorship property is basically the purchase of potential and the results of a sponsorship program are limited only by imagination, creativity and budget. The creation of events, stunts, awards and happenings around a sponsorship makes sense. However it is important that the event has synergy with both the sponsorship and the sponsor, otherwise it will be irrelevant and unlikely to achieve objectives. A caution here - make sure the event doesn't take over to the detriment of the sponsorship and logo.

Whilst managing an Olympic sponsorship for a major corporation we were looking for ways to extend the sponsorship, entertain clients and increase public awareness and media coverage of our involvement.

Subsequently, the Olympic 'Welcome Home Program' was created. That program delivered street parades to acknowledge the achievements of our Olympic team in every city of Australia. Each parade was successful, however, the largest attracted national television coverage, 230 000 on-street spectators and a number of front page articles in newspapers. The program also generated enormous news coverage in every city, resulting in the sponsor achieving a 68% unaided awareness of its sponsorship nationally.

Most importantly, the 'Welcome Home' program also delivered black tie dinners where our executives had the opportunity to offer high level corporate entertaining, and where medal winning athletes were at each table to entertain the company's most important clients in each major city around the country.

Functions

Functions are an excellent way of providing client and supplier entertainment while remaining relevant and tying into the sponsorship. A function could be designed as a fundraiser for the sponsored organisation, thereby creating goodwill towards the sponsor, and providing (usually much needed) funds to the organisation they are sponsoring. To keep the function relevant and tied to the sponsorship, there should be a specific purpose for holding it, and some are:

- Welcome home to a victorious team
- Testimonial year for a hero
- Award nights
- Fundraisers
- Farewell prior to an international tour
- Victory dinner
- Last night celebration

Merchandising

Licensed merchandise (logoed t-shirts, caps, etc.) can be an excellent communications tool, with the added advantage of stretching the life of the sponsorship, because the merchandise may be used long after the sponsorship relationship has ceased. Merchandise also can help a sponsor make her sponsorship self- liquidating.

There are a number of legal matters to consider prior to entering any merchandise program. Be aware of the licence fee as, rightly, it may be payable on every item manufactured or every item sold. The licence fee could either be a single fee or a royalty, or a percentage of the retail price of each item sold or manufactured. The fee could be as high as 30% of retail cost. Royalties can become a troublesome issue, however, due to the strict accounting procedures that have to take place.

If you are considering entering into an agreement with merchandisers, we would advise you to retain the services of a Solicitor to clearly define your rights and the exclusivity of those rights. The control of trademarks and licences must be held either by the sponsor or the seeker. If that control is assigned to a third party, perhaps a merchandiser, all control is lost.

Redemption Offers

This is where the wholesaler offers consumers free tickets, pit passes, free product, and so when they provide proof of purchase of a certain product. These offers quite often include the chance to gain special privileges such as entry into sold out events or into areas not normally accessible, such as the pits at a car race, or rehearsals for the ballet etc. They may also offer the chance to meet high profile personalities at an after event function or the like.

Sales Promotions

Sales promotions are short term incentives which are provided to encourage the consumer to buy a product and are also used to make that product stand out from other products in the category. The strategic use of sales promotions is a common extension in major sponsorship programs. Sales promotions can include the use of such incentives as: competitions, redemption offers, sample refunds, sweepstakes, bonus offers, stamps, and 'scratch it' promotions.

As stated above, Sales Promotions are a common extension in major sponsorship programs, however, it is important to make sure sales promotions interest and attract the right audience. It is also important not to make the promotion difficult to enter or it may result in wastage, in terms of both human resources and budget, and not move stock or meet objectives. The use of toll charged numbers is now common in the use of sales promotions because consumers are far more likely to pick up the phone than to fill in a coupon and post it.

Selling-on

Some manufacturers 'sell on', or give sponsorship benefits they have purchased to their retailers, and in doing so provide the retailer with incentives to increase their customer base. Common benefits 'sold on' include event ticketing, in store celebrity appearances and signage. This activity should not be confused with sponsors running consumer promotions. In the case of selling on, the benefits are handed to the retailer who then acts as a de-facto sponsor. Other sponsors on-sell sponsorship benefits in order to lower the cost of the sponsorship purchase. This can, however, also result in a dilution of benefits to be original purchaser.

Stunts

One particularly successful 'stunt' was for a Dairy Foods Company. They sponsored a major women's sport long term, and held a competition offering a monetary prize for the athlete who gained the most media coverage. One young lady filled her bath with milk, called the local media, bathed in milk, and gained great coverage for both herself, her club and the sponsor – she didn't forget to leave a milk carton on the edge of the bath – logo facing!

Telethons

Telethons and special programs offer the opportunity to gain extensive media coverage for both the sponsor and the seeker. The danger is that it can be extremely boring television. Telethons offer the opportunity to involve large numbers of the sponsor's staff, which gives a boost to morale and creates interest, and often-strong support, for the sponsorship within the company.

Traffic Growth Attractions

Traffic growth attractions can include; having celebrities appear in-store or in shopping centres; displaying a racing vehicle, or, as in Kraft's Indy Car sponsorship, positioning a life size car simulator outside a store. The only way consumers get to ride in the simulator is to purchase a specified amount of product and present their receipt to the simulator operator.

These traffic growth attractions are offered on the basis of the retailer's past performance in moving the product, as a reward, or are attached to an order of a specified value.

Cause Related Marketing

Cause related sponsorships involve the sponsorship of an organisation or cause that will generate emotion, or tug at consumer's heart-strings. This type of sponsorship is designed to generate sales by linking a consumer purchase to funding or assisting the cause. In some cases the money spent on promoting the sponsorship will far exceed the donated amount.

Experiential Marketing

Experiential marketing is a relatively new term which describes the situation whereby marketers have the opportunity to communicate their message whilst consumers (target audiences) are undertaking an experience of their own choosing. There is a theory that this is a more personal, relevant and effective way of getting the marketing message across.

Summary

- Promotional extensions can be a vital part of the success of a sponsorship program. They are designed to drive awareness of the sponsor and the sponsorship and increase sales through sales promotions.

- Cross promotions are programs undertaken by two or more sponsors of one organisation and are used to further the commercial interests of all parties involved.

Chapter 28

Media Management

Associating a Sponsor's Name with an Event

Media coverage in some cases is one of the most valuable benefits being offered in a sponsorship package, however **media coverage without acknowledgment of the naming rights sponsor is of no value to that sponsor whatsoever!**

Many sponsored organisations proudly send along a copy of all media coverage they have received to their sponsor. As the sponsor goes through the coverage, they may realise that they in fact received very little, or no, coverage. Even though positive media coverage is very rarely the only sponsorship objective, it will always be in the objectives somewhere, and realising that only the sponsored organisation gained coverage can prove to be a negative experience for the sponsor.

We repeat – no coverage of your sponsor = no benefit to your sponsor. In such a case, it would be better not to highlight the lack of coverage.

The media's reluctance (sometimes aversion) to naming sponsors in its coverage of an event is a recurring problem for sponsors and promoters alike. The only time you are almost guaranteed of naming rights coverage is if there is a negative angle.

The media are particularly reticent to acknowledge prefix naming rights – even to events with a long tradition. Such events are commonly referred to in the media minus the sponsor's naming rights, which the sponsor has generally paid a premium for. It is really up to the event organiser to liaise with the media over such omissions.

Obviously the media love to report news of big events. It helps to fill their newspaper or news bulletin and it generates sales and ratings.

As the media continue reporting these events, editors need to acknowledge that big events only happen with the support of sponsors and to ensure these sponsors continue supporting events in our country, they also have to start acknowledging them in their publications and programs.

If naming rights to an event are sold to a sponsor, it is up to the owner of the event and/or the promoter to aggressively enforce the sponsor's rights in the media. This requires the use of every tool and sphere of influence available.

Media Reluctant to Name Sponsors

The media will rarely acknowledge sponsors willingly unless they themselves happen to be the sponsor. This is more evident in the arts than sport. The media have this attitude for a number of reasons. Some sub-editors believe that if you want to get awareness in their publication, you should buy advertising. Others believe sponsorship is bastardising the sport or the event. Some papers will acknowledge the principal sponsor in the article, but once only (and often that depends on whether the sponsor is a major advertiser in their particular medium).

The main way of getting a sponsor named is by being both patient and creative. Remember to explain to journalists about the sponsor's involvement in the project and the importance of their cash, and keep on reinforcing it.

Television Telecasts

At one time television stations used to pay for the cost of coverage and sometimes paid the promoter for the rights to telecast an event. The highly competitive nature of the television industry has changed this. Television stations now rarely telecast events without some sort of financial inducement. Outside broadcasts are expensive and if you want your event covered, unless it is extremely high profile, someone will have to pay.

The cost of television coverage varies enormously, depending on the scale of the production and the interest in the sport. It is possible to get a once off event covered and telecast as highlights, perhaps in a sports show, for a relatively modest fee (say, three to four thousand dollars).

If sponsor signage is strategically placed, and there are decals on uniforms for example, it may well be worth the sponsor exploring this avenue, and budgeting to get the coverage.

Television Program Sponsorship

Sponsorship of television programs is basically an advertising extension and television sponsors pay television stations a premium to sponsor a particular program – usually a high profile event. Companies that take out sponsorship of a televised event are often mistaken for event sponsors whether they are or not. Both benefits and costs relating to a television sponsorship package are negotiable but usually include:

- Opening and closing billboards.
- Guaranteed placement in a particular time zone.
- Exclusivity in product category within the program, (stops your event being ambushed).
- Priority placement of advertisements, (usually at the start of breaks or the end).
- Pull throughs.
- In show promotions (such as Cadbury Schweppes Classic Catches in the Cricket Telecast).
- Acknowledgment on stations promotions (commercials promoting the program).

Program sponsorships offer a number of additional benefits and are limited in supply. Naturally they attract a premium on top of the normal advertising cost, which can be anything up to 150%.

Media and Naming / Title Rights

Naming rights are acknowledged more often than non-naming rights sponsors. The Fosters Melbourne Cup, for example, is often, but not by any means always, correctly reported.

Naming rights are rarely reported or acknowledged in the coverage of once off events. The secret to getting coverage is to include the sponsor's name in the event or team name, for example, The Volvo Challenge.

If Volvo is dropped the event fails to be identified by category – 'challenge' is not enough to identify the event as it could relate to any number of events!

Media and Sponsor Signage

Sponsor signage is avoided by the media wherever possible but, here again, there are a number of ways of beating the system and they really come down to an understanding of how an event is covered in relation to camera shots and angles. Photographic editors will chop off a person's body up to the neck to ensure logos are not printed. Make sure your personalities have signage around their collar, or on their heads - e.g, a cap - obviously, if a person is being interviewed, it is very hard for the media to omit their head and shoulders!

Free Media

Regional and suburban newspapers are run on shoestring budgets and often limited journalism staff. They are therefore very receptive to receiving news stories that are relevant to the local area, which can be localised with a photo of a local personality and a local slant to the story. The best way to get these stories published is to provide the newspaper with a ready to print story and photo. Nine times out of ten they will run the story as presented, provided it is well written and fitting. By providing the story you have assisted them in filling their newspaper, and left a journalist free to report on something else. If you have an on going competition (say basketball at your local hall) it is worth supplying copy every week - they might give you a column and credit you as a correspondent. By writing the story and staging the photo it is possible to relay your messages and gain sponsor acknowledgment.

Relationships with the Media

Striking up relationships with members of the media can be invaluable. If you get to know the journalists and management, it makes it far easier to get your message across and get a favourable hearing.

The secret to a good relationship with the media is to be useful to them - become an important source of information - provide them with good leads and stories. Look for interesting photo ideas that will be visually exciting. Journalists need to be in touch with what is happening - keep them informed of any interesting stories or events coming up, and be available to provide further information if it is required.

It must be kept in mind that it doesn't matter how the story is written and presented - the Sub-editor can quite easily either edit the story and remove all mention of the sponsor or drop it completely. With this in mind, make sure you if you foster a relationship it is with the decision makers. Some ways of keeping the media informed and onside are:

- Host media parties and receptions.
- Invite their partner to any after hours events, as they rarely get invited.
- Develop long term relationships with members of the media.
- Make sure media launches etc. happen at an appropriate time for the media.

Some colleagues recommend wining and dining journalists but caution needs to be exercised here. If you know them well that is fine - if you are just maintaining the relationship, but don't use the occasion as a platform for demanding stories to be written. It usually doesn't work and in the long run it may ruin a good relationship. No one likes to be used - the relationship you develop with journalists should be as genuine as other important business relationships.

Manners

Journalists are humans (its true … even though some may debate this!). As people they have feelings. Remember, they are always being asked to cover events and write stories that suit organisations and individuals. So if a journalist comes out to cover your story or publishes a story that shows your organisation or sponsor in a favourable light, pick up the phone and say thank you. People are often quick to criticise the media but, it seems, slow to thank them. Your thanks will be remembered just as, we suspect, will your lack of thanks.

Co-sponsorships with the Media

If you enter into a media sponsorship agreement, make sure your desired outcome is agreed to - in writing. This is just like any other sponsorship agreement with the payment in publicity, so make sure you get paid with enough publicity.

Media who sponsor events generally only acknowledge themselves as sponsors. If the sponsored organisation enters into a media sponsorship agreement make sure it is agreed in writing that sponsors will be acknowledged. If you get involved with a media sponsor be aware you may be shutting out all other media outlets so weigh up the pros and cons carefully.

Accreditation

If you are in the enviable position of running a newsworthy event that occurs in a private venue, make sure that media have to be accredited to cover the event. One of the clauses they should agree to is to report the event by its correct name, even if that does include a sponsor's name.

Think Like a 'Journo'

Journalists have to write or cover stories that will interest their consumers, so use every tool available. Make sure you fit in with their deadlines, give them exclusivity in return for a good article or photo. In getting coverage it is important to know what will interest the public and therefore the journalists. TV coverage requires interesting footage, and if you are only offering a 'talking head' you will receive little or no coverage. In summary, the best way to make sure you receive media coverage is to make covering the story easy. To do this we offer the following checklist:

Media Checklist

❑ Create unique and different photo opportunities or stories.
❑ Create a stunt.
❑ Always have a spokesperson available.

- ❏ Personalities will attract media and even good news stories.
- ❏ Provide event information, athlete profiles, statistics (if relevant).
- ❏ Provide an event logo that contains the sponsor's logo.
- ❏ Be aware of deadlines, and know the hours the media work.
- ❏ Media are always busy - fit in with them.
- ❏ Follow up before and after the event.
- ❏ Provide prepared footage and prepacked television and radio stories and programs.
- ❏ Provide interesting photos with recognisable personalities or local identities.
- ❏ Provide spokes-people for radio and TV grabs and quotes.
- ❏ Write ready to air scripts for radio and ready to print articles.
- ❏ If you are holding a large event that will attract substantial media, provide a media centre with facilities to enable journalists to write and file their stories on site. These facilities could include; phones, desks, faxes, copier, free refreshments.
- ❏ Be aware of deadlines.
- ❏ Know the tone of various publications - know which stories fit which publications.
- ❏ Create heroes and characters to be used as media personalities.
- ❏ When writing a media release keep it relevant and to the point.
- ❏ Provide different angles/quotes/personalities to different journalists.

Pre-packaged Stories

If you have a story you want to get out, a successful tried and proven method is to prepare a ready to print article along with an interesting photo. It is surprising how many publications will print the story. You can do the same for radio and television, however, the production costs are more expensive, so there is more risk involved.

A sponsorship we managed stated as one of their objectives that they required as much media/PR coverage as possible.

This was achieved by the sponsored organisation sending out pre-packaged stories containing relevant information and photographs with a local flavour. We achieved 138 stories, most of which were printed verbatim and 6 stories on television - all of which used the pre-prepared television tape.

Because the information sent to the media was controlled, all stories conveyed the key message that the sponsor was a caring member of the community and the vast majority included wonderful photos featuring the sponsors logo. The pre-packaged stories also resulted in some excellent editorial.

Create a Media Guide for Big Events

When involved with large events or sporting seasons, one of the best tools for assisting a journalist to do their job is to provide a media guide containing all relevant background information and a contact name and number that they can use during the event/season. This can be prepared by either the sponsor, or the sponsored organisation.

A media guide normally contains the following information:

- Details of the competition or event, including interesting statistics and relevant history.
- It contains the draw detailing times of events, venues and who is competing.
- Profiles, including photos of competitors or artists.
- Most importantly, provide contact phone and fax numbers and names of relevant officials who can be contacted throughout the event or season.
- Bromides of event logos and sponsors logos when applicable.

Press Kit

A press kit is a handy item to have when dealing with the media. It can contain useful generic information, statistics, photos, event, team or organisation logos, stock video footage and anything else that would assist journalists to cover your event or activity.

Know Media Tastes

In attracting media coverage it is important to know the tastes of the various publications and media outlets, in other words which stories will suit which publication.   Also be aware which is the appropriate section of the publication for your story, and ensure you are dealing with someone who can use the story. It is pointless dealing with the general news desk if you have a photo opportunity for the social pages.

If you know that there is a Journalist with a personal interest in your event or organisation, invite them and their family along.   Journalists sometimes work very unsociable hours and the opportunity to bring along their partner or family for some recreation may well appeal to them.

Create Heroes, Personalities or Characters

In the long-term interests of gaining abundant media coverage, create heroes and characters who can be used as media personalities, and who your fans can relate to and enjoy. By characters we mean a Ronald McDonald type figure, and by heroes we mean someone like Michael Jordan. The flow on effects will include the use of your personalities in game shows, stories in magazines, press and so on.

There can, however, be a danger that you create a hero who is so strong that they become more important to the media and the public than your sponsors or your event. However if this happens you can get your hero to endorse your event and sponsors. It is a good idea to have a publicist 'mind' your personality and handle any necessary liaison with the media.

Another caution - beware of personalties who are likely to do the wrong thing. If you have amongst your stars people who are big drinkers or are likely to misbehave, think very carefully before selecting them for the role, and if you do select them, make your expectations in relation to the standard of behaviour expected in public very clear.

The Internet / Web

We do not intend to go into this in great detail. Like all other areas of sponsorship, the results achieved are largely a result of the amount of dollars and creativity expended, but following are some ideas:

Create a home page and feed information about your event and sponsor on to the net. Every day more people are accessing the net, which will provide increasing coverage for you and your sponsor.

The web offers the option to run consumer competitions linked to sponsorship activity. It can also provide product sales that are tailored to the organisation's target audience, and allows direct links to sponsor's websites. It also allows the collection of data on fans, which can then be used for direct mail activity (check privacy provisions).

The internet also allows discreet sites for Journalists so that they can gain information and relevant contacts for the production of media stories.

Another benefit of the internet is that a sponsored organisation can create links and direct web traffic to their sponsor(s) site. The sponsor can measure the increase in traffic via a very simple counting mechanism. This can add value in terms of the sponsor having the opportunity to communicate product attributes to a larger audience.

Media Consultants

There are many PR and Media consultants who can assist with the preparation of media items if you don't have the resources or capabilities to do the job. They will charge on an hourly basis to prepare the items, depending on the size of their organisation, and their reputation, and this is a service that we recommend for those of you with few skills in the area.

Media Training

If any representatives of your organisation are likely to be interviewed by the media it is well worthwhile organising media training for those people.

The cost could be included as a budget item in the sponsor's business plan as it is to their advantage to have an articulate speaker(s) trained to include their name in any coverage received. There are a number of organisations that provide media training which includes practical sessions on how to introduce the sponsor's name and not have it edited out, dealing with hostile and studio interviews, etc. The training is conducted with a video in use, which is subsequently used for constructive appraisal.

Media Launch

The launch of the sponsorship will almost certainly be the first acknowledgment of the sponsorship. Launches take many shapes, ranging from a private ceremony to hand over the cheque right through to large media events. The launch of a major sponsorship has the potential to be extremely newsworthy and may be picked up by many media outlets. Local launches should be designed to attract local media, at a time to suit them. There is always the possibility that an election will be announced, or a war will commence somewhere on the planet, and therefore no media may show up, even though they have indicated previously that they will be there. If this happens, don't be too disheartened - privately commissioned photos and a press releases sent to local papers will often result in a good story being published. See Media section for detail on running media events.

Contacting the Media

A Journalist's function is to provide the public with information that they want and that interests them. If you can help a journalist to that, you are far more likely to get your organisation or event covered by them.

Sending an advisory one page media release three months out, giving prior notice of your event and containing some basic (but interesting) information will allow a journalist to, a) enter your event into his diary before it is too full, and, b) put some thought into the sort of angle he could use to make this event really interesting to the viewing or reading public.

You should then send more formal invitations to the media six weeks prior to the event. In the days prior to the event ring all media and encourage attendance.

On the morning of the event it is worth ringing around the news desks to see if news crews and journalists have been rostered to attend the event. As editorial meetings are in progress prior to 11.00am it is far less likely that you will gain good media attendance if your event is held before that time. It is important to arrange the timing of a news conference at a time and venue that will suit journalists. This will generally be close to the city very late in the morning or early afternoon.

To get your team's results into the relevant newspapers, phone either then central agency or phone the publications involved and find out how, when (what time, day of the week) you should provide the results. If you are going to be providing the results on a regular basis, let them know so they can plan to include them.

Note: Journalists receive numerous requests for coverage, so don't get them offside or harass them - there will always be another story for them, but there will not always be another Journo for you!

Writing a Media Release

The art of writing a media release is to keep the information to the point. Use short grabs and positive colourful words. It is crucial that your release contains unique information or a local angle. If it doesn't, it is unlikely to receive any coverage.

It is important that the basic information that a reader would expect is contained in the press release:

- Who is involved?
- What is happening?
- Where is it happening?
- Why is it happening?
- When will it be?
- Contact details, including business and after hours contacts.

Photos

The inclusion of relevant photos with your media releases assists in gaining the interest of the journalist and the reader, and can be helpful in gaining coverage.

These photos should be sent in a digital format, which is easily downloaded by the recipient.

Media Interviews

Tips and rules of media interviews

- Most TV stories use a 20 second clip, so tell your story in 20 secs or less.
- Keep all comments brief, in headline form and to the point to stop reporters covering messages you don't want covered.
- If you have a point you want to get across use it a couple of times whether it answers a specific question or not. Have you ever noticed how politicians get their point across - sometimes giving an answer that has no relevance to the question whatsoever.
- *Never* speak off the record. An interview is never over until the journalist has left. Quite rightly, journalists are never off duty in an interview situation, and nothing can be guaranteed to be off the record remember, their job is to gain as much information as possible - that is their job!
- Preparation is vital. Try to predict what questions you may be asked and have the answers ready and rehearsed.
- Have a theme and repeat the theme regularly. Know your messages.
- Always be polite and friendly. Human nature says they will be less likely to criticise or lampoon you if you have been pleasant and relaxed to deal with.
- Never say "no comment". Answer the question with an answer. For example, "that is confidential information", or "that is subject to legal action so I'm afraid I can't answer your question".
- Offer to review the story for accuracy if it is a technical subject.
- Reverse negatives with positives. Never agree with comments on the negatives, or increase speculation by discussing them.

- Offer good photo opportunities for press and good sounds for radio.
- Be brief. Keep your statement short and to the point in simple terms.
- Reinforce your message with apparel where appropriate. Send to key media in advance of the event, and make it attractive - that way it will get worn.
- To get message across relate the message first.
- Package the message so it contains information of public importance. If you can do that your message has a far greater chance of gaining coverage.
- Maintain eye contact during the interview.
- Look happy.
- Watch the body language.
- Conduct the interview in front of an appropriate media backdrop.
- Look for visual events or create stunts.
- Use the interviewer's first name. All viewers are on first name basis with their journalists.
- Provide good pictures for television.
- For TV don't wear stripes and do wear your sponsor's gear.

Sponsor Mentions

When a seeker is being interviewed it is imperative not only to name the principal sponsors, but also include in the message why they sponsor, ie, helping the community and the benefits the sponsorship provides. Make the mention of a sponsor relevant so that it is included in the final cut.

Negative Stories

A few rules for dealing with negative stories in the media:

- Be human - everyone makes mistakes!
- Either be honest or say nothing -i.e., "Unfortunately, for the moment, that is confidential, and I am not able to discuss it with you."
- Remember, the interview doesn't finish until the journalist has left. Never be tempted to confide in a journo off the record, unless you are prepared for what you have said to gain coverage.
- If you 'screw up' admit it, and state what steps you are taking to rectify the situation.

- Respond quickly to anything that may cause negative publicity. It is a good idea to have a staff meeting to decide on how you are going to handle the problem, and have *every single person* handle the issue in the same manner.

Summary

- **Treat the media with respect - you need them more than they need you.**
- **Maintain relationships with the media so that you know them.**
- **Become a source of information to them.**
- **Plan all media events to suit media schedules**
- **Be politely persistent, but not pushy.**

Chapter 29

Client Entertainment & Hospitality

Hospitality, when used strategically, provides a very powerful cost effective business tool. For hospitality to work it must:

1. Target the right people

2. Be relevant and desirable

3. Benefits accruing from hospitality must be predictable

4. Accrue measured benefits

Providing hospitality that yields no result is pointless, and amounts to a form of very expensive Corporate Philanthropy.

Managing Corporate Suites

Managing corporate entertainment facilities can be extremely time consuming, and they are inevitably subject to inter-company politics and hierarchy. To ensure that the entire area of corporate entertainment is accountable and comes under the heading of genuine business activity, you should ensure that the following procedures are in place:

- Entertainment guidelines
- A bid process
- Standard menus
- A ticket kit
- Host questionnaire
- Official/acceptable wording for company invitation

Entertainment Guidelines

A short set of guidelines outlining the company's policy on entertainment assists in making sure the corporate suite is used correctly, and that the company image is not tarnished by undesirable behaviour.

The guidelines could include the following:

1. Information on an acceptable staff to client ratio. The standard is between 30% and a maximum of 50% staff for client entertainment purposes.

2. A dress code. For example: neat casual, or business attire.

3. Billing details. (Costs may be billed to the user's departmental account.)

4. Rules pertaining to children. It would be usual that no children would be allowed if the suite is to be used for corporate entertaining. You should also keep in mind that corporate suites are generally licensed, and will therefore be covered under relevant legislation.

5. Rules pertaining to staff entertaining staff. (See point 1.).

CORPORATE HOSPITALITY GUIDELINES - Example

Corporate Hospitality, when used strategically, provides a powerful cost effective business tool. Providing hospitality that yields no result is pointless, amounting to a very expensive form of Corporate Philanthropy. To ensure return on investment is maximised, invitations for Corporate Hospitality should be issued six weeks prior to the event.

Under the directive of the Group Manager, Sponsorship, Events and Hospitality, Corporate Hospitality Guidelines have been put in place in order to successfully gauge these benefits to the Company. It is recommended these guidelines are included with each request for ticketing/hospitality.

Corporate Hospitality must:

- provide opportunities to entertain key, current and potential clients, opinion leaders, people with significant political and bureaucratic leverage, media, and to a lesser extent, suppliers and staff;

- build and maintain the desired profile of the Company;

- support the Company's desired corporate image;

- ensure host to guest ratio does not exceed 25%. Over 25% staff attending will result in excessive FBT in relation to food and beverage costs. **NB:** for FBT purposes, staff partners are classed as staff.

To ensure corporate entertainment provides quantifiable returns to the Company, it will be subject to a formal application and review process that:

- provides accountability;
- identifies return on hospitality investment;
- reduces unnecessary entertainment;
- ensures clients are being entertained for commercial reasons;
- reduces hospitality costs

Process

Allocating entertainment facilities or tickets to various business groups or executives becomes even more difficult than usual when the event is highly popular/desirable. The fairest way in these circumstances is to have a bid process where every eligible host bids for the date(s) on which she wishes to entertain. To ensure that entertainment provides identifiable returns to the sponsor, each potential host should use the same bid form, which will:

- Provide accountability
- Identify return on hospitality investment (by department)
- Reduce unnecessary entertainment
- Ensure clients are being entertained for commercial reasons

- Free up tickets for other uses, ie sales promotions
- Reduce hospitality costs

In companies where a formal bid process has been introduced, there has been a significant reduction (up to 40%) in tickets required for hospitality.

Bid Form

A hospitality bid form provides accountability, and ensures that entertainment opportunities are used appropriately and not misused.

Those unsuccessful in their bids could be offered the dates that have not been bid for. By instituting the bid process at the beginning of your contracted period for use of the facilities, you can be sure the facility will be well used and it gives hosts ample time to invite clients who are going to provide benefit to the company.

Standard Menus

Many caterers offer extensive menus. For ease of administration it is very wise to order a standard menu for all occasions, and if an individual host wants to adjust the menu for their use of the facility, it becomes their responsibility to do so. However, by arranging a standard menu, you will avoid the situation where; a) no food is provided because no order was placed (far more common than you would think!), or b) having the caterers harassing you to find out what the host wants.

Host's Kit

The host requires a number of items prior to using the facility. These include instructions about the box, its location, meal times, tickets etc. Therefore the easiest way to ensure that there are no last moment problems is to put together a kit for each occasion. It should include the following:

1. An information sheet for the host detailing:

    - Date and time of game
    - Map of venue and local surrounds
    - Tickets for her/him and all guests
    - Details on when the facilities open and close
    - Advice regarding the standard menu and contact name and number in case a is required (for example a guest is a vegetarian)
    - The time the meal is served
    - Minimum dress code
    - Any rules relating to behaviour, and who has the authority to police the rules
    - Suite phone number
    - Where and when keys can be picked up
    - Emergency contact for problems

2. Maps for guests, mobile number of host or phone number in suite, ticket(s).

3. Cab charge dockets. You will require these for the occasional inebriated guest – your legal people can advise on the liability issues surrounding plying guests with alcohol, and then sending them on their way with no concern for their safety.

4. Programs or program vouchers.

5. Questionnaire for host to fill in as follows

Corporate facility questionnaire should query:

- Cleanliness of the suite
- Staff attentiveness
- Food quality
- Any repairs required prior to next use of the facility
- Any problems experienced

Promotional material in corporate facility

The Corporate Entertainment Suite offers the opportunity to place promotional material and product samples for clients to sample. Keep it up to date, tidy and relevant.

Gifts

An easy way to follow up with the clients who were entertained is to send a gift after the event. The gift might be a related promotional item or a publication such as a cricket almanac which could printed with the company logo and gift wrapped, accompanied by a note saying that (host) enjoyed their company, and hopes they had a good day, or something similar.

Who to invite

Your corporate entertainment facility should be used, on all occasions for the good of the company. This does not exclude staff using the box, however, such occasions would typically be very limited. Generally such a facility is used for high-level networking and to gain leads that will benefit the company – often these will be sales leads.

Client Entertainment

There is very little point in inviting clients to a facility or function, and then not doing your best to ensure they have a great time. For corporate entertainment to be successful, it must be easy for your guests to attend. Ensure that they have their tickets, their maps, a car park voucher if that is appropriate, and a place to meet.

Another secret to successful entertainment is inviting the right people - the decision-makers. Any after hours entertainment should appeal to the spouse due to the fact that diary organising for after hours is generally an equal rights situation.

Always make your invitations non-transferable. If the person you invite initially can't or doesn't want to attend there is very little point in accepting his subordinate as a stand-in.

If you start the invitation process early, this will give you an opportunity to ask your second choice, who will also be important to your organisation.

Client entertainment can be a most effective way of striking up a relationship with a client who has been difficult to woo. If you invite them to the ballet or the opera, or a high calibre sports event that their spouse is also keen to attend, they will almost certainly accept. A warning: don't use this situation for the hard sell – it is not ever appropriate to hard sell when entertaining, although inevitably business will arise in conversation – resist the temptation. Use the note or telephone follow up to make the next move and organise a meeting during business hours.

Host Survey

Requiring hosts to fill in and return a survey form after every corporate entertaining opportunity is a great way to gain an idea of the value of the hospitality. Doing this may also ensure that abuse of the rules relating to facility use do not happen. (See Appendix 9 for a clean copy of this survey)

Client Entertainment Survey - Hosts

How many people did you entertain during the Football?

With free corporate tickets *twenty*
With food and beverages *twenty*

How would you classify the breakdown of the people you entertained?

50% business contacts, 50% their partners.

☒	Current clients
❑	Potential clients
❑	Suppliers
❑	Trade
❑	Executives of major companies
❑	People of influence to our Company
❑	Staff
❑	Friends
❑	Other

What was the reason for selecting your guests for entertainment

☒   Pursue sales
☒   Thankyou
☐   Strike up relationship
☐   Return Entertainment

Would you have entertained these clients anyway had this entertainment opportunity not been available?

Yes   75%
Possibly   25%
No

How many of these customers have done business with you before?

              50%

Will this entertainment result in sales

☒   Yes
☐   No

If so how many (Please enter unit nos.) 50,000

What benefits or possible outcomes will result from your entertaining at the Tennis?

Where possible approximate $ value

Increasing sales in areas with poor growth $50,000

Keeping current customers happy $20,000

Did you find entertaining guests at this and other sponsored events valuable

☒   Yes
☐   No

Guest Follow Up

A short guest survey will confirm the effectiveness of your entertainment – particularly where you are entertaining large numbers of people. (See Appendix 10 for a clean copy of this survey.)

Guest Survey

As part of our ongoing effort to ensure relevance in all business related activities, we would appreciate your taking a few moments this afternoon to complete the following questions:

When I see a company sponsoring events like the XYZ, it gives me a positive image about the company?

- ❑ Agree Strongly
- ☒ Agree Somewhat
- ❑ Neutral
- ❑ Disagree Somewhat
- ❑ Disagree Strongly

When I see Products made by companies who sponsor events like the XYZ, it makes me more likely to choose that brand?

- ☒ Agree Strongly
- ❑ Agree Somewhat
- ❑ Neutral
- ❑ Disagree Somewhat
- ❑ Disagree Strongly

What should The XYZ Company of Australia Sponsor

- ☒ Sport
- ❑ Arts
- ☒ Environment
- ❑ Community Events
- ☒ Education
- ❑ Charities
- ❑ Individual athletes

Hospitality

Think outside the square. Some events just don't lend themselves to hospitality easily, but there may still be an opportunity to provide a quality experience. The Motorola Cycling Team used to entertain their clients by taking them in the team chase car, from where the manager controlled the cyclists and gave orders. This was highly exciting for Motorola clients – they were in the thick of the action, and this was an opportunity that was afforded to very few people – in other words, a premium opportunity.

Remember you can always create hospitality events to entertain clients and the media. Don't forget to use sponsored organisation's personalities (who will often be your guest's heroes).

An example of this is, in managing the Olympic sponsorship for a major company there was a requirement for an event that would allow management to informally meet their top 400 clients in each state. A proposal was put to the Olympic Committee to stage Welcome Home Parades in each city for the victorious athletes, which would be sponsored by the company. This was agreed to, and in addition a dinner was arranged on the evening of each parade. This dinner was attended by Olympic athletes, Olympic Committee Officials, the company's top 400 clients, and their spouses. Not surprisingly, there was a 105% acceptance rate and the business done and relationships cemented informally exceeded all expectations. Our clients got to meet their heroes - the victorious athletes - who were sitting on their tables and mingled afterwards. As an added bonus, the parades (very strategically signed) received enormous media coverage, featuring the company logo.

Access to Personalities

It is wise to make sure contractually that personalities are available when requested for advertising, promotions etc. If there are personalities, for example, rowing team members, ballet dancers etc. who are laid up due to injury or are not required to participate on that occasion, invite them to visit you and your clients at the event. This is a great method of forming a relationship with the people your company are sponsoring. Best of all this should cost you nothing, and it adds a great deal of value in terms of goodwill.

Summary

- **Set hospitality guidelines**

- **Be very organised as far as invitation, tickets, maps, menus are concerned**

- **Make sure the facilities are acceptable – check often!**

- **Any hospitality undertaken should add value to the company**

- **Post evaluate hospitality**

Chapter 30

Ambush Defence Planning and Rear Guard Actions

Ambush Marketing - Sponsorship's Cancer

Ambush marketing is all about stealing rights you don't own. The sponsorship ambush occurs when a company associates itself with an image or an association where it has no right to do so (legal or moral!). Ambush is seen by some companies as a cheap way of getting involved. Ambush provides more money to spend below the line as there is no sponsorship fee incurred. The negative is that ambush devalues sponsorship properties. The result of ambush is a) companies are unwilling to re-sign sponsorship deals where their rights and benefits have been used/stolen by another company - usually their competitor, and, b) the more ambush happens industry wide, the bigger the question mark about the true value of being involved in sponsorship.

The methods for committing an ambush can include: Advertising, telecast, competitor, spectator and property ambush. The ambusher is commonly a non sponsor who has no rights to the property, but is on occasions a sponsor who takes rights they haven't purchased and therefore appears to be a more major sponsor than they really are.

In the vast majority of cases committing the ambush is not illegal. The ambusher may not be breaking any laws, however their company has to make the decision, 'where is the line' and 'is it ethically correct to ambush'. In today's competitive world the reality is that the ambush does provide value for money and has become an integral part of the marketing mix of some companies.

As already pointed out, ambush results in unhappy sponsors and devalues the property.

It is far harder to sell a property that has been effectively ambushed, and it is therefore up to both the property owner and sponsors to protect their assets from ambush.   This will require some forethought, and as a last resort having the willingness to threaten the ambusher with 'lawyers, guns, and money'.

The best method of dissuading potential ambushers from ambushing you is to ensure your target audience knows who your sponsors are. There have even been instances where an ambushed organisation has taken out newspaper advertising pointing out who their legitimate sponsors are, and mentioning that a certain company has associated themselves with the organisation without the right to do so, thereby creating bad publicity for the ambusher.

The advertisement to the left was reproduced with permission of the Australian Commonwealth Games Association and was arranged by Sports Marketing and Management.

Identifying the Ambusher

In any sponsorship there are three types of players - sponsors, non-sponsors and the media. All of these have the potential to become ambushers. The methods for committing the ambush by any of these players can include: advertising, telecast, competitor, spectator and property ambush. All of these will be identified in this chapter.

- **The Trojan Horse Ambush** is named after the famed horse of ancient Troy and is committed by sponsors who ambush co-sponsors and the title sponsor, taking rights they are not entitled to or appear to be a far more major sponsor than they actually are.

- **The Guerrilla Ambush** is committed by non-sponsors who 'steal' the perception of being a sponsor when they have not bought any rights to associate themselves with the organisation in question.

- **The Media Ambush** is committed by media itself. They associate themselves with an event that they are either media sponsor of, or a minor sponsor, and give no other sponsor(s) any coverage – particularly naming/title rights sponsors. They thereby create the impression that they are either the sole sponsor, or a far more major sponsor than they actually are.

Have You Been Ambushed?

The most difficult question is "what constitutes an ambush". Everyone has different views as to where the line is drawn. The best method of deciding whether an ambush has been committed is to define the rights that have been have granted to sponsors, as stated in their contracts, and if one or more of the sponsors have taken rights and benefits over and above those agreed to, this could be considered an ambush.

From the sponsor's point of view this definition is too tight and unrealistic, as they want to make the most of the property they have purchased. If an organisation is fortunate enough to have a number of sponsors with identical rights this reduces the possibility of the Trojan horse ambush, and also gives sponsors a free hand to get the most out of their sponsorships. A good example is sponsorship of an Olympic Team. Each sponsor receives identical rights.

To put it simplistically, they purchase the rights to use the Olympic Committee's symbol, the national flag and Olympic rings, the use of the team mascot, and the right to call themselves an official sponsor of the Olympic Team. How much each sponsor gets out of the sponsorship after signing the deal is up to their budget, resources and creativity and management skills.

Telecast Ambush

The most common ambush to take place is the Telecast ambush. This occurs where an event is televised, and the property sponsor has not purchased the network telecast advertising and sponsorship package. Telecast sponsors have a large advantage over property sponsors as they are getting their message to a larger number of consumers - the television audience.

The telecast sponsors have the advantage of generally being perceived by the viewing audience as sponsors of the event being televised. This perception is heightened because some event sponsors (usually the more major ones) are also telecast sponsors. The use of in-telecast promotions heightens the perception that network sponsors are event sponsors as well, because of the close association with the event through the strategic use of sponsored replays, highlights, sweepstakes, team or player profiles and the like.

Networks and outlets who have the telecast and media rights become ambushers when they promote their association at the expense of the title or principal sponsor and give the perception that it is the network's event. This occurs frequently, although it is often unintentional and is just a case of the network looking after its own interests. It is up to the property promoter to look after their sponsor's rights, without being prompted.

Protecting sponsors from this sort of devaluation of the rights and benefits they have purchased should be done as a matter of course!

Advertising Ambush

The Advertising Ambush is probably the most calculated ambush of all. Even the ambusher can be in doubt that they are perpetrating an ambush.

In the advertising ambush, generally, non-sponsors create a strong association with the property, usually through advertising or sponsoring the telecast, thereby giving a strong impression that they are actually sponsors.

Advertising Ambush Techniques

The following methods of advertising ambush are regularly used:

- Buying the right to historic footage and photographs and integrating into advertisements at strategic times.

- Becoming a television telecast sponsor and using in-telecast promotions to gain association.

- Owning ex champions and using in advertising campaigns and product endorsement.

- Advertising in associated publications including fan guides, event programs, etc.

- Offering individual sponsorship to a team member for use in advertising campaigns.

- Buying signage rights to the venue from venue management.

- Advertising outside the venue using billboards, mobile signage and the like.

Event Competitor Ambush

Imagine if you sponsored a race series and it is won by your competitor's vehicle. The driver, who will be welcomed to the dais by your chairman, will be covered in his own sponsor's signage. Your chairman will present the winner with the cheque, and the winner then gets to have his say. He will thank his sponsor and probably go on to comment that he is driving the best vehicle on the market. The press the next day is likely to feature large adverts. Stating that your competitor's vehicle is so superior that it won your event whilst competing against your models.

Well, that's competitor ambush! Sponsors should think very carefully about sponsoring events their competitors might win, and it is up to the property owner to minimise the opportunity for their sponsor's competitors to get favourable coverage.

Property Ambush

The property ambush is usually unintentional. Basically the property owner, who worked so hard to woo the sponsor, has blown it unintentionally by inviting their sponsor's competitor to be a service provider on site, or by just not controlling their rights properly. These ambushers might also be non-competitive, but are just diluting the value of their sponsors commitment. It gets back to the clutter situation. If you have a very active site it is very difficult for the sponsor to get recognition, it would be cheaper for them just to be an attraction or a service provider themselves.

The property ambush can and has happened in the following situations;

- Invite an attraction, for example, skydivers sponsored by a competitor.

- Not controlling merchandising rights and having competitor's brands sold by fast food outlets. For example, your sponsor's opposition's brand of beer being the only beer available.

- Beverage vending machines and fast food trailers advertising competitors product.

- Competitor equipment sponsored by the opposition, ie, timing clocks, radar guns, referees attire, etc.

Spectator Ambush

Spectators provide an excellent platform for event and telecast ambush.

An excellent way for the ambusher to portray the image to attendees and television audience alike that they are a major sponsor is to have displays set up outside the event giving away significant quantities of merchandise.
For less than the price of purchasing the property, the ambusher can flood the event with their merchandise. Some effective items for outdoor events are hats and sun visors. Depending on the ambusher's budget they can be either material or cardboard.

The best method of telecast ambush I have seen is to purchase a number of strategically placed seats that are likely to get a lot of coverage and place spectators wearing your gear, or spelling out the company word mark with cards, in those seats. Another method I have been told is successful, is to place a few attractive ladies wearing your merchandise close to a camera position. (Cameramen have been apparently been given inducements to ensure they pick the right shot.) Of course, these methods will be equally as effective for legitimate sponsors!

Integrated Marketing

Integrated marketing is an attempt to stop the ambush. It eliminates competitive advertising and hopefully guarantees you won't be ambushed at any level, including the telecast. This form of packaging is being used extensively in high profile sports and obviously attracts a premium.

Integrated marketing is the marriage of the sponsorship and the broadcast coverage, normally through a third party or joint venture. Integrated marketing secures the television rights and broadcast time, the signage, the sponsorship property, and promotional opportunities in a single package.

Integrated marketing makes the job of signing sponsorship for companies far less risky, and less work.

Ambush Defence

The best methods for ensuring sponsors and property assets are not ambushed is for:

- **Sponsors to take ownership.** Ensure the target audience knows who the sponsors are - via conventional advertising if necessary. In fact, conventional advertising can be the most effective method of dissuading potential ambushers from ambushing the property.

- **Clearly define the rights and benefits** belonging to each sponsor and ensure all sponsors are aware of their rights and those of others.

- **Integrated marketing** is the marriage of the sponsorship and the broadcast coverage, normally through a third party or joint venture. Integrated marketing secures the television rights and broadcast time, the signage, the sponsorship property, and promotional opportunities in a single package.

  Integrated marketing makes the signing of sponsorships for companies far less risky and less work. It eliminates competitive advertising and hopefully guarantees you will not be ambushed at any level, including the telecast. This form of packaging is being used extensively in high profile events.

- **Event owners must control the property.** No component of any property should be controlled by a third party. This includes:

  o Advertising in sponsored organisation publications
  o Sale of signage
  o Sponsorship of individuals or team sponsorships

One method of protecting your self against ambush is to familiarise yourself with local 'passing off' legislation which is part of many country's laws. The basis of this legislation is that a company cannot mislead, deceive or make false representations. The Australian Government produced landmark legislation called "The Olympic Insignia and Indicia Act" to protect the rights of Olympic Sponsors and to protect the intellectual property of the International Olympic Committee and the 2000 Sydney Olympic Games.

See your solicitor if you require more detailed information!

Ambush Defence Checklist

- ❏ Is the contract watertight?
- ❏ Be aware of who the sponsor's competitors are?
- ❏ Is the telecast sponsorship tied up?
- ❏ Is telecast advertising tied up?
- ❏ Are in-telecast promotions tied up?
- ❏ Are all signage rights tied up?
- ❏ Do associated publication's advertising rights protect sponsors?
- ❏ Is there an agreement between peak body, state association, clubs, etc, that each organisation's sponsorship agreements will not be compromised?
- ❏ Can you tie the event and sponsor logos in to a single logo (if corporate ID guidelines allow it).
- ❏ Appoint someone to police your event and lock out people and organisations who are ambushing it?
- ❏ Have you ensured that all stars are owned by the event either directly or does their contract protect the sponsor's rights?
- ❏ Identify likely places or avenues for ambush?
- ❏ Restrict airspace by putting your own banner towing aircraft in the sky.
- ❏ Legally establish the image through trademarks and copyright law. See your solicitor.
- ❏ Make sure the public and target audiences know who owns the property.
- ❏ Ensure spectator banners are monitored and controlled if required.
- ❏ Do you control media in your venue?
- ❏ Prevent non-sponsor association with the property via promotions and/or advertising.
- ❏ Can competitors purchase permanent venue signage?

Righting Wrongs

From the Sponsor's perspective, if they have been ambushed, the first question they should ask, the Seeker is "what are *you* going to do about it"? Generally once the ambush has occurred it is very difficult and expensive to correct. The steps you can take to correct the situation include: corrective advertising; warning off the ambusher; or the expensive one - if any laws have been broken bring in the lawyers or certainly threaten the ambusher with them.

If a sponsor has been badly ambushed, they will certainly consider either terminating the contract, or not renewing the sponsorship at the end of the contract period.

An ambushed sponsor should be every property's nightmare. The rights holder has an obligation to their sponsor to rectify the problem and an obligation to their event's future ability to attract sponsors to stop the ambush.

If All Else Fails

- Aggressively enforce the responsibility on the promoters.
- Be the big bully and protect your image and rights.
- Advertise your rights via conventional advertising.
- Threaten with, and use if necessary, 'lawyers, guns and money' as the saying goes!

Summary

- Ambush results in unhappy sponsors and devalues your property. It will be far harder to sell a property in the future if it has been effectively ambushed.

- It is up to the property owner and sponsors to protect their assets from ambush, and this requires extensive foresight and planning.

- As a last resort having the willingness to threaten the ambusher with "lawyers, guns, and money" may be the answer.

- It is up to both parties to police the potential for ambush.

Chapter 31

Evaluating the Results and Benchmarking

Evaluating Sponsorships Using Conclusive Data, Not Guesses, Provides Investment Accountability

Evaluating sponsorships has to be the single biggest headache for any Sponsorship Manager. The most common evaluation method in the past was the use of "go with the gut" - you just knew if it worked! The main flaw of the 'Gut Feeling' method is that you cannot provide any tangible numeric proof that the sponsorship provided a return on investment.

The following statement was made in relation to measurement of temperature, but relates equally as well to almost anything that requires formal evaluation:

> "When you can measure what you are speaking about, and express it in numbers, you know something about it; but when you cannot measure it, when you cannot express it in numbers, your knowledge is of a meagre and unsatisfactory kind; it may be the beginning of knowledge, but you have scarcely, in your thoughts, advanced to the stage of science." **William Thompson later known as Baron Kelvin of Largs. Relating to the measurement of temperature.**

Sponsorship is an integral part of the marketing mix and should now, and increasingly is, be receiving the same evaluation and cost justification as other media buys. It is true that accurate measurement of any mass communications medium is difficult and this includes advertising, PR, and sponsorship. There are however many ways of coming to a very satisfactory conclusion on the cost benefit of sponsorship programs.

You do need to keep in mind that it is almost impossible to measure the results of any program in isolation if you haven't stated the desired outcomes. (See Chapter 24 – "Creating the Sponsorship Plan".)

Methods for measuring return on investment vary from sponsorship to sponsorship. Normally each element or activity is measured in a different manner. In evaluating the sponsorship, break the program up into separate activities and look at the value each returned.

There are three reasons why evaluation is critical:

- To determine whether planned sponsorship (marketing and communications) objectives were achieved.

- To determine whether the return on sponsorship investment was worthwhile in comparison to other marketing and communications activities such as conventional advertising and consumer promotions.

- To help improve the management and the outcome of the company's overall sponsorship programs.

The Process of Evaluating Sponsorships

The ability to predict and measure the impact of a sponsorship program relies on a basic process:

1. A structured selection process to ensure relevant properties are chosen to be sponsored that have the ability to deliver the sponsor's marketing and communications objectives. (See Part 4, 'Streamlining Sponsors Processes'.)

2. The writing of sponsorship business plans that clearly detail quantifiable objectives, detailed tactics to deliver those objectives and the evaluation methods to be employed. (See Chapter 24 'Creating the Sponsorship Plan'.)

3. Continuous review of the achievement of the marketing and communications objectives to ensure delivery of these is on-track throughout the contracted period. (Detailed later in this chapter.)

4. A formal post-evaluation of the sponsorship program to ascertain final outputs and outcomes delivered. (Detailed later in this chapter.)

5. Benchmarking is the comparison of the performance of an individual sponsorship vs. the sponsors other current and past sponsorship properties. This is undertaken to ascertain value for money and delivery of marketing and communications objectives vs. other sponsorships.

Who to Evaluate and How Often - Seekers

Depending on the number, and the financial value, of your collective sponsors, you will have to make a decision on the level of reporting and evaluation you are going to provide for each. However the bare minimum for all sponsors should be a basic post evaluation of the performance of the sponsorship they have purchased.

*   **Standard Report.** This would contain information pertaining to the activities of all minor sponsors, with information relating to all activities of the sponsored property. This report would likely be produced either bi-monthly or quarterly, and is written with a view to reminding sponsors of the value of sponsoring the property. It will also provide information on all relevant activities. This report could be in the form of a newsletter or letter.

*   **Individual Report.** This report would be produced individually for each major sponsor and would detail all relevant activities that are occurring. This would also be used to remind the sponsor of upcoming opportunities and to review all recent activities. Copies of any media received promoting the sponsor, sales of product etc, should be included in this report. It should be written quarterly, or more often if a large amount of media has been received.

*   **Minor Evaluation.** A minor evaluation would generally be quite generic with the same information going to all sponsors. This evaluation would include relevant information on the sponsorship property, including numbers of spectators, hours of television coverage, etc. One section of the report would be personalised; specifically detail each minor sponsor's returns.

- **Major Evaluation.** A full evaluation is custom written for each major sponsor. The information that should be included in a major evaluation is detailed in later pages.

The table below is provided to assist in your decision making process.

Investment	Up to $1,000	$1,000 to $10,000	$10,000 and over
Regular reporting (standard report)	Yes	Yes	Yes
Individual reporting	No	Possible	Yes
Minor post Evaluation	Yes	Yes	No
Individual post Evaluation	No	Possible	Yes

Why Evaluate Sponsorship Results

Evaluating sponsorships is certainly a time consuming task for any Sponsorship Manager. The most common evaluation method in the 1980s was the use of 'gut feeling' - you knew if it worked! The main flaw of the 'gut feeling' method is that you cannot provide any tangible numeric proof that the sponsorship provided a return on investment.

The 1990s was the period when sponsorships were traditionally measured by determining the outputs generated by the sponsorships (ie, media coverage, sales contacts, awareness, publicity etc.)

The 2000s have brought a more developed model that not only measures the outputs, but also the outcomes. In other words, the effect that the sponsorship had on its target audience and whether this was positive or negative for the sponsor. Outcomes traditionally measured include: attitude change towards the sponsor; behavioural change – usually resulting in propensity to purchase a sponsor's product, thereby increasing sales, and lastly, measuring the return on investment delivered to the sponsor through the sponsorship.

Sponsorship is an integral part of the marketing mix and should now be receiving the same evaluation and cost justification as other media buys. Accurate measurement of any mass communications medium is difficult and this includes advertising, public relations, and sponsorships.

Many sponsors find it difficult to quantify the bottom line gains that have resulted from the benefits provided by the sponsorship. Therefore the best way of making sure sponsors understand the returns is to provide a post evaluation report detailing the benefits received. If the sponsorship is worth a large sum of money and is necessary to the sponsored organisation's ongoing operation, it may be worth getting the event evaluated by an independent professional.

The report should detail all the contracted benefits, stating whether they were delivered and providing evidence of delivery. It should contain copies and details of all media received by the sponsor and should also identify any problems and the measures that have, or will, be taken to rectify the problems. This report could identify areas for improvement on both sides and make recommendations on methods to facilitate the improvements. The report should make an attempt to value the benefits delivered, and hopefully the benefits will far exceed the cost of the sponsorship.

Sponsorship managers have to justify to their superiors the value of sponsorship's contribution to their company management. Therefore if you can help them to justify the sponsorship of your property by pointing out the benefits received, you are far more likely to have them re-sign at the end of the contract period.

How to Evaluate the Sponsorship

The planning process that details the quantifiable objectives to be achieved must be undertaken in order to undertake a successful and meaningful evaluation process.

Traditionally the evaluation is reported either annually or at the conclusion of the sponsorship program. However, leaving the evaluation until the end of the program can be dangerous – because you may in fact be achieving little or, worse, causing damage to your corporate image, but if you do not evaluate during the term of the contract, you will not have knowledge of this.

Methods for measuring return on investment vary from sponsorship to sponsorship. Generally each element or activity is measured in a different manner.

The decision has to be made as to which activities are to be measured. Those elements that will identify the ROI and help improve the management and the outcomes of the sponsorship program are most useful.

In evaluating the sponsorship, break the program up into each separate activity and look at the value of each. You may well find some promotions were an absolute waste of time or money in terms of return on investment (even if they were heaps of fun!). Eliminating such elements will help you plan for the future and more accurately predict your results.

Here are some proven methods of evaluating your return on sponsorship investment:

Gut Feeling

You just know if it worked. This method is still distressingly common, and is often made on the "fun factor", which, if we are honest with ourselves, is not always an indication of its success in company terms. 'gut feelings' main flaw is that you cannot provide any numeric proof that the sponsorship provided a return on investment. In the age of corporate accountability answering your boss's question "what did we get out of this sponsorship?" with "I know it worked - it felt good" does not give him sufficient assistance to justify this expenditure to the board. You must be able to provide back up sales figures or comparative figures versus using conventional advertising.

Subjective Report

This was traditionally produced by the Seeker organisation, and contained anecdotal information relating to the delivery of the benefits and the Seeker's view of the success of the relationship. It also usually included examples of outputs, such as media coverage (which may or may not have included the sponsor's image or message).

Measure opinions

Measure your target audience's actions/opinions due to their being influenced by the sponsorship. Do not ask merely whether they attended or saw the event. Instead, ask them whether they purchased the sponsor's product, or, do they intend to? This can be measured by asking your target audiences the following questions on a survey.

Q. **When I see products made by companies who sponsor events like** *(insert your organisation or event),* **I am more likely to purchase the sponsor's brand?   Please indicate how you feel about the following two statements.** *Tick relevant box.*

❑ Agree Strongly
❑ Agree Somewhat
❑ Neutral
❑ Disagree Somewhat
❑ Disagree Strongly

Measure the amount of publicity/media received

Take particular note of whether the sponsor's key messages were accurately transmitted to their target audience.   We keep stressing this – media coverage that does not include the sponsor is of no value to them whatsoever!

This requires the collecting and filing of all media and publicity received. At the end of the period a breakdown of the number and percentage of articles naming the sponsor should be provided, with examples of sponsor coverage included in the report.

It is also worth looking at whether the article was positive, neutral or negative, and whether the sponsor's message(s) was included.

In the past one way of evaluating the value of a sponsorship was to calculate the value of the media coverage by using column inches featured and equating it to an advertising dollar value. The majority of media articles do little more than name the sponsor.   Most sponsors have reasonably high awareness anyway, and are not sponsoring with corporate awareness as a priority objective, so such coverage is not actually worth the same as conventionally purchased advertising to a sponsor.

We have always questioned measuring the value of media as the primary measurement of a sponsorship's success.

The reason is that ultimately a sponsorship should be affecting the target audiences attitudes and behaviours, therefore rather than measuring the medium (output) it is better to measure the change in behaviour towards the sponsor or their product – (the outcome).

There are a number of global organisations that specialise in the measurement of media coverage delivered to sponsors. The techniques utilised are based on a combination of advertising rates, quality of sponsor exposure, length of exposure and placement on the screen/in the publication. If you are going to utilise this type of media analysis, you need to ensure that the same method is being used for each of your sponsorships to enable 'like with like' comparison.

Remember you can't buy a front page or a news story so what value do you put on it? Measurement of media exposure should identify the following?

- Were key messages transmitted to your target audience?

- Measuring the amount of publicity received and particularly on the basis of the number of images achieved.

- Cost per exposure compare effective media exposure received to the cost of similar exposure via conventional advertising, note, you have to agree to the value of editorial and the method for calculation.

- Television audience reach in numbers of people/hours. This can be measured with the following formula time exposed X cost per thousand X spot ad buy cost X % value of time

- Cost benefit in comparison to paid for advertising radio, television press and outdoor advertising; signage.

- Subject or theme by articles and impressions.

- Tone and volume of articles by geographic location and publication or outlet.

- Sponsor acknowledgment by impression, number of articles, publication and outlet.

- Cost per impact.

- Determining quality of exposure

  o influence or tone
  o messages communicated
  o prominence
  o audience demographics reached
  o celebrities or company spokesperson quoted
  o type of coverage

Don't forget – the old saying that "a picture is worth a hundred words" is quite correct in terms of media exposure.

Measure Changes in Corporate Brand and Product Image

The majority of large companies undertake regular brand health or corporate image monitoring which provides an insight into the views of consumers towards a particular company, brand or product.

Sponsorship when strategically used can dramatically affect consumers' views towards the sponsor and its products. It is possible to measure the views of the sponsorship audience and compare this result with the result amongst the general public. Traditionally a question such as the following will be asked. It is important that the same wording used in the corporate image monitoring be used in any surveys directed at the sponsorship audience.

History states that where a sponsor has high awareness and is seen by fans (fanatics) to be adding value to the sponsored activity or organisation, they will usually positively disposed towards the sponsor. However, if the sponsor is not seen to be adding value, and is seen as being commercially exploitative, the fans will at best be neutral, and at worst, actively opposed to the sponsor.

Q. **When I see a company sponsoring events/organisations like** *(insert your organisation or event)*, **it gives me a positive image of the company? Please indicate how you feel about the following two statements.** *Tick relevant box.*

❑ Agree Strongly
❑ Agree Somewhat
❑ Neutral

❑ Disagree Somewhat
❑ Disagree Strongly

Measure Increases in Awareness With Target Audience

Sponsorship is sometimes undertaken to generate some form of awareness. It is only of any value if awareness is low. By asking the following question, you will be able to track the changes in unprompted recall or awareness of a sponsor. This method can be further refined to provide a prompted response. This is where you would ask a second question – ie "Can you name any Dairy Products sponsors"?

Q. Can you name the sponsor(s) of *XYZ event*?

1._____   2._____

3._____   4._____

Identify Relationships

Identify relationships resulting from the property and the resulting benefits to the sponsor. These relationships could be relationships with other sponsors, regulators, media, potential clients delivered through the sponsorship, politicians and so on.

Measure Employee Morale

Identify employee and employer benefits that accrued to the company through the sponsorship. For example, when one major company ran an in-house employee program related to their Olympic sponsorship, they achieved the benefits of less absenteeism, less resignations and less industrial disputes amongst their workforce. The benefits to the employees were a high sense of camaraderie, and the chance to win various levels of packages to the Olympic Games.

Sales Figure Analysis to Identify Sales

Measure action or behaviour rather than exposure received. This means measuring sales. Sales are the most important and sometimes the most difficult result to measure.

One successful method is to measure the difference in incremental sales over the period in question. To do this you will need to predict what the sales would be over the sponsorship period without the sponsorship and take this figure away from actual sales over the period.

To do this you will first need to predict what the sales will be. For example, assume your product is non-seasonal and you move 10 containers of product each month. You can safely guess that, without the sponsorship, you will move 10 containers in the month the sponsorship occurs. If your actual sales during the sponsorship period result in the movement of 14 containers and follow on sales in later months of 12 containers (in a 12 month period) you (the sponsorship) can take credit for providing 28 containers in additional sales.

The next thing is to find out what the return on investment (ROI) was. To be able to do this you need to take the sponsorship costs away from the increased revenue received. Assume each container provides $10,000 profit. Your increased gross profit is therefore $280 000. Take away the sponsorship costs of, say, $100 000, which leaves a net profit of $180 000.

The next thing is to compare this result to using other communications mediums. If you know every dollar spent on advertising returns $1.50 in net profit you know that sponsorship is outstripping advertising in sales by 30 cents in every dollar spent. This calculation is well worth doing as the results may well justify an increase in sponsorship spend.

In short: incremental movement less incremental cost = the sponsorship ROI.

There are also other evaluation methods used, and some of these are

- Sales due to trade and consumer incentive programs run in conjunction with a sponsorship.

- Actual sales at the event (ie, the result of gaining vending rights, or on-site rights for your product via the sponsorship agreement.)

- By establishing a standard in-house methodology and consistently applying it to events over time.

Keeping Tabs

Following every event, make a habit of writing down everything that worked, everything that didn't, and identify possible ways of improving the program. These improvements can then be incorporated in to the next year's Business Plan.

Seekers Keep All Clips That Name Sponsor

Regardless of whether the sponsor has a media monitoring service, you should forward copies of all media stories that report them whether it be TV, radio or print. Often media monitoring services may miss local media reports and the like. Copies of such clips should be provided as they appear in the media, and then should be re-collated for the post evaluation.

Seekers - Report Good News

Make sure the sponsor knows about your property's successes. Everyone likes to be associated with winners, so send relevant information and clips for your sponsor's information. Remember though, media reports that do not mention your sponsor are of no benefit to the sponsor whatsoever, so no matter how good the publicity, if it does not include your sponsor, they are hardly likely to be as delighted with it as you are.

Let the sponsor know about all impending announcements prior to the press being advised. It will make him feel part of the team and assist in the relationship building process.

Cost Benefit Analysis

The evaluation document should result in a cost benefit analysis where all costs are totalled and that figure subtracted from the benefits received. This will provide an indication of whether the activity was a profit driver or a cost centre.

Undertaking the following exercise will result in a cost benefit analysis looking something like the following:

Cost benefit analysis
(Example only)

Costs

Property Cost	$
Broadcast coverage	$
Cost of Below the line spend	
Management	$
Advertising	$
Hospitality	$
Staff Time	$
Ticketing	$
Evaluation	$

Returns

Media Exposure Equivalence	$
Employee Relations	$
Sales	$
Product Sampling	$
Merchandising	$
Relationship marketing	$
Cross Promotions	$
Signage	$

Intangibles

Corporate Image	$N/A

Success or Failure

Net Return or Deficit	%
Total cost (under/over budget)	
Total benefits (under or over achieved)	
Total profit/loss	$

Benchmarking

A benchmark is quoted in The Macquarie Dictionary as being: *"A point of reference from which quality or excellence is measured"*. Sponsorship benchmarking is where you select the most successful sponsorship property of a similar category or event, which has had a similar below the line spend invested in its management and compare the results of your sponsorship to that of the benchmark. This then gives you an indication on how effectively your sponsorship has been managed.

For example, if you are an Olympic sponsor you could compare against the most successful sponsor or all other Olympic sponsors or a sponsor with a similar budget to yours, and compare all outcomes including awareness levels, sales, media clips etc. You would get a very good idea of how your sponsorship management compares.

Benchmarking establishes a basis for setting measurable performance targets, and gives you a point of reference to strive for when setting objectives in your Business Plan. Making the comparison generally improves the level of performance of your Project Manager and gives quantifiable points of reference to compare with.

Writing the Evaluation Document

The post evaluation document should include the following information:

- **Introduction.** Which briefly describes what the evaluation covers and what methods of measurement were used.

- **Situational Analysis.** The situation Analysis should provide a reader who has no prior knowledge of the sponsorship, with a detailed picture of what was sponsored, for how long, and the performance of the sponsored organisation during the period. The situational analysis should include:

  o Copy of the contracted rights, benefits, category of sponsorship, level of exclusivity.
  o The performance of the organisation, event or individual during the period of the sponsorship.

      o   List of other sponsors.
      o   A description of the sponsor's competitors in this area of sponsorship.

- **Sponsorship Analysis.** This area should briefly describe the methods analysis employed in preparing the sponsorship and could include the following:

      o   Description of methods of undertaking any surveys.
      o   Methods of measuring media coverage

- **Objectives.** Detail the planned quantifiable objectives to be achieved through the sponsorship program.

- **Results.** This area should clearly indicate all the positive and negative things that the sponsorship delivered and should make comment in relation to their delivery and/or use. The results section should include examples of publicity achieved, photos that are relevant etc. Headings in this section could include:

- **Sales.** This should include a detailed analysis of direct sales generated for the sponsor through the sponsorship.

- **Media Coverage.** All media coverage received during the sponsorship period featuring the sponsor should be analysed for: number of mentions, the transmission of sponsor's messages, television coverage in minutes (supply a VHS copy if available), copies of articles that demonstrate the value of the property to the sponsor, ie, featuring their name.

- **Sponsor's Image.** Surveys should by undertaken amongst spectators, organisation members and the public, if appropriate, to demonstrate the following:

      o   Awareness of sponsor
      o   Attitude to sponsor
      o   Sales that resulted through sponsorship
      o   Likelihood of future sales due to sponsorship

- **Numbers Affected by the Sponsorship.** Relevant statistics should be included here:

  o Number of people who attended the organisation's events
  o Number of people who saw the event through the media
  o Demographics, e.g., age group, earning capacity, gender, etc
  o Whether the organisation or event is in a growth or decline cycle.

- **Publicity Delivered Through Signage.** Include a list of publicity received, and discussion about the quality of the publicity generated through the sponsorship signage, including number of impacts that saw posters, newspaper ads, tickets etc.

- **Hospitality.** Detail hospitality provided, facilities used and any missed opportunities, for example, empty seats where tickets were provided.

- **Cost Benefit Analysis.** The cost benefit analysis should be an objective financial style report detailing all the property costs and all benefits that accrued to the sponsor.

- **Recommendations.** The recommendations section should clearly detail any improvements that you believe would help the sponsor maximise their benefits.

Example of an Evaluation
(A clean copy of this template can be found in Appendix 7)

Introduction
Briefly describes what the evaluation covers, what methods of measurement were used.

_____

_____

Situational Analysis
Provides the reader who has no knowledge of the sponsorship with a detailed picture of what was sponsored, for how long, and the performance of the seeker during the period.

Sponsorship Analysis
Briefly describes the methods of analysis employed in preparing the sponsorship.

Results
Clearly indicate all the positive and negative things that the sponsorship delivered.

- Sales
- Media coverage
- Sponsor's image
- Numbers affected by the sponsorship
- Publicity delivered through signage
- Hospitality
- Cost benefit Analysis
- Recommendations

Summary

Sponsorship, when used as a marketing or communications tool, must be subject to the same accountability as advertising or public relations. This requires:

- Setting of relevant quantifiable objectives

- A structured selection process

- The writing of sponsorship business plans

- Establishment of acceptable methods of evaluation

- Undertaking ongoing research and analysis

- A formal post-evaluation to measure actual return on sponsorship investment

- Comparison of results to established benchmarks

Chapter 32

The Renewal Process

To Renew or not to Renew - Sponsors?

It is far harder for a sponsored organisation or individual to find a new sponsor than it is to secure the renewal of a current one, so in this respect, they should have done everything in their power to provide all contracted benefits, and to maintain a professional relationship with you the sponsor.

The bottom line in making the decision as to whether or not to renew a sponsorship, is to look at what was delivered during the contract period. Secondly, the relationship between the two organisations should have been cordial and professional at all times. You need to look at whether everything promised in the sponsorship contract was provided, and whether this sponsorship provided a value for money communications tool for your company. Remember, sponsorship is a commercial agreement, and you (the sponsor) should be there because sponsoring this organisation was seen as an opportunity to achieve some of your company's objectives.

If you achieved or exceeded your objectives, the sponsorship has been a success and it should be easy for you to justify continuing the relationship. If you have not achieved the majority of (pre-set) objectives, renewing the sponsorship will most likely be seen as pouring good money after bad!

In fairness to the organisation you sponsored, if you did not plan activities and pre-set objectives and outcomes to be achieved by the sponsorship, it is very unlikely that you will be able to quantify the benefits and justify renewing this sponsorship to your manager.

The only fail-safe way to make the decision as to whether or not to renew is to have had a plan in place – usually for a 12 month period - including pre-set objectives and outcomes to be achieved by the sponsorship, and then to undertaken, or commission, a post evaluation of the sponsorship.

Checklist:

Below is a checklist, which may make the decision making process somewhat easier.

❑ Did you receive service from day one, according to your contract?

❑ Did you feel as if you were a valued and an important part of the sponsored organisation?

❑ Were you involved in all activities?

❑ Did staff at the sponsored property actively help you manage the sponsorship to get the most out of the property? Did they make suggestions as to how you could improve the benefits gained?

❑ Did they acknowledge you in every way possible?

❑ Did they thank you for your commitment, and leave you in no doubt as to the importance of their sponsorship to your organisation?

❑ Did they provide value for money – or did they just "take the money and run"?.

❑ Make sure your property is a raging success whether you are a sport or a medical research unit. Everyone likes winners, especially the sponsor?

❑ Did they meet your needs? Did they make themselves aware of what your objectives were?

❑ Did they offer additional benefits – over and above the contract?

❑ Did they take up every media opportunity to promote you as a sponsor?

❑ Did they make introductions and initiate cross promotions between sponsors?

❑ Did they respond quickly to all requests and try to accommodate them? Were they constructive, not obstructive?

❑ Were you kept informed, particularly if any negative publicity was about to occur?

❑ Did they provide you with an alternative key contact in case one contact moved on, or urgent attention was required during an absence?

❑ Was the organisation you sponsored loyal? They should have looked after your interests above all others if you were their major sponsor?

❑ Did they support any 'spin off' programs that you ran?

When renewal time is imminent, it is worth asking yourself the following few questions:

1. Did we receive value for money?
2. Did the sponsored organisation look after us?
3. Is the sponsored organisation the best method of achieving our objectives?
4. Should we renew?

If you answer "no" or "maybe" or "don't know" to any of these questions you may have a hard time justifying your funds into the sponsorship!

The decision to renew a sponsorship is based on many factors, ranging from the personal relationship of the sponsor and seeker, through to the budget and the perceived value received.

Remember, most sponsorships are entered into to achieve specific objectives for the company which could include anything from moving more product, gaining a relationship with a particular person or target market, positioning a brand or product with a lifestyle, creating or increasing awareness or enhancing the company's image. Even if the main objectives have been accomplished there is still a chance the sponsorship will not be renewed. The reason for this is that most sponsorships have a finite life, of generally between three and ten years, and this will depend on the product or company life cycle. Not too many companies stay with the same advertising campaign over a number of years, and for the same reasons, they will not stay with the same sponsorship campaign for ever either.

Contracts should include termination or 'out' clauses and will also specify when negotiations will be entered for renewal, and this is usually well before the end of the contract. Most reputable companies who have enjoyed a good relationship with the sponsored organisation will advise early if they are not intending to renew, to allow time for a replacement sponsor to be found.

Many sponsors assist in this process by providing suggestions for replacements and providing honest and positive references to potential sponsors

To Renew or Terminate? Checklist - Sponsors

The decision to renew or terminate the sponsorship relationship is made on business grounds that could include:

- Were the stated quantifiable objectives in the business plan achieved?

- Did we receive value for money?

    o Quantified by effective evaluation

- Did the seeker look after us?

    o Did they deliver contracted benefits without us having to remind them?
    o Did they look after our interests in the media?
    o Were their personalities available?
    o Was their membership supportive of us?
    o Did they actively participate in making our sponsorship a success?

- Is the seeker the best alternative?

    o Are they winning?
    o Are they credible?
    o Do they deliver our target audience?

- Is sponsorship the most effective/cost effective method of achieving desired results?

    o In comparison to advertising, sales promotion, direct marketing?

- Can we afford to continue this sponsorship?

    o Is the budget available?
    o Do we have sufficient human resources to run the program?

- o   Do we have customer support through this sponsorship?
- o   Do we have management and staff support for this program?

- Can we afford to terminate the sponsorship at this time?

    - o   Will we receive negative publicity?
    - o   Will our major competitor take up this opportunity?

- Does this sponsorship still fit?

    - o   The current and desired image of the company?
    - o   Is it relevant to the company's overall communications aims and objectives?
    - o   Is there natural synergy with our company/products?

- Was the sponsorship easy to manage?

    - o   Are their personnel professional?
    - o   Do they actively promote us?
    - o   Do they create media events?

Keeping Sponsors Happy - Seekers

It is far harder to find a new sponsor than it is to secure the renewal of a current one, so in this respect, servicing your sponsor is imperative. If your old sponsor leaves the relationship disappointed you will find it very hard to replace them, as many sponsors ask the outgoing sponsor for their opinion of the benefits gained from the association.

The bottom line in retaining current sponsors and gaining new ones is to deliver everything you promised in the sponsorship contract, and return value for money. Remember, sponsorship is a commercial agreement, and the sponsor is there because he has seen sponsoring your organisation as an opportunity to achieve some of his company's objectives. If he achieves or exceeds his objectives the sponsorship has been a success and it will be easy for him to justify continuing the relationship. If the sponsor has not achieved the majority of his objectives, he may see renewing the sponsorship as pouring good money after bad! So, it is very important that you know what your sponsor wants out of the association and to help them to achieve it.

If the company does not have quantifiable objectives (and this still happens occasionally) it may be pertinent for you to sit down with them and develop some.

Checklist to Keep Your Sponsor Happy:

❑ Service your sponsor from day one, according to your contract.

❑ Make sure the sponsor feels like he is valued and an important part of your organisation.

❑ Involve the sponsor in all activities.

❑ Actively help the sponsor manage his sponsorship to get the most out of the property.

❑ Acknowledge your sponsors as often as possible.

❑ Thank your sponsor for their commitment, and leave them in no doubt as to the importance of their sponsorship to your organisation.

❑ Measure their success - ongoing evaluation.

❑ Give value for money - don't just take the money and run.

❑ Make sure your property is a raging success whether you are a sport, a charity, or a medical research unit. Everyone likes winners, especially the sponsor.

❑ Meet the sponsor's needs. Be aware of what their objectives are.

❑ Be flexible; wherever possible give additional benefits

❑ Ensure media promote the sponsor as often as possible.

❑ Initiate cross promotions between sponsors.

❑ Teach sponsors about the value of sponsorship and how to use it if necessary.

❑ Respond quickly to all requests and try to accommodate them - be constructive, not obstructive.

❑ Once again - under sell and over deliver.

❑ Keep in touch with sponsors and keep them informed, particularly if any negative publicity is about to occur.

❑ Establish more than one key contact in case one contact moves on.

Why Sponsorships Fail

Lack of Fit

If there is not some synergy between the seeker and sponsor organisations, it will be very hard to develop an effective sponsorship program.

Bad Contract

A well written and fair contract, which reflects the understandings of both parties is fundamental to a good sponsorship relationship. Make sure the wording is clear and cannot be misinterpreted in any way by either party - this will substantially lower the chances of misunderstandings and bad feelings marring the relationship.

A vague contract that doesn't spell out all facets of the agreement in detail, including the payment terms, will surely cause problems if either party isn't sure of or has different perceptions in relation to what was agreed to. If there is any uncertainty or hostility during the contract phase, the time to fix the problem is then - before you 'climb into bed with each other'. Otherwise the relationship may well end up in a messy divorce!

We often hear people say − "if the contract is right, you can put it in a drawer and never visit it again". We disagree − the contract should become almost a working document − that way benefits promised will be delivered, and neither party will head off on a tangent which will cause misunderstandings − the truth is − the contract must be right, and you WILL have to check it at some stage of the sponsorship relationship.

Not Win Win

If the deal wasn't 'win win' the sponsorship will not last. **Both** parties must to be able to readily identify the benefits that are accruing to them. If the current contract isn't delivering, consider adding some extra dimensions to it, and then renegotiate the deal to ensure you have that desirable 'win win' situation.

Bad Relationship

Bad personal relationships make it highly likely that a sponsorship will fail. It is imperative that both parties like and trust each other and have common goals. If the relationship isn't working change your attitude or, if necessary, change the personnel.

Change Of Personnel

A change of personnel on either side can however, have disastrous consequences. It will mean that new relationships have to be formed, and new understandings will have to be reached in relation to objectives and benefits. If you have a comprehensive contract covering all aspects of the original understanding, it will make these new relationships far easier to form. The disruption caused by change of personnel can't be underestimated – this is why we recommend one point of contact, with a back-up person who is appraised of all the facts as the relationship grows.

Longevity

Sponsorships are generally signed for three to five years (with 'out' clauses included in the contract). The reason for this is that associations and relationships take time to grow, and the longer period is allowed for the public and event audience to see that association amalgamate.

Market Awareness Increases Over Time

Another reason to look at a longer contract period is that if increased brand or product awareness within a particular target market is one of your objectives awareness will grow over time. Sponsorship is one of those business tools where the benefits definitely accrue over time, rather than a short and sharp campaign that brings more immediate results.

Too Hard

If management of the sponsorship is too difficult or too expensive - think twice about being involved again.

Ambushed

If you have been ambushed during the sponsorship agreement period, and the organisation you sponsor hasn't vigorously defended you and the rights have purchased, you would need to consider very carefully whether you wanted to sponsor them again. We would recommend against re-signing. Don't forget properties that are ambushed are devalued – another organisation is using the rights and benefits that you have purchased – without paying for them.

Non Performing in Competition (Losing)

It is more difficult to gain benefits and recognition if the organisation you sponsor is a perpetual loser in their field. It is more and more common for a sponsor to demand performance guarantees are included in the contract and for them to exercise their termination clause if performance is not to the specified level.

Be Loyal

At the risk of labouring the point, if you have a sponsor, you are in a relationship that is both commercial and personal. Stick by your partner and look after their interests. Loyalty is appreciated in any relationship.

Support Sponsor's Related Programs

Willingly assist your sponsor(s) with 'spin off' programs from the main sponsorship if it is possible to provide extra benefits without watering down, or creating a Trojan Horse ambush.

Cost Benefit

Make sure your sponsor is well aware of the benefits they are getting for the cost of the sponsorship. This is an ongoing process of making sure they receive all contracted benefits and any possible 'extras' along the way. As mentioned, it is worth undertaking continuous evaluation, and providing the results of that to your sponsor. The evaluation process also keeps you informed as to whether you are providing the benefits, and therefore value for money.

When renewal time is imminent, it is worth asking your-self a few questions from the sponsor's perspective:

1. Did we receive value for money?
2. Did the seeker look after us?
3. Is the seeker the best method of achieving our objectives?
4. Should we renew?

If you answer "no" or "maybe" or "don't know" to any of these questions you may have a hard time justifying your sponsor's reinvestment of funds into your organisation!

The Renewal

The decision to renew a sponsorship is based on many factors, ranging from the personal relationship of the sponsor and seeker, through to the budget and the perceived value received.

The renewal process is, however, two way. While the sponsor is deciding if you still fit her needs, you should be considering whether your current sponsors are appropriate to your needs and fit your image. Obviously, while you are making this decision, you will have in mind that sponsors are quite often hard to come by. So ask yourself the following questions:

1. Do you still want to be sponsored by your current sponsor?

2. Do they suit your organisation's needs?

3. Has the relationship been 'win win' and are they likely to want to continue the relationship?

4. Is your membership supportive of the sponsor?

5. Is the 'life cycle' of the sponsorship over - ie, has your sponsor been with you a long time, and are they looking for a new fresh program?

Remember, most sponsorships are entered into to achieve specific objectives for the company which could include anything from moving more product, gaining a relationship with a particular person or target market, positioning a brand or product with a lifestyle, creating or increasing awareness or enhancing the company's image.

Even if the main objectives have been accomplished there is still a chance the sponsorship will not be renewed. The reason for this is that most sponsorships have a finite life, of generally between three and ten years, and this will depend on the product or company life cycle. Not too many companies stay with the same advertising campaign over a number of years, and for the same reasons, they will not stay with the same sponsorship campaign for ever either.

Contracts should include termination or 'out' clauses and will also specify when negotiations will be entered for renewal, and this is usually well before the end of the contract. Most reputable companies who have enjoyed a good relationship with you will advise you early if they are not intending to renew, to allow time for a replacement sponsor to be found. Many sponsors will assist in this process by providing suggestions for replacements and providing honest and hopefully positive references to potential sponsors

To Renew or Terminate? Checklist

A company's decision whether to renew or terminate the sponsorship relationship is made on business grounds which could include:

1. Were the stated quantifiable objectives in the business plan achieved?

2. Did we receive value for money?

    o   Quantified by effective evaluation

3. Did the seeker look after us?

    o   Did they deliver contracted benefits without us having to remind them?
    o   Did they look after our interests in the media?
    o   Were their personalities available?
    o   Was their membership supportive of us?
    o   Did they actively participate in making our sponsorship a success?

4. Is the seeker the best alternative?

     o Are they winning?
     o Are they credible?
     o Do they deliver our target audience?

5. Is sponsorship the most effective/cost effective method of achieving desired results?

     o In comparison to advertising, sales promotion, direct marketing?

6. Can we afford to continue this sponsorship?

     o Is the budget available?
     o Do we have sufficient human resources to run the program?
     o Do we have customer support through this sponsorship?
     o Do we have management and staff support for this program?

7. Can we afford to terminate the sponsorship at this time?

     o Will we receive negative publicity?
     o Will our major competitor take up this opportunity?

8. Does this sponsorship still fit?

     o The current and desired image of the company?
     o Is it relevant to the company's overall communications aims and objectives?
     o Is there natural synergy with our company/products?

9. Was the sponsorship easy to manage?

     o Are their personnel professional?
     o Do they actively promote us?
     o Do they create media events?

Summary

- Good relationships are the basis of good sponsorships

- The contract must be right

- Did the sponsorship make financial sense for both parties?

- Did our sponsorship partner look after us?

- Is the current sponsorship the best medium for achieving our objectives?

- Does it make sound business sense to continue the relationship?

Part 7

Appendices

Appendix 1

The Sponsorship Unit Awareness Questionnaire

1. Can you name any sponsor(s) of your organisation?

1 _____ 2 _____

3 _____ 4 _____

5 _____ 6 _____

7 _____ 8 _____

Please indicate how you feel about the following statements.

2. When I see products made by companies who sponsor (*insert the organisation, event, or sporting team*), it makes me more likely to choose that brand?

☐ Agree Strongly
☐ Agree Somewhat
☐ Neutral
☐ Disagree Somewhat
☐ Disagree Strongly

3. When I see products made by companies who sponsor and support
    (*add the category of your organisation e.g., charities, the environment,
    football*), it makes me more likely to choose that brand or product
    over competitors?

    ❑   Agree Strongly
    ❑   Agree Somewhat
    ❑   Neutral
    ❑   Disagree Somewhat
    ❑   Disagree Strongly

4. When I see products made by companies who sponsor organisations
    or sporting teams I don't support, it makes me less likely to choose
    that brand?

    ❑   Agree Strongly
    ❑   Agree Somewhat
    ❑   Neutral
    ❑   Disagree Somewhat
    ❑   Disagree Strongly

5. Can you name any sponsors in the (*insert sponsors product*)
    category.

    _____

    _____

6. Have you used (*insert potential sponsors product category*), if so how
    long ago?

    ❑   Last week
    ❑   This month
    ❑   This year

If relevant include questions relating to demographic and geographic
information.

Appendix 2

Sponsorship Unit Cost Sheet

List all items that will incur either financial expenditure or person hours	
Item and quantity	**Real Cost**
Tickets	
Hospitality, food and beverages	
VIP parking passes	
Event programs	
Additional printing	
Signage production	
Signage erection	
Support advertising	
Apparel for competitors, officials, media etc, featuring sponsor	
Evaluation research	
Media monitoring	
Fax's and phone calls	
Public relations support	
Legal costs contract preparation	

Cost of selling sponsorship staff time and expenses based on hours at $ per hour X 1.9 for real cost of salary	
Cost of servicing sponsorship in staff time based on hours over the season $ X 1.9 for real cost of staff member	
Total Costs	$
Plus profit margin minimum 100%	$
Minimum Sponsorship Sale Price	$

Appendix 3

Sponsor Identification Checklist

This checklist is designed to assist you in identifying potential sponsors in the market place.

1.   Does your property have synergy with a particular company or industry? *(List all potential industries and companies.)*

_____

_____

_____

_____

_____

_____

_____

2.   Does the target market, of any company exactly match the make up of your organisations members or events audience?

_____

_____

_____

3.   Would your organisation's members be relevant to any company's products and services? *(list all products used exclusively or in quantity by your members/event audience)*

_____

_____

_____

4.   Can you offer on site concessions or vending rights to food or beverage manufacturers?

_____

_____

_____

5.   Does your sponsorship have the capacity to help any particular business sell product or make money if so list them?

_____

_____

_____

6. Does your geographic reach match that of any potential sponsors specific market area?

_____

_____

_____

7. What does your sponsorship offer that other mediums (advertising, sales promotion, direct marketing) cannot? *e.g., Networking, media exposure, a particular niche market*

_____

_____

_____

8. Will your property attract potential clients for any potential sponsors?

_____

_____

_____

9. Will your property directly sell products and or services for any potential sponsors?

_____

_____

_____

10.   Will the property increase the sponsor's visibility in the eyes of
        your members/audience?

        _____

        _____

        _____

11.   Will your property buy a piece of the 'good guy' image for
        potential sponsors?

        _____

        _____

        _____

12.   Do you want your organisation sponsored by the companies you
        have selected?

        _____

        _____

        _____

Appendix 4

Sponsorship Assessment Checklist - Sponsors

This checklist is designed to assist sponsors to identify appropriate sponsorship properties.

Fit:

☐ Is the property consistent with our company's objectives?
☐ Does the lifestyle of the event fit the product, brand or company?
☐ Do audience demographics match those of the product(s) to be promoted?
☐ Does the event's geographic reach match your product's requirements?
☐ Does it fit with existing sponsorships - is there synergy?
☐ Is your organisation compatible with current or future sub-sponsors?
☐ Does the property reach the target audience numbers required?
☐ Is this cost effective in comparison to other marketing mediums?
☐ Is it a sustained activity (longevity)?
☐ Will the target audience receive multiple impacts (ie, be exposed to our message more than once)? What is the frequency?
☐ Will it attract consumer attention? Is it an issue of importance?

General:

☐ Is category exclusivity guaranteed?
☐ Degree of clutter - how many other sponsors are there?
☐ What is the likelihood of ambush?
☐ Is the event in a growth or decline cycle?
☐ Is the package tailored with the benefits required? If not, can it be?
☐ Does it have long term potential?
☐ Can the benefits promised be delivered?
☐ Does it enhance our corporate image?
☐ Are we backing winners?

❑   Is the event unique?
❑   Will this activity have staff and shareholder appeal?
❑   Will it open doors to prospects, government departments, legislators
        and the media?
❑   Is there sufficient time to complete the planning processes prior to
        the event/season commencing? (Usually at least three months.)

Seeker Credibility And Track Record:

❑   Is the seeker responsible, able to work with sponsors, flexible,
        creative, motivated to succeed?
❑   Does the organisation want a sponsor or is it simply desperate for
        funds?
❑   Will the seeker win in its competition/be best in its category?
❑   Does the seeker have the resources to run a sponsorship and look
        after our company's interests?
❑   What is their record with finances?
❑   Will it be easy to implement and execute a program which will
        achieve our objectives?

Costs:

❑   Is sponsorship the most cost effective means to achieve the
        company's objectives? If not, consider advertising, direct marketing
        or sales promotions.
❑   Is the cost realistic in comparison to other similar events on the
        market?
❑   What are the below the line costs?
❑   Are there any hidden costs?
❑   Will costs be justified by results?
❑   Cost of not sponsoring (will the competitor grab it)?

Awareness:

❑   Will it reach and favourably influence opinion leaders?
❑   Will the Sponsorship broaden product awareness, and therefore
        stimulate sales?
❑   Is the community interested in this activity? (Check research.)

Promotional Extensions:

❑   Can in store promotions be used?
❑   Can local promotions be created?
❑   Can trade incentives be introduced?
❑   Are compatible co-sponsors interested in cross promotions?
❑   Can advertising programs be created using the event or its
             personalities?
❑   Are there opportunities to create event merchandise?
❑   Are there opportunities for sampling?
❑   Are there display opportunities?
❑   Are there opportunities to get on site concessions?
❑   Is there access to data-bases for direct marketing?

Signage:

❑   Television?
❑   Uniforms/apparel?
❑   What is the clutter like? (ie will there be a duelling logos situation?)

Hospitality:

❑   Is it available?
❑   Is the standard of client facilities acceptable? (Make sure you
             physically check!)

Media Coverage:

❑   Will the media see the sponsorship or the event as newsworthy?
❑   Are there opportunities to get the brand or logo in all media stories?
❑   Is the event broadcast? Are there opportunities for advertising or on
             air promotions?

Staff Involvement:

❑   Are there opportunities to involve staff?
❑   Will the staff be proud to be associated with this sponsorship?
❑   Is there an opportunity for staff discounts?

Appendix 5

Sponsor Plan Template

Sponsor Plan for _____

Introduction

_____

_____

_____

_____

_____

Objectives

_____

_____

_____

_____

_____

Action list/timeline/accountability

Date	Action	Responsibility
_____	_____	_____
_____	_____	_____
_____	_____	_____
_____	_____	_____
_____	_____	_____
_____	_____	_____
_____	_____	_____
_____	_____	_____
_____	_____	_____
_____	_____	_____
_____	_____	_____
_____	_____	_____
_____	_____	_____
_____	_____	_____

Sponsorship Unit Cost Sheet List all items that will incur either financial expenditure or person hours	
Item and quantity	**Real Cost**
Tickets	
Hospitality, food and beverages	
VIP parking passes	
Event programs	
Additional printing	
Signage production	
Signage erection	
Support advertising	
Apparel for competitors, officials, media etc, featuring sponsor	
Evaluation research	
Media monitoring	
Fax's and phone calls	
Public relations support	
Legal costs contract preparation	
Cost of selling sponsorship staff time and expenses based on hours at $ per hour X 1.9 for real cost of salary	
Cost of servicing sponsorship in staff time based on hours over the season $ X 1.9 for real cost of staff member	
Total Costs	$
Plus profit margin minimum 100%	$
Minimum Sponsorship Sale Price	

Evaluation

_____

_____

_____

_____

_____

_____

_____

_____

_____

_____

_____

_____

_____

_____

_____

_____

_____

_____

Appendix 6

Publicity Checklist

The publicity checklist details all likely expenditure items required to be produced or paid for by the business to ensure the sponsorship runs successfully. These additional costs add significantly to the overall price of the sponsorship and should be considered when assessing the sponsorship. In some cases many of these items are included in the purchase price of the sponsorship.

Signage

Production ... ... $
Erection ... ... $
Permits ... ... $
Storage ... ... $
Cleaning ... ... $
Repairs ... ... $
Person hours ... ... $
estimated hours X hourly rate

Sub Total ... ... $

Advertising

Production ... ... $
Placement external ... ... $
Event materials ... ... $
Person hours X hourly rate ... ... $

Sub Total ... ... $

Personalities

Payment	...	...	...	...	...	$
Expenses	...	...	...	...	...	$
Person hours	...	...	...	...	...	$
hours X hourly rate						

Sub Total ... ... $

Event Management

Event Manager	...	...	...	...	$
Person hours X hourly rate	...	...	...	$

Sub Total ... ... $

Media Management

Media consultant	...	...	...	...	$
Person hours	...	...	...	...	...	$
hours X hourly rate					

Sub Total ... ... $

Hospitality

Invitations	...	...	...	...	...	$
Additional ticketing	...	...	...	...	$
Food and beverages	...	...	...	...	$
Follow up gifts	...	...	...	...	$
Cab dockets	...	...	...	...	...	$
Host time	...	...	...	...	...	$
(usually 30 hours minimum) X hourly rate					

Sub Total ... ... $

Negotiation/Contract

Negotiation time	...	...	...	...	$	
(usually 10 hours minimum) X hourly rate						
Negotiation expenses ...		...	...	...	$	
Legal Costs	...	...	...	...	$	
Sub Total	...	...	...	...	...	$

Employee Relations

Staff communications ...		...	...	...	$	
Staff tickets/discounts ...		...	...	...	$	
Person hours X hourly rate	...		...	...	$	
Sub Total	...	...	...	...	...	$

Post Evaluation

Media Monitoring	...	...	...	...	$	
Media analysis	...	...	...	...	...	$
Research (target audience attitudes)	...		...	$		
Sales analysis ...		...	...	...	$	
Hospitality surveys	...	...	...	...	$	
Person hours	...	...	...	...	$	
hours X hourly rate						
Sub Total	...	...	...	...	...	$

Merchandise/Promotional Material

Design	...	...	...	...	$	
Licence fees	...	...	...	...	$	
Stock ...	...	...	...	...	$	
Person hours	...	...	...	...	$	
hours X hourly rate						
Sub Total	...	...	...	...	...	$
Group Total ...	...	...	...	...	...	...	$
Sponsorship Fee	...	...	...	...	...	...	$
Total Cost of Sponsorship	...	...	...	...	...	$

Appendix 7

Sponsorship Evaluation Pro-forma

Sponsorship Evaluation of _____

Introduction

_____

_____

_____

_____

Situational Analysis

_____

_____

_____

_____

_____

_____

_____

Sponsorship Analysis

The following methods of analysis have been employed in preparing the evaluation.

_____

_____

_____

_____

Results

- **Sales**

_____

_____

_____

- **Media coverage** *copies of clips are attached at the rear*

_____

_____

_____

- **Awareness of sponsor**

_____

_____

_____

- **Attitude to sponsor**

  _____

  _____

  _____

- **Numbers affected by the sponsorship**

  _____

  _____

  _____

- **Publicity delivered through signage**

  _____

  _____

  _____

- **Hospitality**

  _____

  _____

  _____

Cost Benefit Analysis

  _____ $ _____

  _____ $ _____

  _____ $ _____

  _____ $ _____

Recommendations

_____

_____

_____

_____

_____

_____

_____

_____

_____

_____

_____

_____

_____

Appendix 8

Client Entertainment Survey - Hosts

How many people did you entertain during the _____?

With free corporate tickets _____

With food and beverages _____

How would you classify the breakdown of the people you entertained

Place the number of couples entertained in each box

❏   Current clients
❏   Potential clients
❏   Suppliers
❏   Trade
❏   Executives of major companies
❏   People of influence to our Company
❏   Staff
❏   Friends
❏   Journalists
❏   Other

Please list others
_____

What was the reason for selecting your guests for entertainment

❏   Pursue sales
❏   Thankyou
❏   Strike up relationship
❏   Return Entertainment

Please list any other reason

_____

Would you have entertained these clients anyway had this entertainment opportunity not been available?

Yes   _____%
Possibly   _____%
No   _____%

How many of these customers have done business with you before _____%

Will this entertainment result in sales

❑   Yes
❑   No

If so how many (Please enter unit nos.)_____

What benefits or possible outcomes will result from your entertaining at the event?

Where possible approximate $ value

_____$_____

_____$_____

_____$_____

Did you find entertaining guests at this and other sponsored events valuable

❑   Yes
❑   No

Appendix 9

Guest Entertainment Survey

As part of our ongoing effort to ensure relevance in all business related activities, we would appreciate your taking a few moments this afternoon to complete the following questions:

When I see a company sponsoring events like the XYZ, it gives me a positive image about the company?

- ❑ Agree Strongly
- ❑ Agree Somewhat
- ❑ Neutral
- ❑ Disagree Somewhat
- ❑ Disagree Strongly

When I see Products made by companies who sponsor events like the XYZ, it makes me more likely to choose that brand?

- ❑ Agree Strongly
- ❑ Agree Somewhat
- ❑ Neutral
- ❑ Disagree Somewhat
- ❑ Disagree Strongly

When I see a company sponsoring events like the XYZ, it gives me a positive image about the company?

- ❑ Agree Strongly
- ❑ Agree Somewhat
- ❑ Neutral
- ❑ Disagree Somewhat
- ❑ Disagree Strongly

When I see the products made by companies who sponsor the XYZ, it makes me more likely to choose that brand?

❑   Agree Strongly
❑   Agree Somewhat
❑   Neutral
❑   Disagree Somewhat
❑   Disagree Strongly

What should The XYZ Company of Australia Sponsor

❑   Sport
❑   Arts
❑   Environment
❑   Community Events
❑   Education
❑   Medical Research
❑   Charities
❑   Conferences
❑   Individual athletes

Thankyou for your assistance in answering these questions.

Please give the completed form to your table host

We hope you enjoy our hospitality

Sign off

Dictionary of Terms

Advertising is where a fee is paid for the right to place advertising. The company retains complete editorial control of the advertisement; by this we mean that all messages are scripted and approved and appear as scheduled advertisements.

Agents or brokers have the right to sell the property and take a commission or receive payment.

Ambush marketing occurs when a company associates with an image or an association it has no rights to.

- **The Trojan Horse ambush** is named after the famed horse of ancient Troy and is committed by sponsors who ambush co-sponsors and the title sponsor and take rights they are not entitled to OR appear to be a far more major sponsor player than the rights they have purchased.

- **The Guerilla ambush** is committed by non sponsors who steal a perception of being a sponsor, when they have not bought any rights to the property.

Arts marketing is a term used by the Arts fraternity to describe the process of exploiting an arts sponsorship for commercial gain.

Assessment checklist is utilised by sponsors to quickly and uniformly determine if a sponsorship property is going to best suit their needs, the checklist reflects elements of the sponsorship policy and the sponsorship strategy.

Awareness prompted is a measure of the target audiences awareness of the sponsors relationship with the sponsored property after having been prompted by the interviewer i.e. 'can you name a beverage sponsor of XYZ organisation .

Awareness unprompted is a measure of the target audiences awareness of the sponsors relationship with the sponsored property without any prompting.

Ballot Sponsorship is where a number of potential sponsors pay a small amount with the hope of being drawn out of the hat to win the major sponsorship for a small wager.

Benefits are rights or items provided to the sponsor by the seeker as a component of the sponsorship agreement. They would typically include tickets, signage rights, sponsor status, etc.

Brokers have the right to sell the property and take a commission or receive payment.

Cause related marketing (CRM) When a company becomes a sponsor of a cause – often a charity or an environmental initiative and utilises it for commercial gain through incentivising consumers who are supporters of the cause. These relationships are typically 'win win' for both parties.

Contra is where a company's products or services are provided in lieu of, or as well as, cash for the payment of a sponsorship. Contra occasionally suits both parties, however there are taxation and valuation implications to consider.

Contract an agreement between the sponsor and the seeker that allows the sponsor to exploit the relationship in return for a fee. The contract details the arrangement and the obligations of both parties.

Corporate image – The perceptions held within the wider community of what a company stands for (in other words – its reputation). This can be affected by marketing activities including sponsorship.

Corporate sponsorship is the provision of financial or material support (cash, services, or product) by a company for an independent activity not directly linked to the company's normal business.

CRM – See Cause Related Marketing.

CRSM – Cause Related Sponsorship Marketing – See Cause Related Marketing.

Cross promotions are where two or more sponsors group together and create a promotion that mutually benefits all parties involved. These are a good way to extend the benefits of your sponsorship.

Definition of sponsorship: Sponsorship is generally recognised as the purchase of the, usually intangible, exploitable potential (rights and benefits), associated with an entrant, event or organisation which results in tangible benefits for the sponsoring company. See also Corporate Sponsorships, Marketing Sponsorships, and Philanthropic sponsorships.

Demographics The vital and social statistics of populations. Might include information relating to your membership such as: age, education, ethnic back ground, family size, income, occupation, sex, and social class

Donations are a gift of product or cash with little or no expected return. Sponsorship is not a donation. Sponsorship is a business tool used by various departments of companies to achieve defined objectives.

Event marketing is a term used within the events and sponsorship fraternity to describe the process of exploiting sponsorship of an event for commercial gain.

Exclusivity is a right accorded to sponsors, which guarantees the exclusion of their competitors from receiving any promotion or benefit or any association with the sponsored activity. This is commonly described as category exclusivity.

Exit strategy is a pre-planned tactic that will handle the termination of a sponsorship. This is particularly important where there has been a long-term relationship.

Experiential marketing is a term that describes the use of a consumer having an experience perhaps at an event and being marketed to during this period.

Fans is an abbreviation for fanatics i.e. football fanatics.

Frequency is the number of times a consumer receives a message or attends an activity over a given period.

Geographic make up pertains to the geographic characteristics of your audience. Would indicate where the audience and its membership resides by region or regions, in your state only, nationally or internationally.

Grants are often once off payments. They are given, generally to assist in the development of a project, or purchase of an artwork and are usually of a non-commercial nature, being given by either government or a trust.

Hot property term to describe a property that is highly sought after by sponsors.

In kind support the provision of goods or services by the sponsor instead of cash to pay for the property. Otherwise known as contra or value in kind.

Integrated marketing program is where the sponsorship property is linked to all available marketing activities, including telecast rights. It is utilised predominantly to prevent ambush marketing taking place.

Leverage is the name used to describe any activities undertaken to exploit a sponsorship relationship in order to deliver the sponsors objectives.

Marketing is the process of planning and executing the conception, pricing, promotion, and distribution of ideas, goods, and services to create exchanges that satisfy individual and organisational goals.[2]

Marketing sponsorships are the provision of cash or contra (free goods) in return for access to the exploitable potential associated with that entrant, event or organisation. Marketing Sponsorships are used primarily to promote products and services to targeted market segments, reinforce a product brand or promote sales activities.

Merchandisers have rights to produce licensed merchandise.

Naming rights sponsor - is an alternative to a principal sponsor and receives identical rights and benefits with the addition of having the right to have the sponsors name added as a prefix to the organisation or event name.

---

[2]Bennett, Peter D., Ed., 1988, Marketing, American Marketing Association, p.54

Niche marketing is communicating to a tightly defined market that is usually a portion of the overall market of the product. Through niche marketing it is possible to gain a position of strength and appear as the dominant and only brand to that segment.

Official supplier - this status provides the sponsor with the right to claim themselves as being an official supplier to the organisation in return for providing free or discounted services and goods, or simply the right to be the sole purveyor of goods in a particular category.

Option for renewal is a clause often included in a contract to ensure the continuity of the sponsorship past the initial contract period.

Outcomes the description of the effects the sponsorship has had on the sponsor's target audience. An example of an outcome is – a change in propensity to purchase a sponsors product.

Outputs the description of the noise created by a sponsorship – ie, media coverage, signage, publicity.

Packaging is the method in which you structure the benefits for a sponsor and the relationship they have to the seeker and other sponsors. There are five methods of packaging sponsorships: the Level Playing Field, the Hierarchal Package, the Sole Sponsorship, the Pyramid, and Ad Hoc. Each provides different benefits to the sponsors and varying returns to the seeker.

Partner is usually sought where an event or organisation requires substantial funds to underwrite a project and the partner will enter into an agreement with the seeker of the funds and will have rights to the project or venue for its useful life or for an agreed lengthy period. Usually funding is once off at the commencement of the project. In some countries the term partner has legal implications.

Partnership is a joint activity in which business objectives of both organisations are met. In some countries the term partnership has legal implications.

Performance based sponsorship describes a means of renumerating a seeker on the basis of their performance in their activity or on delivery of the sponsor's objectives.

Philanthropy is the intersection of societal and corporate needs.

Philanthropic sponsorships make the company feel good and often provide taxation concessions. Philanthropic sponsorships sometimes generates goodwill towards the company, however, few, if any, benefits are returned, or expected.

Policy document is an internal document and contains items such as the approval processes required, levels of expenditure and the rules as to what is allowed to be sponsored and what isn't.

Principal sponsor is the main sponsor who has rights to have their identity on everything and featured at least twice the size of any other sponsor. They pay a premium and get the most and the best benefits. Only one sponsorship can be sold at this level.

Property is the opportunity (proposal) to be offered to a potential sponsor, whether it be an event, organisation or entrant.

Proposal is a document that provides information to prospective sponsors detailing the proposed sponsorship relationship.

Psychographic is a description for the overall indication of your group's lifestyles and personalities.

Reach and frequency is a measure used in marketing to detail the number of people impacted (reach) and how often they are impacted (frequency).

Real price is the real cost to the seeker of having a sponsor.

Relationship marketing is a term to describe a marketing program where the marketer has direct personal contact with the customer.

Rights are the benefits provided to the sponsor through a sponsorship agreement.

Rights holder is another description for the property owner or seeker.

Sales promotions are short term incentives provided to encourage the consumer to buy the product and are also used to make a product stand out from the clutter. The strategic use of sales promotions is a common extension in major sponsorship programs.

Seeker the recipient of sponsorship from a sponsor. Could be an event, an organisation or an individual entrant. Sometimes known as the seeker.

Selling on some sponsors who are manufacturers sell on or give sponsorship benefits they have purchased to their retailers so providing them with incentives to increase their customer base. Common benefits sold on include event ticketing, in store appearances and signage. This activity should not be confused with sponsors running consumer promotions. In this case the benefits are handed to the retailer who then acts as a defacto sponsor.

Signage is any logo or message on a surface

Sole sponsor is the situation where there is only one sponsorship to be sold – it is totally exclusive.

Seeker the recipient of sponsorship from a sponsor. Could be an event, an organisation or an individual entrant. More often known as the seeker.

Sponsor is the purchaser of sponsorship rights. For the purposes of this manual, either a business or a business's representative.

Sponsorcom is the sponsorship and event management software program.

Sponsorship is generally recognised as the purchase of the, usually intangible, exploitable potential (rights and benefits), associated with an entrant, event or organisation which results in tangible benefits for the sponsoring company. See also Corporate Sponsorships, Marketing Sponsorships, and Philanthropic sponsorships.

Sponsorship brokers have the right to sell the property and take a commission or receive payment.

Sponsorship guidelines are designed to give seekers detailed information on what is and is not sponsored by the company, and how to apply for sponsorship. These guidelines commonly list what information is required to assess the proposal.

Sponsorship plan should state how you are going to achieve each objective, detailing activities that will be implemented and it should include a timeline and quantifiable outcomes.

Sponsorship policy is a document that details the company's ground rules for entering into sponsorship arrangements.

Sponsorship proposal is a document that provides information to prospective sponsors detailing the proposed sponsorship relationship

Sponsorship servicing is the activities undertaken by the seeker to ensure the sponsor achieves their objectives.

Sponsorship strategy is the basic approach to sponsorships within a company. It sets the overall course for achieving stated objectives and provides the foundation of all sponsorship business plans.

Sports marketing is a term used within the sports and sponsorship fraternity to describe the process of exploiting a sports property or personality for commercial gain through sponsorship.

Target audience is the group of people that the sponsor is wanting to communicate or market to.

Television sponsorship is basically an advertising package with extra rights ie, pull throughs, opening and closing billboards, exclusivity.

Title rights sponsor is an alternative to a naming sponsor, receiving identical rights and benefits with the addition of having the right to have the sponsors name added as a prefix to the organisation or event name. Title rights is a term used more commonly in the USA, but gaining acceptance in the Australian sponsorship market.

Traffic growth attractions are attractions used to attract store traffic and can include placing personalities in store, displaying a racing vehicle.

Value in Kind the provision of goods or services by the sponsor instead of cash to pay for the property. Otherwise known as contra or in kind support.

Index

A

B

C